Y. A. TITTLE: I PASS

Y. A. TITTLE:
I PASS!

My Story as told to
Don Smith

Revised Edition

Illustrated with photographs

FRANKLIN WATTS, INC.
575 Lexington Avenue, New York 22

FOURTH PRINTING

Library of Congress Catalog Card Number: 64-18950
© Copyright 1964, 1966 by J. L. Pratt and Company, Inc.

Printed in the United States of America

CONTENTS

vi

FOREWORD

ONE SPRING morning in 1965, many months after Y.A. Tittle
had played his last football game for the New York Giants, he and
I walked up Fifth Avenue headed for lunch at the Plaza Hotel. It
was Y.A.'s first visit to New York since his retirement, but if he
thought folks in the "big town" had forgotten him, he was soon
to learn otherwise.

We had gone only a block or so when a policeman crossed the
street, called for us to halt, and then said, "Mr. Tittle, I'd be mighty
proud if you'd let me shake your hand." Y.A. heaved a small sigh
of relief and obliged him.

Next a bus driver, ignoring the honking horns of cars lined up
behind him, leaned out the window and shouted, "Hey, Y.A., how
ya doin'?" Then a couple of pretty secretaries, squealing with
embarrassment, asked Tittle for his autograph.

And so it went. People flocked around Y.A., buzzing with
excitement, waving to him, calling to him, poking their neighbor
and whispering, "Gosh, there's old Y.A. Tittle." And if the neighbor happened to ask, "How do you know?" the answer was usually,
"How do I know? By his bald head—that's how I know!"

"I wish I was wearing my hat," Tittle said to me. "This bald
head sure gives me away. It's kind of embarrassing."

But Y.A. wasn't fooling anyone. He loved every minute of it—

this warm tribute from New Yorkers. They had not forgotten him, and Y.A. was deeply touched. This was still his town, and it would be, as long as the Giants played football up at Yankee Stadium. It quite obviously did not concern Y.A.'s fans that he had quit the previous December—after seventeen years as a professional quarterback—or that he was now an assistant coach with the San Francisco Forty-Niners. What mattered was that he was walking up Fifth Avenue on a bright spring morning, and this was where he belonged.

The sight of Y.A. Tittle stirs many memories for New York sports fans: memories of championship years in 1961–63; memories of a record-breaking barrage of 36 touchdown passes in 1963; memories of a washed-up old quarterback building a winning Giant dynasty with his rubbery right arm.

New York City is a big place, and it has had its share of sports heroes down through the years—but only a very few have captured the hearts or the imagination of its fans as has Y.A. Tittle. Babe Ruth was one and Joe DiMaggio was another. After that, well, you name them.

In the twilight of his great football career, Y.A. became the standard-bearer of a generation of men approaching middle age: men who have bald heads and who need bifocals to read the stock prices in their morning newspapers; men who figured time was about to pass them by until the old quarterback showed them it's never too late.

Everyone loved Y.A.—even old ladies, non-football fans, who used to remark, "He has such a nice country way about him." And he was loved by the younger generation of longhairs who marveled that a guy with a bald head could throw the football so far and so straight.

When Tittle retired after the Giants' disappointing 1964 season, there was a big empty feeling in pro football. The game had lost more than a great quarterback, more than a record-breaking passer. It had lost a warm human being. It had lost a legend that walks up Fifth Avenue and stops traffic.

Little wonder then, that I was delighted when Franklin Watts told me he was planning to bring out a revised printing of Y.A.'s biography, *I Pass!*

This gave Y.A. and myself an opportunity to bring his story up to date, to retrace his steps through his final season as a player—the injuries, the frustrations, the losses, and, finally, the inevitable decision to retire. In this revised edition of *I Pass*, you'll also read about Tittle's first, and often humorous, exposure to coaching in the National Football League.

Of course, all the rest of the Y.A. Tittle story is here, too—the beginning of everything in a place called Marshall, Texas; his triumphs and defeats in high school football and later at Louisiana State University; his troubled days as a professional with Baltimore and San Francisco; his emergence as a great forward passer; and last but not least, the beginning of a new era when he was traded to New York in 1961.

Yes, it's all here, and I sincerely hope you will enjoy reading it as much as I have enjoyed writing it.

Don Smith

New York City, N.Y.
April 1, 1966

Y. A. TITTLE: I PASS

CHAPTER ONE

BEGINNING OF THE END

In November 1960, the San Francisco Forty-Niners were a football team going nowhere. As their quarterback I was headed in the same direction.

The Forty-Niners' situation was desperate. The ball club had lost four of its first eight starts and, with time running out, trailed Green Bay by three games in the National Football League western division race. The outlook was not good.

My situation was almost as desperate. At least that is the way I saw it at the time. I was 34 years old, an age when most professional athletes have an "ex" in front of their names. I was suffering from a bothersome groin injury which had failed to respond to treatment. Fact is, it got worse as the weeks went by. But hurting me more than the injury was my status with the San Francisco ball club. I was riding the bench behind a young quarterback named John Brodie. After thirteen years as a professional football player, I could not help wondering if the end was not in sight. I had seen the parade pass a lot of fellows by over the seasons, and in November of 1960 I felt perhaps my time had come, too.

The season had been a series of disappointments and frustrations for me. I had started out as the Forty-Niners' No. 1 quarterback, a job that had been mine for a long time. But I was suddenly benched by coach Red Hickey after we beat Detroit, 14–10, in our third ball game. No reason was given. I was just sat down and

Brodie was given the assignment. John went bad against Green Bay the following week, and Hickey had brought me back as a starter for a second time. I felt like a monkey on a stick, one week up, one week down. My good fortune did not last long. Against the Chicago Bears the next Sunday, I pulled a groin muscle and was carried off the field. It had occurred to me at the time that it was a one-way trip for old Y.A., and subsequent events proved that premonition to be correct.

I had tried to come back several weeks later but the injury persisted. My leg just would not hold up under me. They say an athlete is finished when his legs go, and it certainly seemed that mine were gone—or at least one of them.

Heading into November, John Brodie was San Francisco's quarterback, and I was . . . well, I was just there.

I had ridden the bench before and had always gotten my job back. I had gotten it back from Adrian Burk and from Earl Morrall and from a lot of other guys too. But this time it was different. I was not a good quarterback any more. I could throw the ball as well as ever but my confidence was gone. I lacked conviction. Technically, I could still run the Forty-Niner ball club. And yet something vital was missing. I went through the motions of being a quarterback. But I was not the quarterback I once had been. Not by a long shot. I was half a ballplayer, a guy with shattered confidence limping along on one leg.

This feeling had nothing to do with my injury. My confidence had been destroyed long before the Chicago Bears did my groin in. Actually, my problems had begun the previous year when Frankie Albert resigned as head coach and Hickey, who had been Frankie's chief assistant, replaced him.

Albert and Hickey were both fine coaches. I want to make that clear here and now. But they were very different. Under Albert I had quarterbacked one way; under Hickey it was another. Frankie and I had come up together as players and later when he became my coach, we developed a mutual understanding. I did not always agree with him but I played my guts out for him. He was that kind of a fellow. You wanted to go out there and win for him! It was this same quality that made him an inspirational quarterback in the early years of the Forty-Niners. Frankie could get a ball club fired

2

up with nothing more than his personality. He was easy-going and re-laxed. He enjoyed football and he made it fun for everyone else too. Hickey was strong-willed and dominant. Even as Albert's assistant, he exerted tremendous influence on the entire San Francisco opera-tion. Football was Red's business. It was his life. His approach was more grim than Albert's. Frankie often had been content to let his ball club run itself. Hickey was the opposite. He was on top of everything. He left nothing to chance. He played the percentages, and the hell with personalities!

The biggest difference between the two men, at least as I saw it, was that you played *for* Frankie Albert, but you played *to please* Red Hickey.

Red did not harass his players. But you always had the feeling that he was over there watching you, expecting one hundred per-cent on every play. His presence could be felt everywhere on the football field. A ballplayer went into every game wondering what would come next. The pressure was there on all sides, and it increased when Hickey became head coach.

I do not pretend to speak for the other Forty-Niner players. Per-haps they saw Red Hickey differently. But in 1959, when Red took over, I began to lose faith in my ability. I could no longer use my own originality. I felt I was little more than a robot. Hickey did not call the plays from the sideline like Paul Brown of Cleveland or as Albert once tried to do. But Red drew up a game plan, and that was it! I would go out there and run right down the list, one after the other, like he said. I did not have to improvise. Now, most coaches have game plans and most quarterbacks follow them. But under Red's system—and I'm not saying his system was wrong—I lost something that had been with me over the years. I lost my confidence. I had no confidence in myself, so how could the Forty-Niners respond?

This was the way the 1959 season ended, and when we resumed in 1960, it was no different. Brodie was now coming on real strong and I had the feeling my days in San Francisco were numbered. No one said as much. No one ever has to—a ballplayer senses these things.

Red Hickey always treated me fairly. I must say that much. But it was a cold and detached fairness. I was a name and a number

3

to Red, as were the other quarterbacks in camp. My years and my experience made no impression on him. Let me point out what I mean: In 1957 I had a great year and I was named the Most Valuable Player in the N.F.L. But the following season when the Forty-Niners played their first game, I was sitting on the bench! I wondered if I was a second-string quarterback. I did not even get a shot at the starting job until later on. True, I had a poor exhibition season, but I sensed from the first day in camp that my job was on the line—and I wondered why. My confidence was shaky because I felt I had to keep on impressing everyone.

Hickey's attitude toward me was impersonal. I do not believe Red ever liked or disliked a ballplayer. He did not see us as individuals but rather as units of his football team. There was no emotion behind his decisions. He did what he thought best regardless of whom it hurt or whom it helped. His assignment was to build a winning team. He went about this task without becoming sentimentally involved. He had a tough job—like every N.F.L. coach. I felt Red was wrong at times. But I did not second-guess him then, and I won't now. He saw it one way and he was the coach. I saw things differently and I was only the quarterback. Unfortunately, in 1960, I was no longer a good quarterback. But I still liked to think for myself!

We opened the season against New York. I was the starting quarterback and the Giants beat us, 21–19. But then we defeated Los Angeles and Detroit. My confidence began to perk up. Then, bang!, I was benched and Brodie took over.

It was that way week in and week out. John and I never knew which of us would play and which of us would ride the bench. It was an awful feeling, and I believe Brodie felt as bad as I did. He was a fine young quarterback but this situation was enough to upset anyone. It is hard to prepare yourself mentally to play a game when you do not know until the last minute whether or not you are even going to get in there. The uncertainty was affecting both of us. We measured every movement, weighed each call. Neither of us wanted to incur disfavor. We were not relaxed. In my years, I have seen this happen to many clubs which tried to go with two top quarterbacks, so the situation in which Brodie and I found ourselves was not exactly unique.

This tension crept into everything we did. The day we played the Packers in Green Bay, Brodie and I were warming up in a pass drill. Hickey, as always, was watching us intently. We did not always know where he was, but we knew he was watching. Red had not yet named his starting quarterback. Brodie and I had been through this before. Both of us were trying hard to look good. This was no place for a fumbled handoff or a bad throw.

I wanted to play, so I was throwing short passes that were easy to handle. I did not want my receivers dropping any. I looked across the field, and Brodie was doing the same thing. Neither of us was taking a chance on throwing a long ball that might miss the mark. It was kind of humorous at that, and I had to laugh.

I yelled across to Brodie, "Be brave, John. Throw that damned ball down the field."

"Not me," he laughed. "I don't want any of these guys dropping one and making me look bad. I aim to start."

John started against Green Bay and I sat down to watch the game. But it was not his day. He went 0-for-13 in the first few minutes and the Packers jumped all over us. Finally, Hickey gave Brodie the hook and sent me into the game. I had a hot second half even though we eventually lost, 41-14. At least I had my job back. That was something. Now Brodie was on the bench.

That is the way it was in 1960—one week Brodie, the next week Tittle.

Then we returned to the West Coast and played the Bears at Kezar Stadium. I got hit from the side in the first period. As I fell, I heard my groin muscle go "pop." I knew right away it was bad. They helped me off the field, and Brodie trotted into the huddle. I forced a smile. Old John was back in there a lot sooner than either of us had expected.

You might as well say this injury finished me for 1960—and, I guess, with the San Francisco Forty-Niners.

It was not surprising, though. My luck had been bad all along.

When we headed east again to play the Baltimore Colts, who had been the league champions in 1958 and 1959, Brodie was the Forty-Niners' regular quarterback. Hickey never said much to me but I guess it did not matter. I was hurt and I could not play anyway. It was just a matter of finishing out the season. At my age, I

5

knew my injury was not going to heal overnight. Since passing my thirtieth birthday I had learned that injuries, even minor ones, stayed with a man longer. A kid can bounce back in a few days but an old codger like me might take weeks.

What was particularly difficult to live with that year was the stigma of being benched. I do not wish to criticize San Francisco, the fans or the writers. They have been more than generous with me over the years. They have been wonderful. But out there, the favorite word, it seemed to me, was "benched." It carried an ugly meaning. Whenever a player was sat down for a game or was injured, the headlines said: "So and So BENCHED!" To a fellow who plays football for a living, this sort of thing connotes failure or inadequacy. Maybe this "benching" thing happens in every big city. It's just that I was more aware of it in San Francisco that year because I was at a crucial point in my career and I may have been over-sensitive about what I read in the papers.

I remember that when Leo Nomellini, the Forty-Niners' great tackle, did not start a particular game, the headlines read: "NOMELLINI BENCHED!"

Anyone who saw this headline almost had to think there was something wrong with Leo's play. There wasn't; he was merely spelled a bit.

In 1960, it was "Tittle Benched" or "Brodie Benched" or someone else benched. It gnawed at your innards. During a ball game I would find myself wondering, "Am I going to be benched if I do not make this play?" From discussions with the other players, I knew they were under the same tension. All of us were looking over our shoulder to see if Red was there. To be benched in San Francisco was like committing sin; none of us wanted to fall into that category. Even to this day, they still talk about ". . . the time Y.A. was benched." I can't get away from this stigma although it all happened years ago.

I am not blaming anyone in particular for this situation. This is just the way it was in San Francisco in 1960. I am sure Red Hickey never stood up and said to the press, "I am benching Tittle." Red was not that kind of a man. I think he tried to protect his ball-players. Maybe not because he worried about their sensitivity so much, but because he was aware that happy ballplayers win more games. The truth of the matter is that with the Forty-Niners that year, you were either playing or you were "benched." There wasn't any in-between.

And on November 22, when we held our first practice at Georgetown University before meeting the Colts, there was no doubt about it—Y.A. Tittle was BENCHED, maybe for good.

That was the day we first heard about the new shotgun formation.

Before the workout began, Hickey gathered us around him. He took a few sheets of paper from his jacket pocket and said, "Gentlemen, we have worked out a new offensive pattern. We are going to beat the Colts with it!"

Some of us exchanged doubtful glances. Could Hickey be cracking under the strain of losing too many? More than halfway through the season was a hell of a time to change our offense. We had enough trouble learning the old one.

Red knew he had a tough selling job, so he went right to work. For over four months he had drilled the Forty-Niner ball club in the intricacies and timing of the standard T formation. Now, with only five games left on the schedule, the familiar T was to be supplanted by something called the shotgun. I have to admit that a lot of us thought our coach was more than a little mixed up.

But Hickey was serious. He drew some hasty diagrams on paper to show us what the formation looked like. Brodie and I took our first look at the shotgun. Hickey's new offense had the quarterback stationed five to seven yards behind the center, with the left end spread 10 to 15 yards from the left tackle and the right end spread three to five yards from the right tackle. The left halfback and the fullback, the two tight or running backs, were one yard outside of and a yard behind the left and right tackles, respectively. The right halfback was split far to the right, about 10 yards wider than the end on that side.

"Looks like we can get a lot of receivers down the field," I observed.

"Right," said Hickey, "but we are going to run from this thing, too. There is no limit to what we can do from such a formation."

It was obvious Red had given this thing considerable thought—which is what our situation needed at the time. Baltimore, a 16-

7

point favorite, was the defending champion and had the best defense in the league. Hickey evidently did not feel we could run the ball against Big Daddy Lipscomb, Gino Marchetti, Art Donovan and the others. The Colts were so well drilled in their 4–3 defense, however, that Red believed we could use the shotgun and spread them out and maybe move the ball on them before they could adjust.

The original plan, as I recall, was not to depend entirely on the new offense against Baltimore, but to have Brodie resort to the shotgun only when he felt it could be put to best advantage. Of course, Hickey was the one who really called the shots. As it turned out, Brodie threw the shotgun at Baltimore right away and stayed in the formation most of the game. It confused the Colts, just as Hickey had said it would, and we whipped them, 30–22, for one of the biggest upsets of the season.

The success of the shotgun both thrilled and disturbed me. It was an explosive formation, and that was my meat. But at the same time I could see it needed a quarterback who could run the football as well as throw it. Brodie was that kind of quarterback, young and strong and big. I was not the right type for the shotgun. I was 35 years old and I could not run. I could not even run when I was Brodie's age. Also, I had a bad groin muscle which made it difficult for me to even jog. I did not need a crystal ball to realize this new formation had not been designed for me.

Sitting on the bench that day in Memorial Stadium, I could see it all very clearly: If Hickey decided to stay with the shotgun, I was gone!

By the time we returned to California to play the Rams, the shotgun formation was the talk of the football world. The newspapers took over. They ran diagrams of Hickey's offense. They called it a revolutionary form of attack. Of course, it was not new. Many teams had put their quarterback in a short punt formation before. But Hickey's version apparently caught everyone's fancy. It was an overnight sensation.

In the beginning, Red may not have planned to utilize the shotgun as the backbone of the Forty-Niner offense. But now that public opinion was behind the thing, he had no other choice.

When we met the Rams at the Coliseum the following Sunday,

I was still riding the bench and Brodie was riding shotgun. The Rams were ready for the passes John threw from the spread, but they were not prepared for a strong running attack. Fullback C.R. Roberts and halfback J.D. Smith ran wild on reverses and counter plays. We won our second straight with the shotgun, 23–7.

This game, I believe, convinced everyone, particularly Red Hickey, that the shotgun was no flash in the pan offense. You could throw from it. You could run from it. And more important, you could win with it.

The shotgun worked well in the beginning because the other teams were so set in their 4–3 defenses that they had trouble making the necessary adjustments. The shotgun changed their keys, their ideas. It interrupted their 4–3 thinking.

But still the new attack was not enough to carry San Francisco to the top in 1960. Green Bay shut us out, 13–0, in the rain and mud a week later. This game may have uncovered one of the flaws in the shotgun. Many of our running plays were wide sweeps and reverses, but on the wet, slippery field it was almost impossible for our backs to keep their footing when they ran laterally. The Packers, with Jim Taylor and Paul Hornung ramming straight ahead on dive plays through the middle, adapted to the poor footing more easily.

Despite this loss, however, and our 7–5 finish that season, the shotgun had instilled new hope for the future—new hope for San Francisco, that is, not Y.A. Tittle.

CHAPTER TWO

"I'LL NEVER PLAY IN
NEW YORK!"

THE SPRING OF 1961 was a period of great indecision and uncertainty for me.

While Red Hickey and the San Francisco organization put their time and efforts into building a ball club that would conform to the new offense, rumors abounded that I was to be traded to make room for backs who could make the shotgun formation click.

The Forty-Niners took the first step along these lines when they drafted Billy Kilmer, an All-American tailback from U.C.L.A. The acquisition of Kilmer, a big, strong runner who could throw the option pass, was yet another indication that Hickey meant to stay with the shotgun. Kilmer seemed to be the kind of player who would complement John Brodie perfectly as the deep man in the formation.

That off-season was a terrible ordeal for me. I felt more expendable each day.

I was torn between two emotions: hurt pride and determination, with perhaps a little anger thrown in for good measure. My pride was damaged because of the way I had finished the previous season, riding the bench with an injury, completely lost in the hysteria of the shotgun, the new trend in pro football offense. People knew I had been injured but no one seemed to remember it. They didn't seem to want to recall that I was the Forty-Niners' starting quarterback against Chicago the day I was injured. All they talked about was that "Tittle was benched!"

It was galling. At times I said, "The hell with it, Yat. Quit this damned game. You have been at it too long anyway."

But the next instant I'd get stubborn: "Come back for another year and show them you're still a good quarterback," I'd tell myself. "Don't let them shotgun you out of football."

Not a day passed that I didn't fight this battle with myself. Sometimes it went on far into the night. I was in a turmoil, and lost a lot of sleep over it.

Finally, I decided to get away from San Francisco for a while, away from the rumors; from the newspapers; away from the whole darned mess. I packed my wife and our three children into the car and drove to Las Vegas for a short vacation. Minnette and the kids had been under a strain too. Since the end of the 1960 season I couldn't have been easy to live with. The rest would do us all good.

The second day in Vegas, I bumped into Elroy Hirsch, the general manager of the Los Angeles Rams. I had known and admired Crazylegs for many years when he was a great end with the Rams.

Elroy and I were not what you would call close friends. But we did have a great deal of respect for one another, the kind of respect that is bred in a game like football where a man continually is put to the test.

I was playing golf—not very well, I might add—when Hirsch ambled up with that boyish grin of his and asked, "What brings you to Las Vegas, Y.A.?"

I told him I needed a little vacation. "Besides," I said, "I had to get away from all those stories about the Forty-Niners trying to get rid of me so Hickey can put in the shotgun on a full-time basis."

"I'm glad you brought that up," Hirsch said.

"Why?"

He answered my question with one of his own.

"Would you be interested in playing for the Rams?"

This caught me completely by surprise. There had been a lot of trade rumors, to be sure, but somehow going to Los Angeles had never occurred to me. But I recovered quickly enough to answer.

"Yes, I would, Elroy."

I still wanted that one last chance to prove myself, to prove I was not washed up as a pro. And if the Forty-Niners were not going to give me that opportunity, then I'd prefer to remain on the West Coast and play for the Rams.

The one thing I did not want to do was to go back East. I couldn't. My insurance business in Palo Alto, Calif., was going good, and it would be unfair to leave my partner, Milton Iverson, to run the show by himself. At least while I was with San Francisco I could give him a hand once in a while. If I left the West Coast, Milt would be all alone, and that would be asking a lot of him. Nor did the prospect of leaving Minnette and the youngsters and our comfortable home in Atherton, Calif., appeal to me greatly.

No, I wanted nothing to do with an Eastern club. I felt I was too old, and had been playing too many years, to make such a radical change at that stage.

I even went so far as to tell Hirsch, "I'll never play in New York or anywhere else. I'll quit if they send me back East."

Elroy cautioned me to say nothing about our informal conversation. He said he would first have to contact the Forty-Niners through official channels before anything could be done. He said he just had wanted to make certain that I would play for his club if a deal could be made with Red Hickey.

"I still want to play for the Forty-Niners, Elroy," I said, levelling with him. "But if they are going to trade me, well, then I would like to play for Los Angeles."

"Fair enough," he said. "You will be hearing from me, I hope."

Back home in Atherton, I waited for something to break, maybe a decision by the Forty-Niners to keep me, or trade me to the Rams. But the weeks slipped by and nothing happened. Meanwhile, in San Francisco, the rumors persisted that I was on my way.

One day I said to Minnette, "I've had enough of this. I am going down to see Hickey and Morabito. I'm going to find out what's happening."

"Don't you think you ought to wait just a little longer?" she asked. Minnette was as upset as I about the situation, but I guess she was afraid of my going off half-cocked and saying something that I shouldn't.

12

"I have waited long enough," I said. "This thing has been eating away at me, honey. I have to go and see them."

I called the Forty-Niner office and arranged an appointment for the next morning.

Vic Morabito, who owned the ball club, was in Hickey's office when I arrived. I was hardly in a mood for cat-and-mouse games, so I came right to the point.

"What's the story, Red?" I asked. "Where do I stand with your football team?"

I felt better as soon as I got this question off my chest.

To his credit, Hickey levelled with me. That's the kind of a guy he is, and like him or not, you have to respect him for his honesty and straight-forward attitude.

"I'm going to be honest with you, Y.A." he said. "We might make a trade for you if we can work things out with Los Angeles. They seem interested in you."

"That's good," I answered, "because I will retire if you try to trade me back East."

Then I asked him, "What if you can't make a deal, what then?"

"We are planning to go all the way with the shotgun, Y.A. I guess you know that by now."

I nodded. How could I help but know it? It had been in the papers every day for a couple of months. Shotgun . . . shotgun . . . shotgun, that's all anyone heard around San Francisco in the Spring of 1961.

"If you want to play more football, you will just have to come to training camp and take your chances. That's all I can tell you right now. I can't make any promises."

So, that's how things stood!

"We will let you know if anything develops on the Los Angeles trade," he concluded.

I felt relieved, as well as hurt, when I walked out of the Forty-Niners' office. At least now everything was out in the open. They *were* trying to peddle me. Okay, if they traded me to the Rams I would go. If they tried to ship me anywhere else, I wouldn't. I could quit and go into the insurance business full time. I felt that I had held up my end pretty well during my showdown meeting with Hickey and Morabito, but as I left the office, I don't mind

13

admitting I had the blues. After years of being part of the San Francisco organization, I suddenly felt alone and on the outside. This had been *my* ball club; now it no longer wanted me or needed me. I was trade-bait, nothing more. It hurt.

A pro athlete has to get used to hurting—physically or mentally. So after a bit I shook off my depression. I was determined I would play football again, maybe for the Forty-Niners, maybe for the Rams. But I sure would play again in 1961. I wasn't going to be counted out without a fight. I had spent too many of my years in competition to throw in the towel—especially in the off-season.

Once I had made up my mind, I set out to work myself into condition. This was important for a 35-year-old guy who, in a few months, would be battling for survival against a lot of younger and stronger men. I worked harder and longer than at anytime in my life. I had a goal now and it gave me renewed hope and determination.

Of course, I was still plagued by the groin injury from 1960, and this worried me. It had not improved much, even with repeated treatments, and at times I found myself wondering if my leg would ever be strong again. I was afraid that I would go to Los Angeles after they had given up a top ballplayer for me, and then wouldn't be able to play enough to give them a fair return.

Injuries are a part of football and I had learned to live with them. Most injuries can be worked off by playing, by getting in there and being hit a few times. At least I had found it so in my case. This groin thing, though, was more troublesome. I hoped it would clear up by itself, as so many of my other muscle strains had. This time, there was no way for me to be sure until I put it to the test in a scrimmage. And, in April of 1961, the nearest scrimmage was four months away.

Physically, I was able to cope with things. I ran hard. I put myself on a strict diet. I built up my endurance and wind. I played two or three sets of tennis a day. After a month or so, I was in perfect condition. I was lean and hard and my legs, despite the tender muscle, were sound. The way I felt, I could have played a ball game then and there!

Psychologically, it was another story. I had heard nothing from either the Forty-Niners or the Rams. My status was still a mystery

14

and this troubled me deeply. Uncertainty is an awful thing. It's like trying to fight an invisible opponent; there is nothing for a fellow to lash out at.

I did not know what to say when my friends asked, "What's going to happen this season, Yat?"

As the training season approached, the San Francisco papers started loading up the shotgun again. Long before we went to camp, they had John Brodie as the No. 1 boy. Kilmer was being hailed as the ideal back for Red Hickey's new offense. Tittle? Why, everyone knows old Y.A. can't run, and you've got to be able to run in the shotgun. Right?

It was as right as it was discouraging. But I had made up my mind to give it another try, so I pretended to ignore all the palaver.

When I reported to camp at St. Mary's College in July, I was ready, I mean ready, to play football. I checked in at 194 pounds, my high school playing weight. My legs were in good condition. And my arm had never felt stronger.

But I was like a rookie looking over his shoulder, wondering when he is going to be cut. I still kept expecting to hear that I had been traded to Los Angeles but until that word came, if it was to come, I was going to give them one helluva run for their money. The shotgun was a very big thing in camp that summer, of course, but I had met challenges before, challenges from Adrian Burk in Baltimore, and Frankie Albert, Earl Morrall and now Brodie in San Francisco. Looking back over the years, it seems there always was at least one crisis for me every season. Now it was Hickey's shotgun.

Every day I told myself, "They are not going to run you off with this shotgun thing. Hang in there."

In retrospect, and I could be way off base here, I sometimes think the Forty-Niners were somewhat embarrassed by my presence in camp that summer. Hickey was undeniably committed to the shotgun at that point, and everyone who had any sense at all knew there was no place in this kind of an attack for an old quarterback with bad legs, a quarterback who couldn't play anything but the T.

But I kept throwing the ball every day anyway. And I was throwing it real well, too, as well as Brodie, better than Kilmer,

15

better than anyone else at St. Mary's. Hickey himself admitted that.

So the tension grew. I now began to feel that Hickey did not want to trade me to Los Angeles, fearing I might come back to haunt the Forty-Niners. At the same time, my presence was creating pressure on Brodie. It was well known that John was the fair-haired boy for 1961, and as long as I was on the scene it was making the situation rather awkward. I sensed the Forty-Niners might have breathed a little easier if I were not around. Of course, I am merely surmising that this was their attitude. No one ever came right out and told me these things. Brodie had finished the 1960 season in fine style, winning three of four games in the new shotgun, and so maybe Hickey and his staff were completely justified in regarding John as their No. 1 quarterback. I had no argument with Brodie. Pro football is a competitive proposition. There is nothing personal between the athletes. If you are good enough, you stay on top. If not, someone else gets the job. There is no malice involved when one player beats out another for a position. At least I never bore any resentment toward a rival quarterback. Maybe I would not be rooting for him to take my job, but I never hated him for trying. It's the nature of the sport. I accepted that fact a long time ago.

There were four quarterbacks in camp, Brodie, Kilmer, a youngster named Bob Watters, and myself. Coach Hickey never treated me as anything more than "just another of the quarterbacks." Our daily relationship was cordial but strained. I suspected then, as I do to this day, that I was a thorn in his side. I was in good shape and I was, to use Cecil Isbell's expression, "Throwing the hell out of the football." I am certain this upset Red's timetable concerning the shotgun formation.

I am also sure that Hickey rather would have played any of the other three quarterbacks during San Francisco's pre-season schedule. But I had looked so strong in camp that when we went to Portland, Ore., to play the New York Giants, he named Brodie and me as the quarterbacks. I guess he had no other choice at the time, even though he probably felt my presence was serving no purpose but to hinder his eventual transition from the T formation to the shotgun.

The pre-game strategy against the Giants was to have Brodie

open the game and run the shotgun at them. Then I would play the second half from the standard T formation.

This latter consideration was no doubt a concession Red was forced to make in view of my passing in the Forty-Niners' two intra-squad scrimmage sessions.

Brodie started the ball game and gave the Giants their first look at the shotgun. Ray Norton, the Olympic sprinter who was a rookie with us that year, surprised New York on a deep reverse in the opening minute of play and went 29 yards for a touchdown. Boy, did he fly! In the second period, Brodie threw a short touchdown pass to Clyde Conner. But otherwise the shotgun did not exactly panic the Giants' defensive unit, which at that time was one of the best in the game. Sam Huff, Dick Modzelewski, Andy Robustelli and the others did a fairly good job against our new offense. If Hickey had expected to rattle the New York veterans with the shotgun, he was mistaken. Except for Norton's opening blast around end and several pass completions by Brodie, the shotgun did not sweep the Giant defense out of Multnomah Stadium that night.

The Giants led by 14–13 at halftime but apparently Hickey wanted more shotgun. When the third period got under way, Brodie was at quarterback and I was still on the bench.

New York added another touchdown for a 21–13 lead and that's how it stood when Red waved me off the bench and sent me in at the start of the final period. I had just fifteen minutes to play my hand.

The ball was on the San Francisco 34-yard line. I sent Bernie Casey up the middle on a trap for six yards. Next J. D. Lockett went around right end for nine yards. Then I completed a 15-yarder to Lockett. We were moving. From the Giants' 32-yard line, Lockett swept right end for a touchdown. Tommy Davis converted and we trailed by one point, 21–20. I was elated over our making a score three and a half minutes after I had taken over.

I had the club moving for the winning touchdown later in the period when one of my passes intended for Monty Stickles was intercepted by Erich Barnes, and our threat ended.

Still I had a good fourth period against the Giants. If I remember right, I completed six of seven passes for 84 yards. I missed my first

17

attempt, a short throw to Stickles when I came into the game, and after that I hit six straight. Just as the final gun sounded, I hit R. C. Owens with a long pass and he almost broke into the clear.

I can't say how impressive my performance against the Giants really was. But the next day the San Francisco papers splashed the trade business across the headlines again. There seemed to be two schools of thought on my personal situation. One was that I had showed so well in the brief time I had played at Portland that Hickey wouldn't dare trade me. The other was that I had done too well and, by staying, I would only put more pressure on Brodie, thereby creating an uneasy situation for Hickey and Morabito.

I think trading me became a necessity. I must be removed to allow Brodie and the shotgun complete freedom. If the Forty-Niners did not peddle me, one newspaper article said, Hickey might be forced to keep the T formation because of my good luck with it against the Giants.

I thought about my predicament on the trip back to St. Mary's. Since reporting to training camp in mid-July, I had given it my best. Yet, my position was no more secure than it had been during the off-season. The tension began to build up again and it was hard to live with. I hoped to remain a part of the San Francisco organization. This had, after all, been my entire existence for the past nine years. But I had no desire to remain under these conditions. Sometimes I felt that I was actually resented. I had now reached the stage where I wanted something to happen, anything to clear the air. Football had always been fun for me; that's why I was still playing at the age of 35. There was, however, no fun or enjoyment in this kind of a situation. It had become a war of nerves, and I was sick of it.

As I have said there was absolutely no feeling of malice on my part toward Red Hickey or the other coaches. I believed then, and I still do, that Red and the others were doing what they thought best for their ball club. I understood this and I respected Hickey for making the decisions he thought would make the Forty-Niners a winning team.

Quite unintentionally, I had backed Hickey into a hot corner with my strong showing against the Giants. It was obvious from

18

that game that I had a lot of touchdown passes left in my right arm. Red was in something of a dilemma, and everyone was waiting to see what he'd do to solve the problem. That included the problem—me.

I soon found out.

CHAPTER THREE

SHOTGUNNED OUT OF 'FRISCO

"RED WANTS to see you in his office."

Chico, the Forty-Niners' colorful equipment man, sounded almost apologetic. He shuffled his feet nervously as I glanced up from the breakfast table at St. Mary's. Chico obviously was the bearer of bad tidings, and he had no stomach for the job.

I couldn't blame him either. Over the years I had seen a lot of players get the message. It was always the same: "Coach so and so wants to see you." There was no tactful way to put it. Somehow, everyone felt it, knew it. . . .

The touch of Chico's hand on my shoulder sent a chill through me. Somehow, ballplayers usually manage to convince themselves that bad news is always for the next guy and not them.

I had prepared myself, or at least I thought I had, for this very moment. All Spring the uneasy trade situation had been always with me. I had convinced myself it would come and that when it happened I would take it in stride, as I had taken other bad moments in my career.

The Forty-Niner players sitting near me at the breakfast table suddenly seemed to be miles away. They knew what was about to happen. They had been waiting almost as long as I had for the other shoe to drop. But it was evident they had no desire to become emotionally involved. This is the way it is in professional sports, and

20

I accepted their detached attitude that morning. A fellow's first responsibility in such a highly competitive game is to himself. You feel sorry when the breaks go against a teammate. But you sure don't want to trade places with him.

It is amazing how fast a training camp dormitory can empty out when the news is flashed that someone, especially a veteran, is about to be traded or released. No one wants to sit around there and watch a friend pack his suitcase and walk out the door. What can you say to a guy at a time like that? "See you around, old buddy" or maybe, "Good luck now." No, the easy way is to be somewhere else when bad news arrives, or else pretend you don't hear it. Then the break is clean and you don't become part of something you can't change, can't help.

Chico was still standing there, so I took off my glasses, got up from the table and followed him down the hall toward Hickey's office. It was on the same floor as the dining room but I found myself wishing it were farther away. I wanted a few more seconds to gather my thoughts and bring my emotions under control. I needed time to prepare Y.A. Tittle's case.

Which is silly, I told myself, because this wasn't going to be a trial. It was an open and shut case. I was going—that's all there was to it.

One look at Hickey's face as I walked into his room was enough to tell me it was all over.

"Well, Y.A.," he said, "it has finally happened."

He seemed relieved to get it off his chest.

I said nothing. There didn't seem to be anything to say. I just waited for him to continue.

"We have just traded you to the New York Giants for Lou Cordileone."

Just like that, I thought. And then I asked myself, "Who is Lou Cordileone?" I smiled. Christmas, they hadn't even gotten a name ballplayer for old Y.A.

Hickey was waiting for me to say something.

"Well, that's fine," I replied rather stupidly because I did not think it was fine at all. Not for a minute. . . .

Red went on.

21

"I have talked to the Giants. They need you and they are very happy to get you. I want you to understand that. They have Charlie Conerly but don't feel they can get a whole season out of him at his age."

"I will admit you have been throwing the ball better than anyone in camp," Hickey said. "But we need a guard desperately so we traded for Cordileone."

Tittle for a guard named Cordileone. Boy, that took me down a peg!

There was another brief period of silence and then Hickey said, "I want you to know, Y.A., that there is nothing personal in this. It's the breaks of the game."

Red sounded like he was apologizing. If so, I didn't want to hear about it. I interrupted him.

"I realize this is part of football, Red, and I don't blame you. I can't say that I like being traded. But if I were in your shoes maybe I would do the same thing. You are the coach. I will never hold this against you personally. I know you too well to think you would ever make a trade or do anything else to jeopardize your ball club. Forget it."

Hickey seemed surprised. I guess he had expected me to react differently to the news of the trade.

As I was leaving, I turned to Hickey and asked, "Do you mind if I talk to the squad before I leave?"

"Certainly not," he said.

Looking back, I honestly don't know what prompted me to make such a request. Perhaps it was because I did not want a lot of talk going around about my being traded. I am not the kind who wants sympathy. I would rather have anything in the world than someone feeling sorry for me. I had gotten too much out of the game to have anyone claiming I had gotten a bum deal from the Forty-Niners. I didn't want them thinking I was a quarterback broke and broken-down. Football players had been traded before me and they would be traded after I was gone too. This is the pattern of existence in pro football. I was no different than the next guy in that respect. My ten years with San Francisco did not excuse me from the possibility of being dealt to another ball team. But I

22

realized too—and with no sense of self-importance—that my career in San Francisco had made me something of a fixture with the fans and the players, and my reason for talking to the squad was to leave everything in good order—on both sides.

As I went back to my room, I must confess I was darn near bawling. I hadn't let Hickey know how deeply this business had affected me. But alone in my room, packing my bags, I almost broke down.

I had no idea what I was going to say to the Forty-Niner squad in a few minutes. I did find myself wishing I had not opened my mouth and asked Hickey to get the players together. But I finished my packing, took a last look around the dorm that had been my summer home for a lot of years, and walked out the door. My car was parked right near the entrance. I threw the suitcases into the back seat and then I drove over to the practice field, a few hundred yards away.

As I walked across the practice field, I was immediately aware of an excited buzz sweeping through the players. I was in civvies, and they all knew what that meant. You never see a ballplayer in street clothes at practice unless he is hurt, or on his way out. And I was not hurt.

Hickey blew his whistle and yelled. "Okay, everybody up!"

I looked around at the players. I was groping for the right words and, again, I wished I hadn't got myself involved in this scene.

Finally I got going.

"Fellows, I guess you all know by now that I have just been traded to the New York Giants. This is part of being a professional athlete. I don't like it any more than you would. But I accept it. I hope none of you will feel sorry for me. I don't need sympathy." It was so quiet, my words seemed to echo in the air.

I took a breath, tried to sense their reaction and wound up again. I hoped I didn't sound corny.

"I have gotten everything a man can get from football. San Francisco has been good to me. I owe everything to the Forty-Niners and to the Morabitos. I don't want any of you, despite your personal feelings, to hold this thing against Red Hickey or his staff. They have only done what they think is best for the Forty-Niners,

23

for you fellows. Maybe if the situation were reversed, I would make the same move Red made today.

"That's all I have to say except goodbye, good luck, and thanks."

It is well I ended my talk then and there, for I was beginning to choke up. I looked around the circle of players and spotted R.C. Owens and J.D. Smith. Both of them were crying. This surprised me a little because we had never been that close, I mean really close where one guy cries when the other leaves. But they had tears in their eyes just the same, and it darned near broke me up. I had not wanted this thing to deteriorate into a sob scene. All I had hoped to achieve was to make certain no one was feeling sorry for old Y.A., and that my friends on the squad wouldn't hold any resentment toward Red Hickey or Vic Morabito. Ballplayers are apt to consider only one side of an issue. I knew an emotional outburst caused by my exit could stir up dissension in the club.

And again, the last thing I wanted was sympathy. I have always been this way.

If I am bald-headed, I don't want folks feeling sorry for me because I am bald-headed. I had been traded. I didn't like it one bit. But I hoped to walk out of camp a big man. I wanted to impress on the Forty-Niners that I was leaving with no regrets, with no ill feeling, with no alibis. As I pointed out to them that day, football has been good to me. It has given me friends, prestige, money, security. A man can't ask much more.

After I finished talking, I felt I had said more than I had intended to say. I shook hands with most of the players and said goodbye. I could tell many of them were deeply moved. Part of the emotion came, I guess, from their putting themselves in my place. Some didn't look me in the eye; they stared at the ground when we shook hands. A few started to say something but changed their minds.

Feeling the thing had gone too far, I wrapped it up quick and walked across the field to my car.

It was all over now. I was an ex-Forty-Niner. I was gone.

Just down the road from St. Mary's I stopped at a roadside phone and called Minnette. I hoped to break the news to her before she heard it on radio or television. It was bound to be a big story in San Francisco that afternoon.

"Why aren't you practicing?" she asked almost before I could say hello. "Are you hurt, Y.A.?"

"Nothing except my pride, honey," I said. "They have just traded me to New York."

There was silence at the other end of the line. Then I heard her voice again.

"Well, Y.A., what now?"

"I don't know . . . I really don't. We'll talk it over when I get home."

"When are you coming?"

"Right now, honey. There's nothing left for me here. I'm all through."

The drive south along U.S. 1 to Palo Alto takes about an hour. I was grateful for this time to myself. A thousand thoughts were tumbling through my brain. I needed time to come up with some answers. My future was at stake. I wanted to make the right move. I had to. I knew I could depend on Minnette to go with whatever decision I made. She is a wonderful woman, strong and understanding. Her encouragement has been a great comfort to me over the troubled years of my professional football career. She would be with me all the way; of that I was sure. That was a great comfort at such an emotional time. Still, the final decision would have to be mine.

On one hand, I had some money, a pretty secure position and friends. There really was nothing to worry about. On the other, here I was driving away from the Forty-Niners' camp and although this thing had not come as a bolt out of the blue, the finality of it was just setting in. My pride was hurt. My own ball club had sent me away. For ten long years I had been the Forty-Niner quarterback, and now they no longer felt I was good enough.

I had been shotgunned out of 'Frisco.

As I neared home, I still had not made up my mind whether to quit or to play for New York, something I had sworn I would never do.

The thought of leaving the West Coast bothered me. But then again I was not entirely certain I was ready to step down either.

"You are NOT washed up," I kept telling myself.

When the possibility of the trade first arose, I had hoped to go to Los Angeles if I went anywhere. It had not worked out that way, however, and now the alternatives were clear to me: retire, or go to New York.

Rosewood Street, normally peaceful and quiet, was the scene of unusual activity as I pulled up in front of the house. A group of men were clustered around the door. Right away I knew they were reporters and photographers up from San Francisco.

Obviously the word was out.

As I shouldered my way toward the door, they closed in on me.

"What are you going to do, Yat?"

"You said you would never go East. Will you stick with it?"

"Give us something, Y.A."

I smiled. How was I going to tell them anything when at that very moment I had no idea about what I was going to do?

"Give me a few minutes, fellows," I asked. "I've got to talk it over with my wife first."

"Okay, Yat, but remember—we're on a deadline."

Inside I found Minnette with her mother and father, Mr. and Mrs. Walter Risch, who were visiting us that week. Minnette smiled but it was a worried smile and I sensed she felt worse about the situation than she was letting on.

The phone rang incessantly and by this time Minnette had let some of the reporters into the living room. The place was a bedlam. Minnette and I slipped into a back bedroom and closed the door. I had promised the reporters an answer in a few minutes. Now Minnette and I looked at each other. She seemed to be searching for an answer in my eyes. She was wringing her hands and obviously was under a strain. This was the first time in almost ten years that the normal happy routine of our lives had been upset. We suddenly found ourselves at an important crossroads. The decision we were about to make could change our lives radically.

"I said I would never go if they traded me to any team but the Rams," I told her. "I don't want to either . . . but."

"I know," she said. "You would like to show them all, wouldn't you?"

"Yes, I would. But I don't know if it's the right thing. I mean leaving you and the kids and Milt and the business. Damned if I know what to do."

Just then Minnette's mother walked into the room. One look was enough to tell her we had not arrived at a solution.

She said, "Well, if you two are worrying about the children, don't. I will be glad to stay here and take care of them. It will give me a chance to spoil them a bit. Minnette can join you in New York in a month or so, Y.A., and then we will send the youngsters back for a week at Thanksgiving."

Grandma made it sound pretty good.

My family is the most important thing in my life. My big objection to going with an Eastern team had been the thought of breaking up my home for six months a year. Minnette and the kids come first, before football, before business, before anything! Maybe some people think I am old-fashioned in this respect, but that's the way I am. I don't give a hoot for anything if it interferes with my family. I was raised in a happy home, one filled with love and understanding. I have tried to pattern my own home along these lines.

But Minnette's mother had offered a workable solution to a football player's dilemma, and now I had to consider the New York trade in a different light. If Minnette and the kids could be with me part of the time, well, maybe it might just work after all. I could play another year (I never seriously thought of playing any longer), show 'em old Yat still could play some, see the sights of New York and retire after the 1961 season.

And I was in such good shape! That was part of it too. I was ready to play football, and if the Forty-Niners didn't want me playing for them, perhaps the Giants would. I never had been in better condition. It seemed a shame to waste all the work I had done to prepare myself for the 1961 season. My groin injury still worried me but not enough to change the course of my thinking. And I knew I could help the New York Giants. I asked Minnette, "How about it, honey, shall we give it a try?"

She smiled, a relieved smile now, and I knew what her answer would be even before she said, "Okay, Y.A., whatever you say."

That was it. We were off on a new adventure.

I opened the door and walked into the living room. The writers and photographers were on their feet in a second. They had been waiting for over two hours, and were impatient to get their stories.

"What will it be, Y.A.?" they asked in chorus.

"I have decided to report to the Giants," I said. "I am going to give it a try. San Francisco is my town, but I am going to New York."

After the writers had gone, I slumped down on the sofa. I was weary, mentally and physically. It seemed like a year ago that Chico had tapped me on the shoulder and said, "Red wants to see you . . ." But it had been barely three hours earlier. . . . So many things had happened to change my life.

The phone rang. Minnette answered it. She cupped her hand over the mouthpiece, turned to me and said, "It's Allie Sherman. He is calling from Oregon."

As it developed, Sherman, the Giants' coach, had been trying to track me down all day, ever since the trade story broke. He had missed me at St. Mary's. Then he had been unable to get through to my home because of all the newspapers calling.

I was anxious to talk with Sherman. I wanted to know where I stood with the Giants. I had just left one bad quarterback situation with San Francisco, and I didn't want to walk into a similar predicament with Charlie Conerly in New York.

Allie sounded very pleasant and after we had exchanged greetings and he said he was very happy to have me, I told him what was on my mind.

"Am I just an insurance quarterback in your plans, Allie, or do I get a chance to play?"

I was not asking for the starting job. In fact, I did not even expect to play all the time. But I did want a shot at playing some of the time. I didn't care to be like so many other players who had been behind me—just sitting there on the bench, or maybe holding the ball for extra points, practically spectators. I now wanted to play a year with the Giants. But I was damned if I was going to continue football as a bench-warmer.

Sherman's answer was right to the point.

"You'll get all the football you want with the Giants, Y.A.," he said. "Conerly is my quarterback right now but I have an open mind. The best man will play. Besides, we have some concern that Charlie can go all the way at his age."

We talked a little while longer and then Sherman said, "Remember, I didn't trade for you to sit you on the bench. We want to win this thing and we think you can do it for us, you and Charlie.

I felt better after my conversation with Sherman, who seemed to be every bit as sharp as they said he was.

I had never gone to a football team with any idea except to play quarterback, and now I felt the Giants were giving me the opportunity that the shotgun had denied me with the Forty-Niners. Sherman seemed to believe there was some football left in old Y.A. I agreed—and wanted to prove it.

A few minutes before, my future had been clouded and uncertain. Now everything was clear.

The phone rang again, and this time it was Frank Gifford calling from his home in Bakersfield, Calif. Gifford, an all-pro halfback with the Giants for many years, had retired after the 1960 season and was doing some television work on the West Coast. We had been friends for many years and it was good to hear his voice.

(Little did I realize as I spoke to Frank that he would make a comeback in pro football the following year, and that he and I would have roles in two straight eastern division championships for the Giants.)

Gifford told me almost the same things Sherman had said earlier.

"Charlie Conerly is my closest friend, Y.A., but I don't believe he can do it by himself this year. The Giants definitely need another experienced quarterback. They need you!"

Frank's call buoyed my spirits even more. Yesterday I would not have gone to New York for all the money in the world. Now I could hardly wait.

Minnette helped me pack my bags the next morning, as she had done so many times over the years, and then she drove me to the San Francisco Airport, where I caught a plane to Portland, Ore.

I looked at my watch as I fastened the seat belt. It was eight o'clock, just twenty four hours since I had stepped through the doorway into Red Hickey's office at St. Mary's College. Events had moved swiftly.

For better or for worse I was on my way to becoming a Giant!

CHAPTER FOUR

A STRANGER IN CAMP

EVEN WITHOUT PUSHING, I made the 65-mile drive from Portland to Salem in five minutes!

But lest anyone get the idea I am a speed demon, let me explain. Portland was on Pacific Standard Time and Salem was on Pacific Daylight Time. So it was twelve noon when I rented a car and drove out of the airport, and it was five after twelve when I arrived at Willamette University, where the Giants had their camp.

Sixty-five miles in five minutes!

Things were still moving fast!

The day was warm and lazy and I was struck by the beauty of the Willamette campus. Everything was peaceful and quiet. Big and very old trees stood along the stone walks, spreading their shade across bright green lawns that formed the center of the school's quadrangle.

I found it difficult to believe this was the training camp of a professional football team.

"But it is, Y.A., old boy," I reminded myself, ". . . so get your butt moving. You are here to play football, not to admire the scenery."

Someone pointed out a dormitory at the end of the quadrangle and said, "That's where the Giants are staying. It's a girls' dorm, but they are all home on vacation now."

"I am glad to hear that," I said.

I parked my rented car behind the dormitory and lugged two suitcases around to the front. It was lunch time, so I knew the club would be in the dining hall, wherever that was.

Suddenly I feel a strangeness come over me as I stand there on the steps. Why, I don't rightly know. But I am aware of an uneasy feeling in the pit of my stomach, like a kid going to school for the first time or something. I was a Giant now. The papers had said so this morning, and Allie Sherman had told me over the phone. But I sure don't feel like one at this very minute. I am more like a visitor. This was to be my first meeting with the Giants off the football field. There had been plenty of run-ins with them *on* the field, but now I am frankly worried because I had heard this was not an easy ball club to get to know. It was an older ball team with set ways and a lot of guys who had played together for a lot of years. I understood; some fellows are never accepted, I mean really accepted, by these Giants and that bothers me. I know it isn't going to be just a matter of walking in and saying, "Hi, boys, old Y.A. is here so everything's going to be okay." No sir, it doesn't figure to be that simple with the New York Giants.

Standing there in front of the dormitory at Willamette, it dawns on me that I really don't know anybody on the Giants except Billy Stits. He was with the Forty-Niners briefly. I hadn't been very close to Billy, but right now I was anxious to see him—one familiar face among the strange ones. This first meeting with the Giants is a big moment for me. I won't go so far as to say they are a cliquish bunch. But they are an older team, as I have said, and they are a harder bunch for a newcomer, or even an oldtimer like myself, to crack. Much harder, say, than San Francisco. With the Forty-Niners it is different. A new guy comes along, everybody says "hello," and the next thing you know he's sitting there playing cards like he'd been around for years. We didn't have any leaders with the Forty-Niners, so it was easy to become one of the gang.

With the Giants, well, it is another thing. The defensive guys, I hear, are a unit all their own, Robustelli and Huff and those fellows. They don't give a hoot or a holler for the offense or anyone else. Hard to crack? I'll say they are. They haven't had a new face in their group for four years. There is a saying around the National Football League that a rookie is just wasting his time if he is trying to make the Giants' defensive team. Boy, that's a closed corporation, and don't you forget it! And on the offense, here is Charlie Conerly and Pat Summerall, and of course here is Kyle Rote and Alex Webster and all the rest. They have been playing together for years, maybe as long as ten or twelve years and no newcomer is going to walk in and make himself at home. anxious to know *their* thinking too.

There is no resentment toward me. I am pretty sure of that. But neither is there a reception committee with signs reading: "WEL-COME, Y.A."

"You going to stand out there all day, or do you want to have some lunch?"

Allie Sherman was standing in the doorway and his voice jolted me out of my daydreaming. I felt embarrassed as I fumbled with my luggage and hurried up the steps to shake hands with my new coach. I wondered how long he had been watching me.

My first meal with the Giants could hardly be called a memorable event. Sherman sat me down with him and we talked some football. Then he turned me over to Don Heinrich, who was the back-field coach, and we talked more football, nothing very technical, just general stuff. I suspected they were feeling me out. I was anxious to know *their* thinking too.

Billy Stits came over and said hello after lunch. But there was not much response from the other Giant players. Most of them acted as if I weren't even there.

Heinrich helped me find a room and then we drove downtown for a beer and talked football again. Heinrich had a reputation as a sharp young football mind, and I quickly saw why. He had a wonderful grasp of offensive football. He had played as the No. 2 man behind Conerly for a few years and then he had been with Eddie LeBaron at Dallas. He was younger than me but he knew his stuff.

Don drove me back to Willamette and left to attend an afternoon coaches meeting. I looked around for some of the Giants. I figured this was as good a time as any to introduce myself around the squad. But there wasn't a soul in sight. The campus was like a cemetery. The Giants were on one-a-day practices at this point and the fel-lows had the afternoons pretty much to themselves. They had

33

disappeared completely, which is not unusual for football players on a one-a-day schedule.

So I walked up to my room, which was directly across the hall from Lee Grosscup's, and I sat down. And there I sat, staring at the wall, waiting for someone to drop in and say hello, wondering if I had, after all, made the right decision in joining the Giants.

After a while I got up and closed the door. I was embarrassed to have people see me sitting there reading the paper—all by myself with my glasses and my bald head.

It is customary in most professional football training camps for the ballplayers to pile into cars an hour or so before dinner and ride into town for a couple of beers. It breaks up the routine of camp life and besides, with meetings scheduled after dinner, there seldom is a chance to get to town later on. With Baltimore and with San Francisco, I had always looked forward to these afternoon outings. They were good fun. The Giants may have been a different ball team in a great many respects but I was certain they adhered to this daily ritual in training camp.

So there I sit, waiting, wondering if some guy will stick his head in the door and ask me to join them. But nothing happens. Nobody knows me. I am too old for the young guys to come and say, "C'mon, Y.A., let's go have a horn." I am sort of in between.

As for the veterans, well, Summerall and Rote and Webster are all Conerly's buddies and maybe they feel it would be disloyal to Charlie to just grab me and make me one of the group. Let's face it, I am a quarterback and Charlie is a quarterback and for all they know, I am here to knock him out of a job. They have nothing against me. But at the same time they are not going out of their way to make me a member of the fraternity.

And the defense? They are sort of strange anyway and I don't really expect them to make me feel at home.

I am still sitting in my room when the players head for town later that first afternoon. And I am still sitting there the next day and the day after that.

My acceptance by the Giants obviously would not be an automatic thing. My doubts grew that first night as I tried futilely to sleep. I had heard much about the Giants' great togetherness. Now I had seen it firsthand.

Nor did the situation improve greatly the next morning at practice. Nobody was bothering with me. I was just standing around in the back of the group watching things. Then Sherman says, "Get in there, Y.A., and throw a few." I believe that is the first time some of the Giants even realized I was on the field. I had my old baseball cap on and none of them was able to spot my bald head, I guess.

I tossed a couple of passes, not very well because I was nervous and tight, and everyone hollers, "Nice going, Y.A., that's the way to throw the ball." It was almost as if they did not expect me to complete a simple pass in a warm-up drill. They were trying hard to be nice as a group, and I appreciated this gesture. But individually they were still beyond me. I was in the Giants' camp but I felt like a stranger.

Next we went to a team meeting, or rather the Giants went and I tagged along. I sat there next to Conerly and Grosscup, not really knowing what was going on, as Sherman got his ball club ready for the game with the Rams down in Los Angeles later in the week. With the pressure of the game, Allie did not have much time to tutor me privately. I understood this. His first responsibility was to the team. I did not expect any special treatment. It seemed more important at the time to get Conerly ready. He was the club's meal-ticket and he would have to carry the load by himself until I learned what it was all about.

Nevertheless, I tried hard to pick up as much as I could against the time when I would be asked to step in and take over for Conerly or Grosscup.

The most difficult phase of my adjusting from San Francisco to New York was in learning the play calls. I had been with Forty-Niners for ten years and we had used the same numbering system all the way up from the time Buck Shaw had been my coach. When Red Strader took over, he kept Shaw's numbering system rather than change over. And of course Frankie Albert, having played under Shaw and Strader, also used Buck's system when he took over. So, for almost ten years, everything was the same. The odd and even numbering of the holes on the offensive line was the same; the pass terminology was the same, X and Y instead of L and R as with the Giants. In San Francisco we called our halfbacks odd and even; with the Giants we call them A and B. The flare pass in New York was known as a circle pass in San Francisco; the flare pass in Giant terminology was a swing pass to the Forty-Niners.

For me, everything with New York seemed backwards, for a time at least.

The manner of calling plays, the cadence, was different and so was the system of using automatic calls at the line of scrimmage.

It was quite a job for me during that first season with the Giants to go into a ball game and call the automatics, which is changing to a new call at the line of scrimmage by the use of key numbers or colors. Truthfully, I just couldn't automatic in the first few games. Everything had to be completely memorized, and of course in the heat and excitement of a ball game, memory is not always that reliable.

Now that I understand the Giants' system—and I must say, it took a long time—I don't have any trouble. But, boy, it was tough that first week in Salem, Ore., and later when we got back to New York. I was groping in the dark most of the time, trying my darndest to change lifetime habits and absorb a completely new system.

Let me give you one example of the problems I encountered as a quarterback with the Giants:

In all my San Francisco backfields, the left halfback was always designated as "two" and the right halfback as "four." It didn't make any difference which man was in that spot; if he was left half, he was "two" and that's all there was to it. He was "two" whether he liked it or not. But the Giants do it another way. They designate a man as the "three" back, say, Alex Webster. He is the "three" back in this formation where the flanker is out to the right. Now, if you move the flanker somewhere else, the backs stay in the same spots, but now Webster is not "three" anymore. This man over here, maybe Phil King, is now the "three" back and Webster is something else.

In San Francisco, Webster would always be the "three" back no matter what the formation was or where the flanker back was stationed. Out there it was "two" and "four"—"two" here and "four" there, and you could always count on it without even looking.

With New York—as I learned that first week in Salem—the

backs' number designations change with the formation. Webster might be a "three" back on one play and a "four" on the next play and something else on the following play. Thus, I had a difficult time trying to remember which was my "four" back because one minute it could be King and the next minute it might be Webster. All sorts of numbers were spinning around in my helmet when I tried to call a play.

Now I don't even try to figure out the number designations. I just know the overall play and what happens within it. I have been a Giant so long that I "feel" the play rather than memorizing it step by step. A slant-34 is, WHAM!, the fullback over this tackle and through the hole. I don't bother saying to myself, ". . . now this is the 'three' back going into the number four hole." I just call the play and hand the ball to Webster or King. The numbers don't worry me anymore. But they sure did in the beginning.

I was trying so hard not to make mistakes. The more I pressed, the harder it got. Pretty soon, I had a mental block. I would stand there over the center and I couldn't even remember the first thing about the play or the backs or anything. What an awful feeling, standing there with 64,000 people looking down at you and drawing a complete blank. Boy, sometimes I felt like crawling in a hole!

Learning the automatics was tough, too.

In San Francisco, we called an automatic and a fake, or phoney, automatic every now and then; with the Giants, we call an automatic or a phoney automatic on *every* play! This puts considerably more pressure on the quarterback. With the Forty-Niners we used what we called a "live" color to designate an automatic call—red, green, blue, white or some other color. We would start off in the first half with red as the "live" color. This meant that whenever the quarterback came up to the line and yelled out, "Red" an automatic call was to follow. Everyone would be on his toes when he heard the word "red." If I called "Green" it meant nothing. If I called "Blue" it was also a phoney call. But when I said "Red" they knew an automatic call was coming, and they got ready. We might come up to the line and say, "Blue, eighty-one." Nothing! "White, eighty-one." Nothing! "Red, thirty-four." That was it, a new play.

But in San Francisco we did not do this kind of stuff on every play. Sometimes we went through an entire game without using a color, live or otherwise. With the Giants we are always looking for that change off at the line of scrimmage. Everytime we come up to the line, we throw in a fake automatic number. (The Giants use numbers instead of colors.) We like to keep those defensive linemen and linebackers guessing.

In the beginning, though, I was guessing more than the defenses I was trying to fool.

There was a difference in cadence too which caused me great trouble. In San Francisco we used what is called a non-rhythm count, in other words, each play was called with a varied cadence. The tempo of the quarterback's call was always changing, speeding up, slowing down. The word "go" replaced the usual numbers in our system of cadence. If, for example, the snap number was one, it was, "Set. . . . GO!" If our snap number was three, the call might be something like this, "Ready, set . . . go . . . go. . . . GO!" The line would be moving on the third "go."

In the non-rhythm system, the cadence of this call could be varied from play to play simply by changing the timing of the interval between the "go" signals. This was good in a way because it allowed the quarterback to change his timing if the defense started moving around. For instance, if the snap number was two, I might start the call by saying, "Ready, set . . . go. . . ." Then, if I saw the defense starting to shift around, I could hesitate before calling the second "go." Sometimes this interval might be as long as three or four seconds, and by that time the defense would have to settle down in one spot. Then I could complete my call by saying, ". . . . GO!"

When I joined the Giants in Salem in August of 1961, I was exposed to an entirely different theory of calling cadence.

Every call was snapped off in the same crisp rhythm: "Hut one . . . hut two . . . hut three." No matter which quarterback was calling signals, the rhythm was always the same, or at least Allie Sherman strove to have it the same. He wanted to achieve an overall team rhythm where every man would be prepared to move at the same instant with no hesitation or indecision.

In addition to my problems of adjustment the first week I joined the Giants I was greatly concerned by the condition of my injured groin. I still did not know if it would hold up once I started playing for keeps. I strapped it like a demon every day before practice and it felt okay. I had been worried about it in Portland the week before but it had held up while I was in there in the fourth quarter. It held up, I believe, because I really didn't get hit hard that night. I wasn't hit hard enough to put my leg to the acid test. (Maybe some of those big defensive guys had word that I would be on their side in a couple of days.)

Mentally I felt I could play quarterback as good as ever as soon as I absorbed the Giants' offense. The groin was another thing. I would need two strong legs under me. I found myself wishing Sherman would schedule some contact work so I could give it a few good licks and see how it stood up.

The day we flew to Los Angeles, Sherman said to me, "How would you like to go in for a few plays tomorrow night, Y.A.?"

"Sure, Allie, but I don't know any of the plays, I mean good enough to call in a game."

"Sit next to Heinrich on the plane this afternoon," he instructed. "He will help you."

I was glad to be sitting with Heinrich on the flight to Los Angeles. First, because I wanted to make sure I knew what I would be doing the next night if Allie used me in the ball game. Second, because I still didn't know anybody. Oh, I knew the Giants well enough to say, "How are you, Alex?" or "Nice going, Charlie." But I remained on the outside for the most part, and nobody was making any overtures to me.

It was the same in Los Angeles:

The plane lands. A bus takes us to the Ambassador Hotel. It is early evening. After checking in, most of the Giant players go out to dinner. This is a tough experience for me. Here I am a 14-year veteran of the National Football League, and I am standing outside the hotel by myself while the rest of the guys walk by in groups on their way to dinner. Heinrich is the only one I really know. But he is a coach. He coaches me, leaves me in my room and goes off with Sherman and the others. I can't go with the coaches. I have got to go with the guys. But who am I to go with? No one knocks on my door to invite me to dinner; the phone doesn't ring. The fact is, I don't know anybody, so where am I going to eat? I don't

want to eat in the hotel by myself. I go downstairs and I start hanging around the entrance to the Ambassador near the parking lot.
I am just standing there and, frankly, I am quite embarrassed by
my predicament.

A couple of guys come out of the hotel and they see me there.
It is kind of hard to get around me because I am standing right
in front of them, so they have to say something.

"Where you going, Y.A.?"

"Oh, I am waiting on somebody, fellows."

Of course this is not the case. Actually, I am trying to figure out
what to do with myself. I am hoping the fresh air in the parking
lot will clear my head and make it easier.

It is downright humiliating. Here I am waiting on somebody
who isn't going to show. Oh, I know some folks in Los Angeles but
I don't feel like calling them. I want to be with the Giants this
night.

The players are still filing out of the Ambassador, walking right
by me, and now I hear one of them say, "Everyone is down at the
Bull and Bush," which I know from my Forty-Niner days is a
restaurant on Wilshire Boulevard not far from the hotel. So I give
them time to clear out, and I head for the Bull and Bush. I walk in
and I am looking around like I'm trying to find somebody. By this
time everyone in the place is staring at me. I feel awful silly, but I
can't back down now.

A bunch of Giants are sitting at a table right in front of me. Lee
Riley is there and Eddie Sutton and Billy Stits, my old buddy from
the Forty-Niners. Anyway, there are six of them at the table and,
by golly, there is also one empty chair.

"Y.A.," I say to myself, "that is your seat there but how in hell
are you going to get into it?"

Finally, one of the guys at the table looks up and asks, "Who
are you looking for, Tittle?"

This is it—the opening I have been waiting for! But, hold on
there, Y.A. You can't look too anxious now. You have to be cool.
After all, you are a veteran and you've been around for fourteen
seasons, and you don't want these guys to know how really bad
you feel.

"I am waiting on a friend," I lie. "But I guess he isn't here."

"Are you going to eat?" Riley asks.

"Might as well," I say, trying my darndest to act nonchalant but almost vaulting into the empty chair before the invitation is barely out of Riley's mouth. Whew, I have never worked as hard for a dinner invite in my whole life.

After dinner, everyone gets up and walks outside. They are talking about going to some other spot in town but I am not included in the conversation. So back to the Ambassador I go. I am alone in my room again but at least I have accomplished my mission. I have eaten dinner with the team!

The next night, Saturday, August 19, we played the Rams at the Coliseum, my first real game as a Giant, and of course I guess everyone knows what happened—BANG! two broken transverse processes for old Y.A. right off the bat. At the start of the fourth quarter with the Giants leading by 17-3, Sherman looks down the bench, spots me sitting there next to Conerly and motions me to come over to the sideline.

"You ready to go in?" he asked.

"I don't know any plays, Al, but I'm ready to play if you want me to."

"You know the thirty-seven slant, don't you?" he inquired.

"Sort of," I answered.

"Well, go in and call a thirty-seven slant then, just to get the feel of things."

With that, he slapped me on the rear end and I was on my way out to the center of the field. En route, I passed Grosscup heading for the bench and Lee said, "Go get 'em, Yat," and grinned at me.

Go get 'em, hell, I thought. I'm lucky if I don't mess things up.

The ball was on the Giants' 46-yard line when I stuck my head into the huddle for the first time and said, "Thirty-seven slant . . . on three."

Ray Wietecha snapped the ball on "three" but I never got the handle. I was all thumbs. I bobbled the exchange and then dropped the ball. When I scooped it up and started to run, I saw two of the Rams, big ones at that, bearing down on me. Now, I never had been famous for my broken field running and I did not intend to establish a reputation at that particular moment, not with those big tackles heading my way. So I simply fell to the ground and pulled

41

the ball to my chest, hoping that I would not compound the felony by fumbling too.

As I hit the ground, the Rams hit me, knees first, square in the back. The transverse processes crackled like egg shells!

I feel a jagged pain leap up my back and I know right away it is something bad. I just lay there on the field with my nose pressing into the dirt. Golly, how embarrassing! One play, a stinking thirty-seven slant, and I am out. Here I'm worrying about my leg and now my back is gone. I am an old man anyway by pro standards and I had been hurt with San Francisco the year before, and here I am again, stretched out on the Coliseum floor like I have been shot through the head. If there is a hole around here, Y.A., I think to myself, I oughta crawl into it.

By this time the Giants' trainers, John Dziegel and Johnny Johnson, are out on the field to see if I am still alive. They take me in tow and haul me back to the bench like a sack of wheat. What an exit! I am ashamed. I am also afraid to glance in Sherman's direction.

I bet Lou Cordileone would have looked mighty good to the Giants right then.

That was my debut for the New York Giants. After the game, which ended in a 17–17 tie, I was packed into the club's chartered plane with the rest of the excess baggage and we flew north to Salem. My back was so sore I couldn't even sit down. I was hurtin'. I was tired. And I was discouraged.

And I still didn't know anybody!

CHAPTER FIVE

BUS RIDE TO FAIRFIELD

THE NEXT morning the bad news was made official.

Dr. Francis Sweeny, the Giants' team physician, took me to Salem Hospital for X-rays. They showed clearly that two transverse processes were broken.

I shuddered when Doc Sweeny told me, "You will be out at least five weeks."

FIVE weeks!

"Are you sure, Doc?" I asked, hoping against hope that he might revise his estimate and say something like three weeks or maybe two weeks.

"Yes, I am sure," he said flat-like. "I have seen a lot of these injuries, Y.A., and there's no way to speed the healing process. All we can do is wait."

Then, taking another look at me from behind his square-cut glasses, he smiled and added, "And don't forget, it takes even longer with us old fellows." The doc, a little wisp of a man, was 68 then.

At that moment, I did not appreciate being reminded of my own age. But I knew Doc Sweeny meant well. I guess I was just on edge; I was actually mad at myself for getting hurt. Here I had been in the best physical condition of my life only a short time before, and now I had a lame back and a bum leg. It looked like I would not be able to play again for over a month.

Damn it, why does a guy get breaks like this?

That night I wrote to Minnette and told her not to worry, that I would be back playing in another couple of weeks. But I don't suppose I sounded too convincing and, when I could hardly bend to untie my shoelaces later in the evening, I knew Doc Sweeny's estimate was more professional and more accurate than mine. It sure as hell would be five weeks; at least that's the way I felt right then.

Now I couldn't even practice. I was back in street clothes watching practice at Willamette University, and sitting in the back row at the team meetings.

But there was one consoling development along about that time—some of the Giant veterans finally showed signs of accepting me into the inner circle. The first two, as I recall, were safetyman Jim Patton and his sidekick Dick Nolan, a wonderful fellow and a fine football player who is now coaching at Dallas. They came to my room one day and asked me to go along with them for a beer. Gradually, the others warmed up to me once Patton and Nolan had broken the acceptance barrier. Of course, I was still good friends with Heinrich, who had been tutoring me. But he was a coach and coaches do not drink beer with the ballplayers in training camp. Don did his tutoring every day and then left me on my own. I didn't mind, though, because finally I felt as if I belonged.

We broke camp in Salem on a Friday and boarded the Giants' special charter plane, headed for Albuquerque, N.M., where we were scheduled to play Dallas the following night.

My back had not improved at all. I was more at home with the Giants, but I was terribly ashamed of myself. I had always pulled my weight with every football team I had played on. But I was dead wood with the Giants. This bothered me. I was unable to help Conerly or Grosscup in the pre-season games. I could not even take my regular turn in practice. With all this, I felt I had thrown Allie Sherman's timetable off. He was depending on me to help the Giants in 1961 and naturally he was anxious to see what I could do at quarterback. So far, though, all he had seen was a fumbled thirty-seven slant. I was eating good, studying hard and talking it up on the bench like crazy. But otherwise I was a big fat zero. I could not blame Sherman and Wellington Mara for wondering if

44

they had made such a shrewd deal when they took me off Red Hickey's conscience. After all, I was 35 years old with a case history of injuries and, as we landed in Albuquerque, there was no certainty that I would ever play again. A bad back can be a permanent thing no matter what the doctors tell you.

With my bald head and my glasses, I must have looked like Ol' Man Mose hobbling in and out of airplanes, buses and whirlpool tubs.

Some quarterback, I thought to myself.

I did not play against Dallas on Saturday, of course, but I was not missed. Conerly and Grosscup dispatched the Cowboys, 28–10.

After the game I was sitting next to Alex Webster's locker as he peeled off his pads and headed for the shower. "Boy, will I be glad to get home," he said. "We have been on the road almost a month. I'm dying to see the kids."

Webster's remark got me to thinking. So much had happened in those first two weeks that the full impact of being away from Minnette and the youngsters had not yet hit me. But when Alex started talking about his family, well, a wave of homesickness swept over me. When we got aboard the charter plane an hour later, my spirits sank. It had not been bad as long as the Giants were training on the West Coast, or even playing in Albuquerque. It did not really seem as if I was too far from Atherton. But all of a sudden that plane took off and headed east, toward New York. Then it dawned on me. By golly, I was gone, really gone. It was only August and that meant it would be five months before I came home again. In all my years in football, I had never been away from Minnette and the kids that long. I do not intend this to sound as if I am the only ballplayer who ever left home. It happens all the time. It's just that I am a family man before everything else, and so it bothered me. Corny or not, it bothered me as the plane flew away from California.

Between my groin, my cracked transverse processes and my homesickness, well, I imagine I was a sad looking sight when we got off the plane at Idlewild Airport in New York the next morning. It did not help, either, to see my teammates in warm reunions with their families. I was so darned lonely I felt like getting right back on the plane.

At that moment, you could have had New York City and twenty points!

A bus was waiting to take us to Fairfield University in Connecticut, where the Giants had their permanent training camp. I did not know where Fairfield was, and at that precise moment I did not care. I climbed aboard, tossed my suitcases on an empty seat and sat next to a window. For a time, I was the only one on the bus; most of the veterans had their own cars waiting for them and had already left with their wives. Even the rookies, or most of them, were heading for New York City since Sherman had given the club two days off, and they were not due back in camp until Tuesday. Finally, a few guys got in and we headed north along the New England Thruway toward Fairfield. I sat staring out the window, lost in my thoughts of Minnette, the kids and California. The only other veteran on board was Andy Robustelli, the big defensive end. But in Stamford, Conn., Andy's hometown, the bus pulled over to the service road and he grabbed his bags and jumped off. I watched as his family greeted him. Andy has eight children, I think, and the little girls were hugging and kissing him. I was feeling bluer every minute. Andy's youngsters reminded me of my own. I was almost relieved when the bus started up again, leaving Stamford and the Robustelli clan behind.

Now I was the only veteran left.

The few rookies in the back of the bus slept the remaining twenty minutes to Fairfield. I was tired too, dog tired. But I could not sleep. My nerves were ready to jump through my skin. Again I found myself wondering if coming to New York had been the right thing to do. Every turn of the wheels took me closer to a strange new existence. I had been with new clubs before, several of them, but the New York Giants were not just another ball club. They were different.

Fairfield University is a beautiful school set above Long Island Sound on an old estate. It looked more like a country club than a university. It was about noon when we arrived but, being that it was Sunday, there was not a rustle of life anywhere on the campus —just the hot sun beating down and a few priests strolling along the walks behind Loyola Hall. The bus pulled into the parking

46

lot and we took our luggage and got off. The bus drove away, drenching me in the hot exhaust, and I was left standing there with two suitcases and not the faintest notion of what to do next.

The other players disappeared mysteriously into Loyola Hall. They had not said a word to me; they just picked up and left. I followed, struggling up the steps with my bags. It was dark inside, dark for a summer afternoon, and even quieter than it was outside. I had not been assigned to a room, and I could not find anyone to help me find one. The Giants' officials had gone directly home from the airport. The coaches, too, and the trainers. Everyone.

Even the university people in charge of Loyola Hall, the Giants' dorm, were nowhere to be found. The place was deserted.

One of the rookies, I forget which one to tell the truth, appeared just as mysteriously as he and his friends had disappeared when we got off the bus. I asked him about a room.

"You're on your own, Y.A.," he said. "Try the second floor. No sense looking down here. The veterans have all these rooms sewed up."

With that he was gone, and I was alone again.

So the veterans had the first floor all sewed up! What the hell did they think I was with fourteen years in professional football? But I did not seem to have much of a choice. Putting a suitcase under each arm, I walked to the end of the dimly-lit hall and climbed the stairs to the second floor. The first door I tried was locked. So was the second, and the third. They were all locked. These obviously were rooms which had been assigned to the Giant players before they made the trip west, and they had locked them and taken the keys.

I plunked my bags on the floor and sat down on them. By this time I was pretty depressed. It was quite a gloomy feeling to be 3,500 miles from home . . . hurt, sitting in a dark corridor, unable to find an empty room or even an unlocked door. If I had had an out at that moment, I would have gone back to California. My introduction to Willamette had been bad. But this was worse!

The fact remained, however, that I had to find myself a room, so I started twisting doorknobs again. Finally I made my way around to an empty wing of Loyola Hall and found a room that obviously

47

was not occupied; it had no sheets on the bed and no towels. But it did not matter to me right then. I put up my suitcases, took off my shoes and flopped on the bed.

"What now, Y.A.?" I asked myself.

I heard a car start up. I got up and walked over to the window, which looked down on the parking lot. The rookies who had come on the bus with me were piling into a little sports car. They turned left out of the lot and drove up a hill, finally disappearing around a big dome-shaped building that I guessed was the Fairfield University gym. No doubt they were heading for town to have something to eat and maybe kill the afternoon by drinking a few beers. I would have welcomed the chance to go with them. But once again, I had not been asked.

I put my shoes on and walked around the dormitory looking for someone to talk to. But the place was as empty as a barn. I even went outside, figuring that maybe I would run into one of the priests I had seen when we first arrived. Again no luck. The walks behind Loyola Hall were deserted.

This was awful. I went back to my room and sat there at the desk looking out the window. I tried to read a paperback novel but I could not concentrate. I tried to sleep but that too was futile.

Boy, I had been in some stiff places in my time but never anything to compare with the Giants' training camp that first Sunday. After a couple of hours of talking to myself I knew how soldiers felt just before they "go over the hill."

What bothered me more than the loneliness, which I knew was only a temporary situation, was the gnawing fear that my bad back might mean the end of me as a football player. In my present condition I could not practice when the squad returned on Tuesday. I could not throw the ball, or even run. I had nothing to contribute to the ball club, and this is what made it bad for me.

The next morning I made my way down to the Loyola dining hall in the basement of the building and was relieved to find Cliff Livingston, one of our linebackers, having his breakfast. Cliff was one of the few remaining bachelors among the Giant veterans and it was indeed strange for him to be the first one back in camp. Strange or not, though, I was glad to see him. It had been a long night—and with no sheets.

48

Cliff was surprised to see me slide into a chair across the table from him. He asked me where I had been. I told him I had not been anywhere and that I had not seen anyone for a whole day, and that I was damned glad that at least he had come back to Fairfield before Tuesday.

"You must be the only veteran in history who spent Sunday afternoon in camp," Livingston chuckled.

"I did not have much choice," I replied, trying to force a smile.

Cliff filled me in on the routine at Fairfield.

"It's a great camp, Y.A. Sherman runs the show the way it should be run. We do everything on a minute-by-minute schedule. But I will say this—Allie is fair. He gets us into shape without killing us. The spirit here is excellent. This is a great crew, believe me."

The Giants resumed practice the next morning. But I was not part of it. Sherman would not even allow me to put on sweat clothes. I stood around like a spectator, watching the team run through drills and dummy scrimmage for an hour. Gosh, it was embarrassing! My first practice in New York, and I was not even permitted on the football field. Sportswriters kept asking me about my back and things like that, but I did not have any answers for them. They kept after me, though, until I finally eluded them by sneaking into a group of players who were standing behind the offensive huddle.

One day later that week, I got word that Allie Sherman wanted to see me in his room. My heart sank. My thoughts raced back to St. Mary's College the day Red Hickey summoned me with the same message. Golly, the Giants could not be giving up on me already. Or could they? I certainly was not doing much to earn my keep at Fairfield. But Sherman had not told me to bring my playbook—a sure-fire indication that a player is on the way out— so I figured it was nothing as fatal as a trade. At least I hoped it wasn't.

When I walked into Sherman's first floor room he motioned me to sit on the bed and then he asked, "What do you think of Del Shofner?"

Shofner was the Los Angeles Rams' end and obviously the Giants were interested in making a trade for him. As was Sherman's custom, he was meticulously sounding out his players and coaches who had played with or against Shofner.

Before I could answer, Allie continued.

"We might get Del in a deal, Y.A., but first I'm trying to find out what his trouble was in Los Angeles last year. He was great his first three years but last season something went wrong out there. He caught only twelve passes for them. The year before that he had forty-seven. It doesn't add up."

"I spoke to him at the Pro Bowl game last January, Allie," I said. "As far as I know, he dropped a couple of passes against San Francisco last year, and the club lost confidence in him. Then he lost confidence in himself, and they put him on the bench. He had a couple of bad muscle pulls, too. But he is as good as he ever was."

"Do you think he could help the Giants?" Sherman asked.

"He sure as hell could. There's no receiver in the league I would rather throw to . . . when I am able to throw, that is," I added with a smile. "I remember the first time I ever threw to Del in practice for the Pro Bowl game. I sent him down on a deep pattern and threw the ball with everything I had. It fell ten yards short. He just ran right out from under it. I never had thrown to anyone with his speed. With the Forty-Niners we had some great receivers, but nobody who could run like Shofner."

Sherman thanked me and I returned to my room, relieved that the summons had concerned Del Shofner and not Y.A. Tittle.

A few days later I picked up the morning paper on the way to the Loyola Hall dining hall and a headline hit me right in the eye: GRID GIANTS GET SHOFNER!

The story read that New York had closed the deal by promising the Rams two future draft choices in return for Del. They were to get a first Giant draft pick one year, and a second pick another year. It was a high price to pay but to my way of thinking, it was well worth it.

The trade was good news to me personally too. Now I had a buddy who was in the same predicament as I was. Del didn't know many guys either.

Things were better for me the minute Shofner arrived. I will never forget the day. They had loaded Del on a plane in the middle of the night in Los Angeles (things move swiftly when you get near the opening of the regular season) and he had not slept a wink all the way to New York. After landing at Idlewild, he took a cab into Manhattan and boarded the New Haven Railroad local bound for Fairfield. Only the train did not stop at Fairfield; instead it went on north to Bridgeport, where he got another cab and came back to the university.

Now, Shofner is not the healthiest looking guy in the world when he is at his best. For one thing, he has ulcers; for another, his skin is naturally sallow. But if you could have seen him that morning, you would not have believed it. He looked like death warmed over, as they say. His eyes were sunk back in his face, his complexion was paler than usual. He was drawn and tired looking. His hair was mussed, and he reminded me of a walking scarecrow.

Swede Svare, the Giants' defensive coach who had known Del at Los Angeles, took him around the dorm that morning to introduce him to the fellows. Some of them had a hard time believing this guy was really a football player.

"He looks more like a clarinet player after a hard one-night stand," one of the fellows cracked.

After the preliminary introductions, Shofner was taken down the hall for an examination by Doc Sweeny, a ritual every man must undergo before he can step out on the practice field. Doc blinked when he saw the emaciated figure Svare had hauled into his room, but he braced himself and put Del through the physical. Somehow, he passed and then they assigned him to my room, probably figuring that misery likes company. He was such a pathetic sight that I momentarily forgot my own troubles. At least now, I thought, the loneliness won't be so bad. Having Shofner as a roommate eased my situation considerably, although I am not at all certain that the feeling was mutual. I had known Del slightly when we were rivals on the West Coast, and this helped. So did the fact that he was a fellow Texan. He hailed from a town called Center, which was not a great distance from my hometown of Marshall in East Texas, and so we had a great deal in common right from the start.

As I said, my outlook changed the minute Del came along. Suddenly, things did not seem so bad. I even forgot my transverse processes for a while. He was good company—and still is. He was single then but he was different from most of the single guys in camp. He was older and more settled. On Wednesday nights when Sherman gave us off from team meetings, Del did not want to run into Fairfield with the boys to have a few beers and go to a movie. He liked to lay around the room and talk or maybe read a western or something. This was just fine with me. I had spent too many nights sitting there by myself looking at the ceiling. Now at least I had someone to talk to, someone with whom I could share the experiences of becoming a Giant, someone who, because he was in the same boat, could understand the difficulties I faced trying to make the adjustment.

This is not to say that Shofner was talkative. He was not. At times I had the feeling I was still alone in the room. Del never said anything unless it was worth saying. We often went hours on end without so much as a word passing between us. In fact, we still are that way. But we understand each other, and it works fine. There were times at Fairfield that summer when our entire conversation for the evening might consist of a few well-spaced grunts and an occasional "yeah" or "no."

Again, though, Del Shofner was my kind of guy and his presence in camp was a great tonic for me.

Unfortunately, he could not do anything to speed the healing of my cracked transverse processes. I continued to watch practice from the sideline. My back was not getting any better, it seemed to me, and my frustration increased daily. The club went to Green Bay on Labor Day night to play the Packers, but again Sherman told me not to bother suiting up. It was depressing, believe me.

Next we met the Baltimore Colts at the Yale Bowl, the first professional game ever played there, and I was still on the bench in street clothes. Shofner had a fabulous debut with two touchdown catches and a total of 220 yards, so at least I had something to celebrate that evening. Maybe I was not doing a damned thing for the Giants, but Room 218, Loyola Hall, was well represented on the big scoreboard at one end of the Yale Bowl. It was difficult for me to be held out of the action that afternoon, a sweltering day when the temperature almost hit 100 degrees. Conerly got hurt early in the first period and Sherman had no one else to use but young Grosscup. Lee did a fine job, all things considered, but Gino

Marchetti and Big Daddy Lipscomb and the rest of the Colts climbed all over him and gave him a fearful beating. He was reeling in the end, bruised and bloodied. I wanted desperately to get in there and help but my back was so sore I could hardly get off the bench to shake Shofner's hand after he caught one of Grosscup's passes for his second touchdown.

This is when the Giants needed me. This is why they had traded for me, to back up Conerly and win the games that Charlie could not win. But here I was—an old bald-headed, beat-up cripple.

CHAPTER SIX

"WE NEED YOU MORE IN DECEMBER..."

THE DOG DAYS of August dragged by at Fairfield University. I dragged too.

I may not have been a forgotten man but I sure felt like one. I lived at Loyola Hall, went to practice every day and sat in on the squad meetings at night. But more and more I was an outsider again.

Football breeds a great relationship among athletes. But you have got to be in there, banging away, getting hit every day to be part of it. If you stand on the sidelines you get left out. You are not part of it. That is how I was beginning to feel—left out.

I did not want pity or sympathy. What I wanted was a chance to play football, a chance to earn my money as a quarterback. But until Doc Sweeny gave me the go-ahead, I was just taking up space. As the weeks went by in training camp, people almost forgot I was there. I couldn't blame them. I think everyone was sort of embarrassed by my predicament. I became an object of curiosity more than anything else.

Through it all, Allie Sherman was just great. He seemed to understand my situation. He knew what was going on inside of me because he had been a fierce little competitor himself at Brooklyn

54

College and later with the Philadelphia Eagles. He was never a great quarterback as far as the records go, but he was a competitor just the same. Again, I hesitate to make my situation sound so tragic. It was not a tragedy. I am merely trying to relate what happened and what my feelings and my anxieties were during the time my back was injured. Every so often when Sherman sensed that I was down in the dumps, he would walk over, put his arm around my shoulder and say something like, "Just take your time, Y.A., and get ready for the big push. We're in no hurry. We'll need you more in December than in August."

It was not long before I developed a keen admiration for Sherman. Despite his youth—he was only 39, and that is young as pro coaches go—Allie had a wonderful insight into the problems of his players. He did not look on the Giants as a team, as a unit. Rather he saw the Giants as forty men, each with his own mentality, each with his own temperament. Sherman was shrewd all right. He knew success depended not on adapting men to a system, but on adapting the system to his players.

"If we do not have a back who is fast enough to run the ends," he once told me, "we will not put any end run plays into our offense. We are not going to have a play on the board just because every club is supposed to have such a play. I want to learn my men first; then I will put in the plays."

Sherman's patience and understanding did much to make my situation more bearable.

Aside from Allie and my roomie, Del Shofner, no one paid much attention to me. I appreciated that. I felt most of them probably thought I would never play football again. Sometimes I had the impression they lowered their voices when I was nearby, like you do when you are talking to someone in a funeral parlor.

There was not much about Y.A. Tittle in the newspapers either. I was an old story by that time, one that had been re-written and hashed over a dozen times. Everyone was tired of hearing about my transverse processes. Most folks, in fact, did not know what in the hell a transverse process was or how one gets cracked like an egg shell, or why it should affect a quarterback's passing arm.

People who talked to me at training camp were careful not to open the conversation by inquiring, "How's the back, Y.A.?"

I became more self-conscious and irritable every day. I was not a quarterback for the Giants; I was more like an equipment man. I had not thrown a football or even handled one since my miserable debut in Los Angeles five weeks before. And five weeks can be a long time to a quarterback in a pro training camp, especially a quarterback who is new to the team, the system and the personnel. Those lost days and weeks can't easily be reclaimed.

Soon after the New Haven game, the Fairfield University student body returned for the fall semester and the Giants broke camp and moved to New York City. We practiced at Fordham University and a lot of the guys, including Shofner, Conerly and myself, lived at Concourse Plaza Hotel, which is a couple of blocks up the hill from Yankee Stadium. My spirits improved at this point. I was still unable to take my turn at quarterback. But living in the city, a new experience for me, was enough of a change to take my mind off my problems. When the Giants started practicing at Yankee Stadium after the World Series was over, it was only a short walk down the hill to practice every day. Then too, our hotel was convenient to downtown Manhattan by subway. A couple of Texans like Shofner and myself got a big kick out of riding the subway; I must have gone uptown and downtown a dozen times just for the ride the first week we moved into the Concourse. It was quite a thrill. We did not have anything like it in the town where I grew up.

Things began to look up for me the week before our opening league game against the St. Louis Cardinals. Doc Sweeny gave me permission to take part in practice. My back was not completely healed but at least I was able to do some light work. This was a great psychological lift for me. I ran a few plays and handled the ball some. Boy, it felt good to be in there again. I had done an awful lot of studying during the weeks at Fairfield and at Fordham but I was nowhere near ready physically. I maintain it is impossible for any player, particularly a quarterback, to get ready for a ball game without some kind of actual work on the field. He can study for ten years but he can never get from his playbook or from the blackboard what he can get from three practices on the field. There is simply no substitute for running and passing and getting the feel of the game. It can't be done in a meeting room or on a projection screen. You've got to be in there.

Thus, while my head was crammed with plays and formations, my body, my arms and my legs, were a month behind the rest of the ball club. That is a lot of time for a veteran to give away.

I remember how awkward I was the first day at practice. I muffed the first few snaps from Ray Wietecha, the center, and my thoughts raced back to the Los Angeles disaster. I needed extra work on the ball exchange to improve my timing. A quarterback and his center must develop precise co-ordination. I asked Ray to stay out after practice and work with me. He readily agreed.

Wietecha typified the New York Giants. He was a genuine pro, dedicated, business-like. Ray never said much, but there was not a thing he did not know about offensive line play. After several sessions together we were working like a real team.

By Friday, I was telling myself that maybe I would be ready for the St. Louis game on Sunday. My back felt good—finally. So did my leg. I was throwing the ball well.

I told Shofner, "I will be there, Del," and I wrote to Minnette saying I was certain I would be able to play. Even the newspapers sensed my confidence. One headlined a story: "Tittle Ready—at Last!"

By Saturday morning I had sold myself completely on the idea of playing. I did not see how Sherman could possibly keep me out of there.

"Be nice to me, Del," I kidded Shofner, "and maybe I will throw you a couple tomorrow."

"It will be the first time one has ever been thrown from the bench," Del cracked right back.

Shofner was closer to the truth than he imagined.

The Cardinal game the next day, my first as a Giant, was another disappointment. We got whipped, 21–10, and I did not play.

Conerly opened at quarterback. But things did not go well. We looked as bad as we had against Baltimore the week before. The Cardinals were using a safety red-dog. The play wasn't exactly new

57

in the league, but it was not common either. They shot Larry Wilson, the little safetyman, through there a few times and he nailed Conerly for big losses. The rest of the Cardinals kept the pressure on too. Luke Owens dropped Charlie twice in the first period, and linebacker Bill Koman got him for minus ten on the next series. In the second period, St. Louis' defensive end Joe Robb busted through and tackled Conerly on the Giant two. On third down, Bobby Gaiters fumbled in the end zone and Willie West recovered for a St. Louis touchdown.

The Cardinals kept hammering away at Conerly in the second half. He took a fearful beating. Apparently it killed his legs, and he could not maneuver to sidestep the St. Louis red-doggers. He was a sitting duck.

I knew what Charlie was going through out there. It had happened to me often enough. Those big ends and tackles break through the line and wallop you just as you raise your arm. Or maybe a linebacker shoots the gap and slams into you from the blind side. Sometimes you wonder where all your blockers are. Every time you hit the ground, you ache a little more. You get up slower. You feel like saying, "The hell with this, there must be an easier way to make a living."

Eventually, the Cardinals wore Conerly down. Charlie was wobbling around like a drunk. His passes had no zip behind them; the ball was fluttering in the air like a bird with one wing. Sherman motioned to Grosscup. It was Lee's big chance but I could not help but think it was a terrible spot for the kid. The Cardinals were swarming all over us. They had the momentum and the lead. Grosscup fared no better than Conerly.

It just was not the Giants' day, or Y.A. Tittle's either.

I kept hoping maybe I would get a shot toward the end of the ball game. They were ahead of us by 21–10 and Grosscup was in trouble. But Sherman acted as if I were not even there. I kept walking in front of him to let him know I was around. He ignored me.

Naturally, I was disappointed over not playing. I had built up a lot of anticipation during the week. So it was a big letdown when I did not get into the game. Still, Sherman was the coach and he ran the team. He made the decisions, just as Red Hickey had, and that is all there was to it. I was certain Alllie had his reasons.

I reminded myself too that Sherman must have been even more disappointed than I was. This had been his first Stadium game as head coach of the Giants, and he had lost it in front of 60,000 hometown fans. He had lost it with a ball club that played poor football. The Giants were a bad team that day. It was a bitter defeat for Sherman. To his credit, though, he took the loss manfully. If he felt bad, he hid it pretty good.

In fact, Allie was too busy trying to cheer up his players to be concerned with personal feelings. He walked slowly from one locker to the next, talking quietly to each man, letting them know he still had faith in them.

When he got to where I was slumped on a stool, Sherman bent over and talked into my ear. I guess I didn't hide my disappointment as well as he did his.

"I had a reason for not sending you in there today, Y.A.," he said. "We have a 14-game schedule ahead of us. I could have used you today but the way things went, it probably would not have done any good. And it might have done a lot of harm."

He paused and slapped me on the back.

"One game does not make a season, Y.A. We've a long way to go. You'll be ready when the big push starts."

Sherman's words made sense when I later considered the logic. It also told me a lot about Allie's character. Most coaches may not have played it the way he did under similar circumstances. They would have said, "We have got to have this one, and we will worry about the next one next week." And truthfully, I had more or less looked at it that way myself over the years. To me, today's game, the one right now, was more important than anything in the world. Win this one, never mind next week! I had played many times with painful injuries because it was important to me to win. Next Sunday always seemed too far off to worry about.

Despite this attitude, I was convinced Sherman's decision had been sound. Using me probably would not have changed the course of the game, not the way the Cardinal defense was shooting through there. And who knows, maybe one of those safety red-doggers

59

might have tagged me like they did Charlie and, with my egg shell back, that could have been the end of it.

Sure, I was anxious to play. But Sherman was smarter. He obviously had the entire season laid out in his mind. He was not going to allow one defeat, especially in the opening game, throw him into panic. It took nerve to make such a decision. Allie Sherman, as I was to discover, not only was smart enough to make decisions but had the courage to go with them—no matter how difficult.

We went out to Pittsburgh the following week to play the Steelers and Conerly was the starting quarterback again. I was physically ready to play but this time I had not worked myself up about playing. Sherman was calling the shots. If he needed me, I was ready to play. If he did not need me, I would not let it get me down as I had the week before. I was learning to trust Allie's judgment.

Conerly threw a touchdown pass to Shofner in the second period at Pitt Stadium, and it was 7–7 at halftime. Then Pat Summerall kicked a field goal and we went ahead, 10–7. Charlie was running the ball club real well, and I had resigned myself to another long afternoon on the bench. Grosscup had drawn the job of manning the headphones which connected to end coach Ken Kavanaugh in the scouting booth upstairs, so I had nothing to do except watch the ball game.

All of a sudden, Conerly was in trouble. Lou Michaels and Joe Krupa, the big Steeler linemen, cracked through and belted him hard for a six-yard loss. Conerly got to his feet slowly. He was shaken up. On the next play, Big Daddy Lipscomb hurled 290 pounds into Conerly and dropped him seven yards behind the line of scrimmage. It took Charlie even longer to get to his feet this time.

Sherman waved for Kyle Rote to call a time out. The trainers ran onto the field to see if Conerly was okay.

"Start warming up, Y.A.," Allie snapped, "you're going in for Conerly."

I leaped off the bench and grabbed for a football. Oddly, at this particular moment, I began to worry about my back. I still was not sure I could throw long. I had prepared for this moment for the past six weeks, and now I was unexplainably filled with doubts. But I felt better as I threw a few warm-up passes.

"This is your shot, Y.A., old boy," I told myself. "Make it good."

There was kind of a questioning air in the huddle. This was my first test under fire, and the Giant players were waiting to see how I handled myself. It was a big moment for them as well as for me. I was stepping into Charlie Conerly's shoes, something a lot of good quarterbacks had not been able to do. The Giants played for Charlie Conerly, and they won for him. But it was not necessarily this way with other quarterbacks. Previously, only Don Heinrich had ever moved the Giants when Conerly was not in there.

The next few minutes would have a tremendous bearing on my future as the Giants' quarterback. I knew this. So did the players leaning into the huddle waiting for my first call.

I decided not to take any unnecessary chances. There was too much at stake. I would play it close to the vest until I got the feel of things.

"Go with your percentage shots," Sherman was fond of saying, and that is exactly what I intended to do.

Shofner was my man. I had no doubt about that. He had great hands and was a cool one. He was my best percentage shot. With first down on the Pittsburgh 42, I passed 12 yards to Del on a square-out pattern. Next, I hit him on a quick slant for a first down on the Steeler 18. Then I passed to him again over the middle and we were on the five-yard line. It was time to run the ball. I tried Alex Webster around right end but Michaels stopped him for no gain. On second down, I used Shofner as a decoy left and passed to Joe Morrison on a swing pattern to the right for the touchdown.

I had thrown a lot of touchdowns in my career but none had given me such a thrill. I was overjoyed: I had come in for Charlie Conerly. I had taken *his* Giants in for a score.

The Giant defense held the Steelers off after our score and we won the ball game, 17–14. I finished the day with ten completions in a dozen tries for 123 yards. I hit my first six passes in a row on that first scoring march. That day, that game, I remember right well.

Sitting in the crowded dressing room under Pitt Stadium I was the happiest guy in the world. My back had passed the test of body contact. Those Steelers had given me some healthy licks in the last period and the back had stood up. My groin had not bothered me either. And, most important, I had helped to win the game for the Giants. They pay quarterbacks for winning. I had won. Maybe after all the dismal time, I was a decent quarterback again.

CHAPTER SEVEN

"PUT IT IN THE AIR"

THE PITTSBURGH game which established me with the New York Giants had some after-effects which went pretty deep.

Some of the newspapers called my performance against the Steelers, ". . . the beginning of a new era for the Giants." This of course was silly. You can't base a man's value to a team on one ball game. I knew better than anyone else that the next time out I might be a cripple, or a bum. Just as easily, Charlie Conerly could be the hero.

I did not like to see these newspaper references to Charlie, especially when they suggested he was on his way out. It was unfair. Conerly was still a fine quarterback, and what writers doing Steelers' post-mortems seemed to forget was that he had given the Giants a 10–7 lead before I had gotten into the game.

This was not a completely new situation for me. I had encountered it many times in my career, only this was my first experience at being on the other side of the fence. Usually it was some other quarterback who had a hot game and put old Y.A. on the bench. Now they were writing off Conerly the same way.

This created an uneasy atmosphere when we resumed practice at Fordham the following Tuesday. It was something none of us talked about, but it was there just the same.

That morning, Sherman walked out to where Charlie and I were throwing passes in a warm up drill. He called us aside and said, "I want to see you fellows in my office before you shower."

Allie did not say why he wanted to see us. But we both knew. He was visibly upset by the situation.

Allie's office at Fordham is a small, cluttered room which is shared by other members of his staff. It has three or four old metal lockers against one wall, a desk and a blackboard opposite the lockers and a couple of showers in a small adjoining room. Boxes and crates were piled all over the place, and I wondered how a coach could operate in such a drab cubbyhole.

Sherman asked Ken Kavanaugh and Ed Kolman to leave. He closed the door behind them and turned to us.

"Fellows, I asked to see you this morning because there is something which needs saying. I want to say it and now." He referred briefly to the newspaper speculations and then said: "I would not be talking like this to any other quarterbacks in the league. But I feel you two are mature enough and have been around long enough to appreciate the ticklish position we are in. You have both been starting quarterbacks for years. Now I must ask you to make sacrifices and put your faith in me. I will be making a lot of moves and, barring injury, there never will be a time when one of you isn't playing. It isn't going to be easy for any of us, but it will be a lot harder if we do not have complete understanding."

I nodded and so did Charlie, whose expression, as always, was unchanging. A man never could tell what Conerly was thinking by looking at his face.

"This can be very good," Sherman was saying, "or it can be very bad. Working with two quarterbacks is difficult. But we can make it work because I have faith in you men. I hope you have faith in me."

Allie lit a cigarette, drawing the first puff deeply and following the smoke with his eyes as it drifted up in small swirls.

"There will be things in the press, and comments from people even closer to the ball club. Some may be nasty things that can tear us apart if we let 'em."

It was plain to see what was worrying Sherman.

"But I will tell you right now—you are both number one with Al Sherman, no matter who starts. Remember this and we can do

64

it, the three of us. If you have anything to say, let's hear it now. Once we walk out that door, I will consider the matter closed."

Conerly scraped his cleats on the rough wooded floor and, without looking up, said, "Hell, Al, I have had my share of good years. I don't care who starts as long as we win this thing."

I was glad to see this reaction by Charlie. I felt the same way. I said, "Same here, Al. I want what is best for the ball club."

Sherman seemed relieved. He shook Charlie's hand and then mine.

"You're real men," he said. "With men like you, we *can* win it."

This was the kind of thing which made playing for the Giants something special. They developed a warm and human relationship that included players, coaches and front office. It was something I had seldom felt on other ball clubs. The Giants treated every athlete like an individual, like a man. A fellow always knew where he stood.

From that day on, the expression "Number One quarterback" never was used by Sherman or anyone else connected with the Giants.

Conerly and I went along knowing we both would play a lot of football. It was going to be a long season and there would be chances for both of us. Neither of us was a kid looking ahead to a brand new career. Charlie was 40 and I was 35. We both were going from year to year, or maybe from game to game. We were not out to make reputations for ourselves. Conerly wanted to go all the way because that is the way he played the game. So did I, and in addition, I wanted a championship. In thirteen years, I had never played in a championship game—and it was getting late.

There had been times in the past when I had resented not starting a ball game, like in 1956 in San Francisco when I was unexplainably benched. With the Giants in 1961 it was different. Allie Sherman made sure of that.

My relationship with Charlie Conerly that first year when we split the quarterbacking job was good. Charlie is by nature a quiet fellow. He earned respect through his actions, and not with a lot of palaver. At no time when I was playing in his place did he ever say anything more than, "Real nice game, Yat. You did a helluva job out there." He never gave any indication that he was disappointed in my success even when it kept him out of games. I am certain he wanted to play more; any great competitor would. But this desire never showed. No matter what his inner thoughts, Charlie was outwardly stoic. He was a pro all the way. Socially, too, he was a wonderful person. He never talked football off the field. This was fine with me because I am a lot like that myself. Charlie and his wife Perian lived at the Concourse that year and, when Minnette came back east, the four of us became close friends and spent many pleasant evenings together at dinner and the theatre. Charlie and I were rivals for the same job on the Giants. But there was no rivalry between us away from Yankee Stadium. Conerly left his football problems in his locker. I soon learned to do the same.

Sherman had asked us to have faith in him the day we had our closed-door meeting in the coaching room at Fordham. Charlie Conerly needed that faith the very next Sunday!

The Giants took the train down to Washington to meet the Redskins in the first game ever played in the new D.C. Stadium. The Redskins fumbled the opening kickoff and we recovered. Conerly took the club right in for a score, passing 17 yards to Kyle Rote for the touchdown. He made it look easy.

If Charlie had a hot hand, the chances were I would not get to do much quarterbacking. I could not expect Sherman to use me when Conerly was moving the ball team. But just the same, Allie had me throwing behind the bench.

But just as quickly the tide changed. Washington stormed back and tied the score when Norm Snead passed to Don Bosseler in the end zone.

Then came the play that almost touched off an explosion on our club. With the ball on the Giants' 45, Conerly under-threw Shofner on a long pass, and the ball went smack into the hands of Dale Hackbart, the Washington defensive back. He ran it back 48 yards for a touchdown. We were behind almost as quickly as we had gone ahead.

Sherman had told me a few minutes earlier to start warming up. "Just be ready in case I want you," he had said.

After Hackbart's interception, Allie waved me into the game and called Conerly to the sideline. It was a quick hook, I admit, but sometimes a coach must act on the spot. A ball game can turn on one play.

Charlie was a little hot. He thought Sherman had yanked him just because of one bad pass. It was the first time I ever saw Conerly really angry. He stormed past Allie, slammed his helmet onto the ground and sat at the far end of the bench.

The Giant players sitting on the bench were aware of the tension. They looked from Charlie to Sherman and back again. They seemed to be waiting for another spark to ignite the fuse.

But Charlie, typically, said nothing. His only outward expression of anger had been throwing his helmet down when he walked off the field. Whatever his thoughts, they were his own. There was disappointment in his eyes but if I know Charlie, he probably was just as angry with himself for having thrown the ball to Hackbart.

It was all settled in the dressing room before we boarded the Pennsylvania Railroad special bound for New York.

Sherman pulled Charlie aside and said, "I had intended to use Tittle anyway, Charlie. I did not yank you out of there because of the interception. You believe that, don't you?"

"I understand, Al," Charlie replied. "It's okay. Forget it."

This was tantamount to a speech for Charlie, a man of few words. Luckily a nasty situation was avoided. The Fordham meeting had paid its first dividend.

I finished the game that day and we beat the Redskins, 24–21. I was still a little uncertain with the Giants' offense, so I stuck mostly to passes. I threw screens, flares and short patterns. In all, I threw the football 41 times and completed 24 for 315 yards.

That is a lot of passing, but to me this game always has been putting the ball in the air.

CHAPTER EIGHT

EVERYBODY PLAYS FOOTBALL
IN MARSHALL

"Putting the ball in the air" was the way I learned to play football in Marshall, and it has been my motto ever since.

To me, football is passing. I am a passer before everything. This is what I do best. Give me my choice, and I am going to throw the hell out of the ball. This is the easiest and fastest way to score points. If you score points you win. And winning is another thing I've always believed in and dearly liked.

Naturally, my great liking for throwing the ball sometimes has given my coaches headaches, and I have had to make concessions along the way. But to this day, twenty-five years after my first forward passes, I still put the ball in the air whenever I can.

If you were a male Texan and grew up in the town of Marshall in the late 1930's, you came by football naturally. Perhaps it was the times—there wasn't enough money to go tearing around. Then, in the town itself, there weren't that many things to do for amusement. Marshall in those days was no Disneyland or Coney Island. Besides, all we wanted to do was to play football anyway.

Marshall is a town located 150 miles east of Dallas and 35 miles from Shreveport on the Louisiana border. When I was a kid the population was around 17,000 and it has not grown much since.

Pine lumber is the main source of economy in Marshall today. But once it was a thriving railroad town for the Texas & Pacific line, and a big foundry is still standing in town.

Marshall is not the kind of Texas town you might see in the movies. There are no big cattle spreads around that part of the state. Only a few large ranches and farms. The land is hilly and the soil is mostly clay, which makes growing things hard in many sections.

There were other houses near where we lived, but ours was not a residential community by today's standards. You could drive down a country road and run across two or three houses or farms, and then you might go another half mile or so and there'd be a house up on a hill. Texas-like, everything was sort of spread out. We never got in each other's way. And there sure was a lot of room to play football—which is what we mostly did.

Everybody wanted to be the passer on our scrub teams—and for what we figured were the very best of reasons: our neighbor, Sammy Baugh, the greatest passer of them all, was an All-American at Texas Christian University around that time. He was the idol of practically every kid in the state, and nowhere was he idolized more than in my home town. Everybody wanted to be like Slingin' Sammy—we wanted to be like him so much that I don't think it occurred to any of us to put the ball under his arm and run. We all threw it.

Every kid in town had an old tire hanging from a tree in the backyard. We all spent countless hours pitching footballs through the loop as we had seen Baugh do in the newsreels. The fellow who could hit the tire most often got to play quarterback when we chose up sides for a game. Naturally, we all worked hard at threading the needle because we all wanted to be like the great Baugh.

I was more fortunate than some of my friends. I had two brothers who contributed a lot to my early football schooling.

My brother Jack, seven years older than me, was a star player at Marshall High School when I was in the lower grades. He got me interested in football in the first place. He taught me how to hold the ball and how to throw it. He tried to teach me other things too, but I always got back to passing.

"You have to learn the rest of the game too," he once warned me.

"I know, Jack," I said, "but first I want to be a passer."

Jack used to throw up his hands at this. He did not agree with me but he worked hard and patiently to help me be a better passer than the other kids. Jack was my inspiration in those early years. He was a football hero around Marshall and my secret ambition was to be as good as he was. In fact, I wanted to be better in everything. There was a keen personal rivalry between us, as there is between most brothers. I never did give up trying to whip him in football, in marbles, in wrestling, in anything we did.

When Jack beat me, which he usually did, I would keep him out in the backyard until I got even. I would try to wear him down if I could not do it any other way. I hated to lose—even to my brother—and the years haven't changed my outlook much.

Once Jack had provided me with the fundamentals, I set out to find someone to practice on. A passer, even a nine-year-old passer, needs a receiver.

That is where my kid brother Don, three years younger than me, came in. I convinced him that running was the most important single thing to consider if he ever hoped to become a football player.

"That's what the coaches look for," I told him. "Those legs have to be in shape. You have to run and run if you want to make it in high school.

Gullible Don accepted my brotherly advice and I don't think he ever suspected my real motives.

"That's the boy," I said. "Now, as long as you are going to run, you might as well catch passes for me."

He thought this was a fine idea, and I had myself a pass receiver. This beat the old tire routine all to heck. I ran Don ragged most days, but he never said anything because I had impressed on him that dedicated football men accept physical punishment as part of the game.

"A guy who complains never gets anywhere," I said authoritatively.

Don nodded bravely. He would not have hollered "uncle" then if it killed him. And it all helped to make both of us better football players.

As I have said, Jack was an outstanding football player at Mar-

70

shall High, and later at Tulane University, where he was a 205-pound blocking back in the single wing. Don, who followed Jack and me, could have been a better athlete than both of us. But he never had much interest in the game after playing in high school. I have often wondered if I burned him out by running him so much when we were kids.

In the beginning, my father, Yelberton Abraham, Sr., a rural postman in Marshall, was opposed to having his boys play football. He was born in Sulphur Springs, a town of 8,000 located in north Texas, and he worked too hard as a young man to have time for athletics. I guess it was no easy matter to scratch out a living in the early 1900's. There apparently were more important things for a boy to do than play games. That is the way my father was brought up, so it was not surprising when he objected to Jack going out for the football team at Marshall Junior High. My mother, Alma, was against it too, but for another reason: she considered football too rough a game for her son.

Jack persisted, though, and they finally gave him permission. My father was a strong-willed man, but he was fair. I guess he realized times had changed since his boyhood.

Jack's football didn't interest my parents at first. They agreed to let him play, but still were not completely sold on the idea. This improved as time went by because folks in Marshall got to stopping my father on his mail rounds to ask him how his son was doing in football. Some would even tell him what a fine player Jack was and that he ought to be proud of him.

"Of course I'm proud of him," Dad would retort. He was, too. And then his natural pride as a father was extended to Jack's football playing ability. It was a lucky thing for me that my brother's success turned Dad into a pretty good football fan. If I thought parental permission was going to be automatic when my turn came to play football at Marshall Junior High, I was sadly mistaken. As a child I suffered with bronchial asthma and my folks were skeptical about allowing me to play such a rough game. The asthma bothered me all through high school. Sometimes I could hardly breathe out there on the field. But I never let on about my condition; I was afraid they would make me quit. I fought the thing and I outgrew it.

71

I can still remember my mother's reaction when she overheard me asking my father about football.

"Certainly not!" she said.

But Jack, whose playing sort of paved the way, joined the battle on my side. Eventually we wore them down. It was my first experience with the old double-team.

Jack's playing ahead of me contributed to my development in still another way: it gave me something to shoot at. It helps to have a goal. Mine was to surpass Jack's achievements. I pushed hard all the time to top whatever he had done. I did not always succeed, of course, but trying made me a better competitor. I was proud of him when someone said, "Your brother did this or that." And it made me work all the harder to be as good or better than Jack.

It was my father, though, who was my real inspiration—not as an athlete, for he wasn't an athlete, but as a warm person. He was a simple man, a good man. His first and only love was his family. He worked hard every day of his life to give his three boys and my sister Huline the best things in life. We were never rich but as Marshall families went, we were well fixed. We had a big brick home on ten acres about three miles outside of town. We had some cows and chickens and pigs, and a garden that supplied most of our vegetables. We had two cars and a few dollars in the Marshall bank. We never really wanted for anything.

Most of all, we had family love, the kind I have tried to bring into my home with my own wife and children.

Dad seldom hid his pride in us. He thought his boys were the greatest, and he let everyone know it. One day he drove me into town to buy me a pair of shoes. We walked into the store and Dad stuck out his chest, put his arm around my shoulder and said to the salesman, "Come on, now, I want you to get my big football-playing boy a pair of those shoes over there."

Everyone in the store looked around, maybe expecting to see Sammy Baugh or some other great star, and I was kind of embarrassed. But that is the way my father was. "My boys" were everything to him.

Dad was quite a "doer" as they say in Texas. After he finished his mail rounds every day, he built or remodeled houses and stores around Marshall. As I recall, he had two or three pressing stores,

72

a couple of cafes—nothing fancy, just coffee and sandwich shops, and some houses. He always seemed to be working to make extra money for us.

Sometimes as I look back I feel a little guilty. Dad did all of this extra work in addition to that required by our own place. Ten acres take a lot of working, and I must confess I was no great shakes when it came to doing chores around the place. Dad probably had too much understanding of my great desire to play football to be what you'd call a disciplinarian.

My father died in 1949. I've always been glad that he lived to see Jack play for Tulane, and that he saw me play for Louisiana State. He also attended a few games when I was with the Baltimore Colts, so I've always felt good over the fact that, after all the work and sacrifices he made for us, he saw them begin to bear fruit. My mother may have had a notion along the same lines, but she passed away in 1945 after my freshman year at LSU. By then, Mom had become quite a fan.

My parents are buried in Marshall, and although I have not lived there for a long time, if I died tomorrow, I should want to rest there in my home town beside them.

Among the many things my Dad taught me was this important lesson: no matter what you do, work hard at it.

This is the way I have approached football. I study hard. I practice hard. I play hard. And I lose hard.

Aside from family considerations, football has been the greatest thing in my life—ever since I was in the fourth grade . . . I organized a team and we whipped the fifth grade. I was the "promoter," the coach and, naturally, the quarterback. That was the start of it all, and even then I liked to "put the ball in the air."

CHAPTER NINE

OTIS MITCHELL:
"I WANT GOOD WINNERS"

I WAS IN THE SIXTH GRADE when I discovered I could throw the football better than the other kids in Marshall.

Unfortunately, the Marshall High School Junior Mavericks, coached by Joe Magrill, were not a passing team. Magrill had somehow escaped the influence of Sammy Baugh. He remained of the unshakable belief that single wing running and blocking were still the best way to move the ball.

Despite our different views, I considered Joe Magrill a fine coach.

Joe had coached my brother Jack and when I came out for the team at Marshall Junior High, he made a big fuss over me. There was a ceremony. They presented me with Jack's old shoulder pads and this, of course, was a very big moment for me. The folks around Marshall considered Jack a great football player and I was proud to be wearing his equipment.

The pads were too big and I could not throw very well in them, but this did not matter much in the sixth grade. The Junior Mavericks were not a passing team. Joe Magrill made me a tailback in the double wing and I soon learned there was more to the game of football than just throwing. A lot more.

I did not play much that first year. I was only a substitute. When I did get into the game, I seldom got a chance to do anything noteworthy. But my desire must have impressed Magrill. One day I overheard him tell my arithmetic teacher, "You watch ol' Y.A., he's going to be better than his brother Jack." I do not know what prompted Magrill to say something like that. I certainly had not done that much on the football field. But still it made me feel good to know he thought that much of me.

Most of my football playing in 1938 was done away from Marshall High—in the sandlots and fields where we chose up sides on the way home from school and played tackle. In the beginning, my parents had worried about us getting hurt in football. But by this time they were used to the idea. They did not baby me when I came home with a cut knee or a sprained ankle. They were not as protective as parents are today. In Marshall, you learned to take care of yourself. If you couldn't, well, you had no business playing football. It was great training, believe me, and I am sorry things are not still like that. Modern day parents are making ninnies out of their kids. That goes for me too. I have two boys, Mike, 12, and Pat, 11, and I worry about them playing tackle in the lot next to our house. I am afraid they will get hurt or something. Imagine that—a professional football player worrying about his boys playing tackle!

In Marshall, people either played football or they watched it. Football was the biggest thing in town. As far as I know, it still is.

The sports life of our town centered around Marshall High School and its two football teams. Friday night games brought out half the town. We always had a capacity crowd of 8,000 in Marshall Stadium. A football game was an occasion in those days. We had parades. The stores closed down. School got out early. No college town ever had a more loyal or rabid following. Residents of Marshall were not only familiar with our teams, but with teams from other parts of the state as well. They knew, for instance, who the up-and-coming halfback was with Longview High School, or which tackle on the Tyler team was a sure thing to make all-state.

Our rivalries with teams from Longview, Kilgore, Gladewater and Tyler were something—even on the junior high level.

There were two clubs out of Tyler, Hogg Junior High and Roberts Junior High. The Roberts team had a fellow named Bill

75

Johnson playing center and fullback. I remember playing against him in my very first ball game. It was not the last time I saw him. We faced each other for the next two years in junior high, and then for three seasons on the varsity level. When I played at LSU, Bill was with Texas A&M and we knocked heads a few more times. In the pro ranks, Johnson went with San Francisco in the All-America Conference and I was drafted by Baltimore, so for the next three seasons we continued our personal rivalry. By this time, we were close friends and of course we grew even closer when I joined San Francisco. Bill was one of my coaches. He is still with the Forty-Niners as line coach.

Joe Magrill was still my coach when I returned for my second year at Marshall Junior High. He stayed with the single wing, so my emergence as a forward passer was further delayed. This was a running offense and I was a passer. But I was learning. Magrill used me as a corner back on defense and I discovered, to my surprise, I must say, that it was a pleasant sensation to drive my shoulder into a ball-carrier and knock him down. My present teammates with New York probably would laugh to read this, but Y.A. Tittle was considered a pretty fair country tackler around Marshall. I like to recall one game where the Longview coach instructed his backs to, ". . . run the other end, away from that guy Tittle." How about that?

I do not think for a moment that this will cause John Lo Vetere or Jim Katcavage any worry over keeping their jobs. Anyhow, my defensive aspirations are a thing of the past. At 38, I have no inclination for further demonstrations. But if they want to make any bets, the file room of the Marshall News-Messenger has all the old newspaper clips on Y.A. Tittle, defensive specialist.

Two changes had taken place by the time I was in my third year at Marshall. One, I now weighed a solid 145 pounds and stood six feet tall. Two, Joe Magrill was replaced as head coach by Robert (Cracker) Brown. The latter development was significant.

Cracker Brown was a fellow who believed in throwing the football. This alone was enough to make him coach of the year in my book. He put in the single wing formation—no one used the T in those days—and installed me at tailback with instructions to "throw the ball whenever you get the chance."

I took Cracker at his word. I threw the ball enough to create quite a stir in Marshall, which was a town unaccustomed to wide open football. The papers built me up as a hot-shot passer. One even said I threw the ball as well as Sammy Baugh had when he was in high school. At the time, that was the nicest thing anybody had ever said about me.

Although my passing was an artistic success that year, the Marshall Junior Mavericks did not have a good season. I often had cause to wonder if "putting the ball in the air" was really the way to winning football. Cracker Brown had given me the green light to throw the ball, but we still lost a lot of games.

In 1941, my first year in high school, Otis Mitchell, out of Pampa, Texas, came to Marshall as head coach and brought with him a winning attitude. Otis, now head coach at North Texas State, was a forceful man in every respect. He exerted a great influence on my career. Up until that time, Marshall High had gone through a long siege of losing football. Longview was the best. Tyler was the best. Or maybe Kilgore was the best. But Marshall was always at the bottom. The picture changed when Otis Mitchell showed up. It did not change immediately, of course. But he put us on the right track.

I remember my first meeting with Otis Mitchell.

The varsity squad was practicing across the street from Marshall High. He walked out on the field and blew a whistle to get the squad together. He stood there for a minute, looking us over, and then he spoke.

"Gentlemen, my name is Otis Mitchell. I am your new coach. I think it will be better for all of us if I tell you right now that I have not come to Marshall to coach a losing football team."

He sure sounded like he meant business.

"There is no such thing as a 'good loser.' I do not want good losers on my football team."

This came as a surprise to many of us. We had been brought up in the belief that it was proper to be a good loser. But Mitchell was telling us something entirely different.

"If any of you are satisfied to finish second," he said, "turn in your suits right now. I am looking for boys who want to win it all. The world is full of good losers. I want good winners!"

77

This, then, was our first exposure to Mitchell's philosophy. His positive approach was contagious.

Mitchell's words reflected my own sentiments. I always have wanted to win. I always will too. I never set foot on a gridiron without recalling Otis' remark that "the world is full of good losers."

Marshall High did not immediately become a football power in east Texas. But under Otis Mitchell, things were beginning to improve. We all felt it was only a matter of time before his winning approach would pay off.

Mitchell was a firm believer in physical training and conditioning. This too had a lasting influence on me. It has carried over to this very day. Otis felt that football players must necessarily pay a price. It could be mental or physical, or sometimes both. "It is not an easy game," he used to remind us, "and there is no easy way to prepare for it."

It was Mitchell's contention, and it became mine too, that a coach can get a player ready physically, but mentally the player must do it for himself.

"Discipline is necessary in football," he once told me. "A player must discipline himself; he must follow the rules and train himself to live by them."

I tried to follow Coach Mitchell's teaching in this respect. It is what I live by today with the New York Giants, twenty-three years after my exposure to Otis Mitchell. I believe in paying the price. More than anything else, I want to win, and to win you have got to pay a price somewhere along the line.

Some of my teammates on the Marshall varsity smoked cigarettes. I did not. I was not a goody-goody by a long shot. But if Otis Mitchell said a football player should not smoke, well, by golly, I was not going to smoke no matter what the others did. Football is tough enough without making it tougher on yourself by not being physically ready, or by not disciplining yourself to do the things that will give you the best chance of winning. Otis Mitchell was a winner. When he said "no smoking," that was good enough for me.

It has been my experience that there are athletes who can disregard training and relax their mental discipline, and still be great players. I have played with men like this, and I have marveled at them. As for myself, I feel I need every edge I can get. I want to be at my maximum if at all possible. The best way to achieve this is by following the rules the way they are set down. If I lose, I do not want to lose because I cut a corner somewhere. Now, I sometimes smoke a cigarette, and I will have an occasional drink. But I will not do either if there is the slightest suspicion in my mind that such a thing might lessen my chance of winning.

Mitchell impressed on me the importance of practice. "You play like you practice," he said.

He was right. I have always practiced hard, as if I were playing a game. I do not want to let up for a second if I can help it. I do not feel right about missing a practice because of a small injury. The rules say you should practice and by golly, old Y.A.'s going to be there somehow.

Otis Mitchell was a winner, but he also made football fun. We started to throw the ball around a lot in practice, and this of course appealed to me. Mitchell kept our practices from becoming strictly body contact sessions. He was firm but he was no slave driver. He conditioned the Marshall squad without making it drudgery.

I never left practice in an exhausted condition. I suppose when you are fifteen or sixteen years old, tiredness is not part of your make-up.

In fact, there were times on a Friday afternoon when we got home from school at three o'clock, played touch tackle for a couple of hours, and then piled into my father's car and drove back to Marshall Stadium to play a game that same night.

The only time I have ever been overweight in my football career, strangely enough, was my first year in high school under Otis Mitchell. How that came about is a funny story.

My father thought I should be bigger if I was going to go out for the varsity team. "They will run right over you at a hundred and forty-five pounds," he warned. "You have got to be bigger, Y.A." With that, he put me on a diet of egg nogs and milk. Every afternoon when I got home from school, my mother would pour a couple of egg nogs into me, followed by a quart of milk. Sometimes I felt like I was going to blow up and bust right at the kitchen table. When I reported for spring practice, I had ballooned to 175 pounds, winning myself such nicknames as "Fatty" and "Lard Butt." It was fortunate I had a good arm and could throw the ball. With all that extra weight, I sure was not going to outrun anybody in Marshall.

Despite my reputation as a non-runner, Mitchell used me at fullback and halfback in the double wing that year. I even played one game at end. I guess you might say I was the "Marshall Joe Morrison." Through no fault of my own, I was named the Mavericks' Most Valuable Player.

This was kind of embarrassing because the award was given by the Sullivan Funeral Home in downtown Marshall and my sister Huline, my greatest fan, was a secretary for George and Bill Sullivan, who ran the undertaking parlor. Well, when they handed me the trophy at our football dinner, I was really embarrassed. I could just hear everyone saying, "How do you like that? Huline Tittle works for the Sullivan Funeral parlor, and Y.A. wins the trophy!"

I am certain Huline did nothing illegal to swing the award my way. I am just as certain, however, that her great pride in her brother Y.A. and her enthusiasm for football in general went a long way toward helping George and Bill Sullivan make their final choice.

The funeral home award may have been symbolic. The Marshall Mavericks did not fare well that season, nor did their supposedly most valuable player.

But in 1943, my senior year, Mitchell's coaching program turned out one of the finest high school teams in east Texas. We won every game in District Two, and got even with such old tormentors as Tyler, Kilgore, Longview, Gladewater and Texarkana. But we lost to Lufkin in the state championships.

I do not care to dwell at length on this period of my career because there are more important events to be covered. But I must say that in 1943 I was blessed with what was to be the fastest high school backfield in Texas history. I was the tailback in Mitchell's double wing offense. My three other backs were Byron Gillroy, Bobby Furrh and Billy Dinkle. They were like greased lightning. They were one, two, three in the district in the hundred-yard dash and, while they did not approach the 9.3 or 9.4 times of today, they could all run the hundred in less than 10 seconds.

Gillroy weighed only 145 pounds but he was dynamite in the open field. He was all-state the following year and later became an outstanding player at the University of Texas. Furrh made the all-state second team, and Dinkle was all-state and then earned Little All-América honors at North Texas State, the school now coached by Otis Mitchell.

The 1943 Marshall High squad also had two fast ends, a boy by the name of Roy Moore, who now lives in Longview, and James Taylor, who is the principal of the high school in Hallsville, only 15 miles from Marshall. Moore and Taylor were rangy kids who could really get out there and run. They gave me five great receivers to throw the ball to, and all of them could go the distance when they caught it.

That must have been the passingest high school team in the state that year. On Mitchell's order, I threw the ball 25 or 30 times a game. Nor did we play it close to the vest like a lot of high school teams. We threw from our own end zone. We threw from our own 10-yard line. We threw on first down. And we threw on fourth down.

And usually when I threw the ball, Gillroy, Furrh or Dinkle or one of my ends was there to catch it. I was completing 18 or 20 passes a game.

We did not throw long. We just shot those fast little wingbacks out there in the flat and hit them with quick passes. Then they took off and, boy, this was something to see. Nobody could catch them once they got in the open. It was like a track meet.

If memory serves me, Marshall survived the final two games of the 1943 season without the services of Y.A. Tittle. I wrecked my knee in the next to last game, against Longview, and Furrh moved in to my tailback position and won the game for us. The next week Furrh was still the tailback and we closed with a win over Tyler to earn a shot at Lufkin in the state championships.

Lufkin was a team we could never beat during my years at Marshall. Lufkin is a little town of about 8,000 located 75 miles south of Marshall but it was always a power in Texas football. Schools were assigned to districts in those days on the basis of total enrollment. And Lufkin pulled the kids in from all over the county.

They hauled them into town in school buses, trains, cars, wagons, anything. And they turned out one fine football team after another. The 1943 Lufkin squad was no exception.

My leg was still in a wire splint, which prevented me from bending my knee, but I pleaded with Otis Mitchell to let me play against Lufkin.

"It's my last chance," I told him, "my last shot at these guys. I just have to play."

Otis finally agreed, against his better judgment.

Although I could not run and could barely walk with the wire splint on my leg, I played the entire game against Lufkin. I caught the snap from center and threw passes until I got knocked down. When that happened, somebody had to pick me up because, with one leg in the wire cage, I could not get up by myself. They knocked me down every play. Gillroy and Furrh propped me up again, and I kept throwing the ball off one leg. I did not throw it well enough, though, because Lufkin knocked us off, 19–7.

Maybe I should not have tried to play on that injured knee. But when you are fifteen years old, a championship football game can be a very important thing in your life.

I have always wanted to play every minute of every game. This is my nature. This is why I am still in the game today.

My first year at Marshall, I played very little. I was the fifth man in the backfield. It bothered me that I was not in there more. I felt I was better than the others, particularly M.L. Branford, a senior who played my position. I could throw the ball better than Branford but Otis Mitchell did not see it that way. Branford played and I rode the bench. This was a frustrating experience for me and it took me a while to get over it.

A lot of folks may consider me a modest player, and in some ways I try to be modest. But I am really not that way. This is a confession I have never made before. I am a team man, but at the same time I have always found it difficult to cheer for a fellow who is playing my position and maybe taking my job away from me. I like to be on a winning team; every athlete does. But, damn it, I want to have a hand in winning. I would not be telling the truth if I said I am delighted when another quarterback does the job while I am sitting on the bench.

At the same time, I have never criticized or second-guessed a coach for not playing me.

A coach has to call the shots as he sees them. It is not always easy. Otis Mitchell taught me to put a checkrein on my impatience. He showed me the value of hiding my frustration and anger. But neither Otis nor anyone else ever has taught me to like sitting on the bench.

CHAPTER TEN

BAREFOOT IN AUSTIN

A NUMBER of colleges in the southwest were interested in me when I graduated from Marshall High School in June of 1944.

This interest was based on two factors. One, I was a 185-pound tailback who could throw the hell out of the ball. Two, as an asthma sufferer (I still had not completely outgrown the condition), I was likely to be 4-F in the draft. With World War II in full swing and manpower scarce in the college ranks, my draft status was understandably more important to the college recruiters than my passing records. What impressed them most, I believe, was the prospect that, good or bad, I would at least be around for the full four years.

I received grant-in-aid scholarship offers from all the Texas schools—T.C.U., Texas A&M, University of Texas, Rice, Southern Methodist; and from Tulsa, Louisiana State and Tulane, where my brother Jack had played. Many of these offers took the form of letters or phone calls from the coaches. But often the schools delegated the direct recruiting to prominent alumni who lived in or near Marshall.

Myron Blaylock, presently a prominent attorney in Marshall, was a Texas alumnus, and he gave me a pretty strong pitch during my last semester in high school.

There were others, too. They visited the high school, and they came out to the house for dinner, armed with pamphlets and other propaganda material. It was a steady parade of scouts and coaches.

My parents were impressed by all this. They thought it was quite wonderful that so many important colleges and universities were interested in their boy Y.A. They really enjoyed entertaining the scouts at dinner. As for me, well, I really was not that interested. I wanted to play football in college but up until the time I graduated, I did not think much about which school I would like to go to.

College football recruiting in the southwest in 1944 was a free-wheeling affair, completely lacking the strict regulations that exist today. It was perfectly legal to have a prospective scholarship player visit the campus. I spent considerable time on trips to schools in Texas and Louisiana. I visited the Louisiana State campus at Baton Rouge several times and got to know Bernie Moore, the head coach, quite well. He struck me as being the kind of man I would like to play for. When the time arrived to make a decision, I chose L.S.U.

I must admit my decision was influenced by more than just my regard for Bernie Moore. L.S.U. was one of the few all-civilian schools in the southwest in those war years. Most of the colleges had service programs, such as the Navy's V–12, and this meant that the guys playing football were older and more experienced. My chances of playing were better at L.S.U. where my competition would come from other 17-year-olds plus some 4-Fs. At a place like Texas, I might have to compete against fellows two and three years older who had played varsity ball at, say, Georgia Tech, Notre Dame or Ohio State, before entering the officer training programs.

Bernie Moore sent me the grant-in-aid papers and I signed them around the middle of May, a few weeks before I was to graduate from Marshall High School. My scholarship would entitle me to tuition, room and board and books. It was the standard type of scholarship being offered at the time. I was happy to be going to Louisiana State because I liked Moore and I knew a little about the school. L.S.U. and Tulane were great rivals, and I had seen several games when Jack was a blocking back for Tulane.

Right here, though, I must tell a story of which I am not overly proud. Still, it deserves telling.

85

Even though I had committed myself to L.S.U., the University of Texas people did not abandon their efforts to make me change my mind. Myron Blaylock was constantly talking to me. And if I remember correctly, Blair Cherry, one of the Texas coaches, might have been on the scene. They did a terrific selling job, and eventually they convinced me that my real football future was with the University of Texas.

Two days after my graduation, and three days before I was to enroll at L.S.U., I was on my way to Austin.

Everything happened so fast that to this day I do not know what made me change my mind. The shame of violating my written and spoken agreement with Bernie Moore has been with me ever since. It happened a long time ago but it still weighs heavily on my conscience. As a plea in my behalf I can only offer that I was immature and probably not too smart.

Anyway, there I was in a car with a couple of assistant coaches from Texas heading for Austin on a scorching hot June afternoon. I was not yet fully aware what was happening. But apparently everything had been laid out very nicely. The plan was to enroll me in summer school, get me a part-time job and keep me hidden from the L.S.U. counterspies until fall practice got under way.

We arrived in Austin that evening and the car stopped in front of a large frame building on the fringe of the Texas campus. A large sign over the door read: "Mrs. Poole's Boarding House."

Mrs. Poole was not unused to having all-state football players deposited on her doorstep. She quickly ushered me into the front room, had me sign the register and then showed me upstairs to my room.

"It's nice and quiet here," she said. "You'll like it at the university."

I wish I had been as sure of this as she seemed to be.

The door to the room next to mine was open. After unpacking, I stuck my head in and said, "Hiya, my name is Y.A. Tittle."

The fellow lying on the bed was husky and blond. He rolled over on his side, looked at me for a second out of half-closed eyes and said, "Glad to meet you. My name is Layne . . . Bobby Layne."

Layne had never heard of me. But I knew all about him. He had played at Highland Park High School in Dallas. He had been

86

the first team All-State quarterback. They said he was the hottest damned schoolboy player in the whole state of Texas.

"They got you too, huh?" said Bobby. "Man, they don't miss anybody." And then he chuckled.

Layne was my age, or close to it. But he seemed much older, more confident. I liked him from the first, but he made me uneasy in a way that I could not explain.

That night I took stock of my situation. With Bobby Layne on the scene it would not be easy to make the Texas ball club. His reputation made him the top freshman in the school. Obviously the rest of us would be at a disadvantage. I was concerned, but I was not going to be scared off. Layne would still have to prove he could throw the ball better than me. I was sure he couldn't. I was not cocky. It's just that I had confidence in my ability as a passer. I was not about to be psyched out by Bobby Layne or anyone else.

The next morning, Blair Cherry came and got me at Mrs. Poole's and took me across the street to the C. and S. Sporting Goods store, which was run by a great little guy called Rooster Andrews, who today is one of my closest friends. They had a job for me there that would keep me busy until summer school started. I was to work two or three hours a day stacking boxes, sweeping and running errands.

Other football players from all over the state were similarly employed around the campus. They were big and tough and there were a lot of them. Layne had been right; the Texas scouts had done their job extremely well.

As might have been expected, Bobby Layne was not involved in any of the menial tasks that befell the rest of us at Austin the summer of 1944. Bobby was a great baseball pitcher, and he had hooked up with a well-paying semi-pro outfit that had a franchise in Austin. While the rest of us were sweeping and stacking, Layne was sleeping so he would be rested for the game that night. I kind of envied Bobby. He sure was a lot smarter than the others, including Y.A. Tittle.

At first, Layne and I were together a lot. But later on he was off playing ball most of the time and I was left with nothing to do after I finished my job at Rooster Andrews' store across from

Mrs. Poole's. I had not made friends with anyone else on the campus, so there was not much to do until Bobby came back. I do not know why we hit it off so well. Bobby was a city-slicker from Dallas; I was a green-eared kid from Marshall. We did not have much in common except for football. But we did respect each other and got along fine.

In the evenings when Bobby was not pitching baseball, we often got out in the street in front of Mrs. Poole's and ran races. We ran in our bare feet because we thought we could run faster that way. We ran right down the middle of the street with everybody looking at us like we were crazy. Maybe we were, at that. But at least it was competition, and Bobby and I thrived on competition of any kind. We just had to be competing.

Whenever I run across Layne today, which is not as often as it used to be since he retired after the 1962 season, we sit down to have a few beers and the conversation always gets around to our days at Mrs. Poole's.

"I can still outrun you, Tittle," he says in that gravel voice of his. And I say, "Like hell you can."

I think Bobby really believes he used to beat me in our races. But actually I whipped him most of the time. Neither of us ever amounted to anything as runners in pro ball, so I guess it does not matter too much who won the barefoot races in Austin.

After a few weeks, I was ready to leave the University of Texas. I was sorry I had gone there in the first place. The rest of the high school players on campus seemed much older and more experienced. They were different than the kids I had played with in Marshall. Then too, I noticed a lot of officer training fellows signing up for football.

"Y.A.," I said, "you will never get a chance to play in this kind of company."

About this time back in Marshall, my mother put in a telephone call to Bernie Moore at Baton Rouge.

"Y.A. is down at Austin," she told Moore. "But I am not so sure he likes it there."

"Do you think he still wants to come to Louisiana State?" asked Bernie.

"Yes. He won't admit it of course, but I believe he would."

Moore thanked my mother for calling and said he would do whatever he could. Mom did not realize it, of course, but what Bernie meant was that he was going to recruit me right back off the Texas campus. In his opinion, turnabout was fair play. Texas had grabbed me away from the L.S.U. camp, so Bernie was prepared to resort to the same thing. Recruiting in those days was a case of every coach for himself.

Bernie called in his line coach, Red Swanson, and told him, "Go to Austin and find Tittle. Don't come back without him."

Swanson showed up in Austin on a Sunday morning and called me at Mrs. Poole's. He said he wanted to talk to me. I was so lonely that I was happy to have anyone to talk to. I told him I would meet him at the hotel for breakfast. It did not even occur to me to wonder why Red had suddenly appeared in Austin or how he had found me so easily.

At breakfast, Swanson was tactful enough not to pressure me on why I had wound up at Texas instead of going to Baton Rouge as I had agreed. I was glad he did not bring up the subject of my defection. I was still embarrassed by the whole incident. I appreciated his thoughtfulness in not mentioning it over coffee and toast that morning.

"You like it here, Y.A.?" he asked me point-blank.

"I thought I would, Red," I replied. "Now I am not so sure."

"Why?"

"To begin with, I do not think I will get a chance to play much here. It seems like every high school kid in the state is here. It's like an Army camp."

Swanson could see I was unhappy at Austin, so he made his pitch right away.

"Do you want to reconsider and come to Louisiana State?" he asked.

"Would they still want me back there, Red?"

"Why do you think I am here?" he said. "Bernie Moore wants you to play tailback for us."

"That's great," I said. "I'll go back to Mrs. Poole's and pack my bag right away."

"Whoa, hold on there. Not so fast, boy. There's something you have to do first."

89

"What's that?"

"You've got to call Mr. Bible and tell him you are leaving. It's the right thing to do. You just can't walk out of here. I'm not taking you back until you tell him you changed your mind about playing at Texas."

Dana X. Bible was the head football coach at Texas, one of the most respected men in his profession, and I was certain he would not be happy to learn I was pulling out. The thought of calling him scared me to death. I tried to wiggle out of it.

"He won't be in his office, Red," I stammered. "It's Sunday, you know."

"I thought of that too," said Swanson, "so I took the trouble of looking up Mr. Bible's home phone number. You can reach him there."

I was trapped. I took the slip of paper with Mr. Bible's number on it and walked over to a phone booth. My heart was pounding. I did not have the slightest idea what I would say to him. I dialed the number and waited. It rang once. It rang twice. Then two or three more times. Happy days, no one was home! Or maybe they were asleep. At any rate, I had tried. My intentions had been good. I felt as if a heavy weight had been lifted from my shoulders.

Later, there was considerable bitterness between D.X. Bible and Bernie Moore over my return to L.S.U., even though this sort of thing happened all the time during that period. To put the record straight, though, I did try to call Bible that morning. And it was Red Swanson, the L.S.U. line coach, who insisted that I make the call. That's more than the Texas people did when they talked me out of going to L.S.U.

Swanson took me back to Mrs. Poole's. I packed my suitcase and we left. Layne and the others did not even know I had gone.

We drove all the way to Baton Rouge, a distance of 450 miles, stopping in Houston briefly to take on another passenger, a kid by the name of Jim Cason. He was from Victoria, Texas, and though we did not realize it at the time, we were to become fast friends in the years ahead. Jim and I played together for four seasons at L.S.U. and later with the San Francisco Forty-Niners. I guess our friendship began that first day on the ride from Houston to Baton Rouge. Jim was only sixteen and we were both frightened. For most of the trip we sat in silence and stared out the window as Swanson pushed the car eastward.

I have often stopped to wonder what might have happened had I stayed at the University of Texas that summer of 1944. Maybe pro football never would have heard of Yelberton Abraham Tittle, or perhaps Bobby Layne's career would have been different. We were both quarterbacks and we might have eliminated each other entirely. It is odd how fate steps in and changes the course of a man's life. In my case, fate was called Red Swanson. Bobby Layne went his way with Texas and I went to Louisiana State. Our paths were to cross many times over the next twenty years, but in 1944 we headed our separate ways.

CHAPTER ELEVEN

FRESHMEN AND 4–Fs

RED SWANSON delivered Jimmy Cason and me to Baton Rouge just in time for the start of summer practice.

Bernie Moore welcomed us to the fold and, being a gentleman, never mentioned my Texas escapade. From the beginning, I knew things were going to be better at Louisiana State.

For one thing, the rest of the football players seemed to be my age. They were mostly freshmen and 4-Fs. There were none of the older guys I had seen hanging around the campus in Austin. L.S.U. did not have an officer training program. At least I would not be competing against graduate students from other colleges who had played varsity football.

Despite this, there was no shortage of football talent. In addition to Cason and myself, the freshmen group that first summer included Red Knight from Bossier City, La., outside of Shreveport, and Ray Coates from Jesuit High School in New Orleans, a great tailback and perhaps the finest high school player in Louisiana.

Coates was being groomed as the No. 1 tailback by Moore when I arrived that June. He was a strong runner and a fair passer, and he had the knack of getting yardage. Red Knight was versatile. He could run and he could kick. Cason was a blood and guts guy at 150 pounds. He was a tiger on defense and a tough little runner. Me? Well, I could not run a lick as tailbacks go. But I was the best passer of the bunch.

Four years later, Bernie Moore called this group, "the finest back-field I ever coached."

But in June of 1944 we were a rag-tail lot and Bernie probably wondered if we would ever amount to anything. The talent was there but it would take a lot of coaching to bring it to the surface.

Moore did not wait long to begin. The day after Cason and I arrived at Baton Rouge we were thrown into our first practice. Bernie Moore's practices were anything but brief. We went at it most of the afternoon, took a breather around supper time, and then turned on the lights in Tiger Stadium and scrimmaged into the night. What a grind! By the end of the summer I was down to 175 pounds, ten less than I weighed at Marshall High School. But I was a better football player.

Most of the football players lived in G Building, a brick dormitory, and except for classes, which ran until 3 o'clock every day, we stayed pretty much to ourselves. The way Moore worked us, there was no time for anything but football and studies—and often the studies ran a poor second. L.S.U., like most colleges at that time, operated on a quarterly schedule with classes the year 'round. Cason and I were enrolled in the physical education course but I must confess that we were not at the head of our class. We were too busy trying to make the ball club.

Practice started every day on the baseball field outside Tiger Stadium. Everyone wore shorts and T shirts because it was so damned hot. The temperature hit 100 degrees in the afternoon. We worked until early evening and then we put on the pads and crawled, and I mean crawled, into the Satdium to scrimmage a while longer. Anyone who was not in shape did not last long under Bernie Moore at L.S.U. Some nights we had all we could do to drag ourselves back to G Building.

"The hell with this," some of the guys would moan. "It's not worth it."

But a good night's sleep usually brightened the outlook and everyone was there again the next day, sweating under the hot sun, banging heads, working like dogs. At least that is the way it was with me. Making the team at L.S.U. was very important to me. I would not allow myself to consider failure. So, along with the others, I endured the heat, the physical punishment—and even the classroom.

By the time Coach Moore had us ready for the first big intra-squad game, Cason, Coates, Knight and myself had established ourselves as the best of the tailback candidates. We all played that night, and I was lucky enough to have a hot hand throwing the ball. I completed my first twelve passes and moved the offense in for two scores.

I must have made a good impression. The next day the papers gave me a lot of copy. They said I might be the best passer to play for L.S.U. since Leo Byrd and Abe Michael, two great tailbacks. Byrd had thrown to Ken Kavanaugh, now my end coach with the New York Giants. Michael's batterymate had been Gaynell Tinsley in the mid-1930s.

Naturally, I was flattered to be put in the same class with these fellows.

But college football in those days, and even today to a large degree, was not a passing game. "There is more to it than just throwing the ball," Bernie Moore used to tell me. He was right, of course, but there was not much else I could do but throw the football. That was *my* game—and still is.

I was not an outstanding runner in the class of Red Knight or Ray Coates, and my freshman year at Baton Rouge was not a stupendous success. I played as much tailback as the others; in fact, I think I started four of our nine games. But we did not win many in 1944 and I doubt if anyone was predicting greatness for Bernie Moore's club.

Two games stand out in my memory that year. One was the opener game against Alabama; the other was the last game of the schedule against Tulane. Alabama had the great Harry Gilmer at tailback and was the class of the Southeastern Conference. L.S.U. was not given much of a chance against the Crimson Tide in the first game, but I was more interested in the prospect of playing against Gilmer. They were calling him the finest forward passer in the nation, and I was anxious to see just how good he really was. I found out! Gilmer was everything they said he was. He could run and he could pass. He was the best tailback I had ever seen. But I was hitting that night, too, and we held Alabama to a 27–27 tie which was definitely an upset of sorts. I got into the game in the second half and threw a couple of touchdown passes. One went to my roommate, Clyde Lindsay, from Kilgore Junior College. The other was caught by Rip Rowan, a big halfback from Memphis who later captained the team at West Point.

Even then, my running prowess was not legend. I remember that when I went in against Alabama, they backed right off that line and waited for me to throw the ball. They just sat there in the secondary, daring me to run.

Things have not changed greatly over the past twenty years, either.

My outstanding day as a freshman, and perhaps the greatest day of my college career, occurred against Tulane, my brother Jack's school, in the final game of 1944. I completed 15 of 17 passes for three touchdowns and 300 yards, and we whipped them by 25–6. Maybe college football was not a passing proposition in those days but for one game at least I changed the script. Bernie Moore gave me my head and I really put the ball in the air. Fewer games have given me greater satisfaction. Tulane was a bigger, tougher ball club made up of servicemen, some of whom had played with Jack three years before.

Jack was in the stands that day and I knew he was proud of me, even though it must have hurt his pride to see his old school get whipped by an underdog L.S.U. team with a freshman back-field.

My brother Jack went into the U.S. Naval Aviation Physical Training program under the guidance of Navy's Tom Hamilton, after leaving Tulane. He coached up at Norman, Okla., and later at Milliken College in Johnson City, Tenn. He played too but he hurt his ankle and the Navy sent him back to New Orleans, his wife's home town. This transfer gave him a chance to get to Baton Rouge in 1944 and 1945 to see me play. The whole Tittle family was there the day I beat Tulane. My mother and dad drove the 250 miles from Marshall and my sister Huline came with them. They saw most of my other games that first season too. My mother died in 1945 but at least she had seen me play tailback for L.S.U.

Although my parents are both gone now, the rest of us are still close. Jack is in the insurance business in New Orleans. Don owns a hardware store in Durant, Okla., and Huline is married and lives in Marlton, Ark., where her husband manages the local J.C. Penny store. They all follow my pro career and Huline clips every word that is written about me and adds it to her collection of scrapbooks.

My scholastic achievements as a freshman were even less spectacular than L.S.U.'s football record.

Everybody who went to college in those wartime years was waiting to be drafted, and so no one really bothered too much about marks. They were not going to do a guy any good in the Army. Even though I had asthma, I expected to be drafted along with the others. I did not feel this condition would keep me out of service. As a result, I did not concentrate too seriously on my studies and if Bernie Moore had not talked me into going to summer school, I would have been ineligible to play football as a sophomore at L.S.U.

When I was called up for my draft physical in the spring of 1945, they classified me 4-F. This was very embarrassing at first. I had always heard that 4-Fs were skinny little guys with horn-rimmed glasses and fallen arches, and I did not relish being put into this kind of a category.

It helped, though, when Cason, Coates, and Knight also turned up as 4-Fs.

CHAPTER TWELVE

MEET MELVIN DIDIER, CENTER

THE T FORMATION came to Louisiana State in 1945 and changed the course of my football life.

I had heard a lot about the T. So had the other guys. But none of us had even seen it in person until the day Bernie Moore showed up at practice and introduced us to a fellow named Carl Brumbaugh.

"Mr. Brumbaugh is here to help us install the T formation," Bernie explained. "I want you to listen carefully to everything he says. This is going to be a big change."

Brumbaugh had been a quarterback with the Chicago Bears in the early 1930s, and so I guess it was kind of natural that he should come to Baton Rouge to teach us the T. The Bears had made the formation popular a few years before when they murdered the Washington Redskins, 73–0, in the N.F.L. championship game. The T was not exactly new. It had been used in the early days of football. But it had fallen out of style until George Halas, the Bears' owner and coach, resurrected it around 1940. Halas brought in Ralph Jones from little Delaware College and Clark Shaughnessy from the University of Chicago, two of the smartest coaches in football. They re-designed the T for the Bears. They added a man-in-motion and a counter play. They gave it deception and speed. Then Halas used it to whip the Redskins for the championship.

97

Following that memorable rout, the T formation was No. 1 on everybody's hit parade, in college ball and in the pro league.

Shaughnessy left the Bears in 1941 and went to Stanford University where he built an undefeated club with Frankie Albert and Norm Standlee which went to the Rose Bowl.

As I recall, Rice University was the first Southwestern Conference team to switch to the T from the single and double wing formations that were popular at the time, and then Georgia followed suit in the Southeastern Conference. Louisiana State was the next school to make the changeover.

When Moore hired Brumbaugh and brought him to Baton Rouge, he sent two of his L.S.U. assistants, one of them Slick Martin, to South Bend, where Notre Dame was also putting in the T. Bernie wanted to learn as much about the formation as possible—and as quickly as possible.

Moore's biggest problem was what to do with his backfield. He had Ray Coates and Red Knight and Jimmy Cason and me, but we were all tailbacks.

"I guess there's no choice with Tittle," Bernie said to us one day. "He can't run worth a darn and he can't block, so we've got to make him the quarterback. Besides, he can throw the ball pretty good."

Well, at least Bernie thought that much of me!

When the juggling was completed, our three tailbacks, plus newcomer Dan Sandifer from Shreveport, constituted the starting backfield. Red Knight, a hard runner with a quick start, went to fullback. Ray Coates was the left halfback. Sandifer and my old buddy Jimmy Cason shared the right halfback job.

The T was a strange and puzzling thing to all of us right from the start, and Carl Brumbaugh had his hands full.

Nobody in my part of the country had ever taken a direct handoff from center. It just was not the thing to do. We stood back there seven yards and let the center snap it to us. When Brumbaugh showed me what was expected of the quarterback in the T, I scratched my head and asked, "How am I going to get back out of there to pass?"

"Oh, you'll get back all right," he said. "Don't worry about it. I've never lost a quarterback yet."

Then he lined us up in the T—me with my hands under the center's crotch and the others, Cason, Knight and Coates, strung out in a straight line behind me. Being natural-born single wing men, we all felt kind of silly standing there like that. None of us knew what was coming next. I was worse off than the others because I could not see any of them without looking over my shoulder. After years of being a tailback, it was strange to be up there so close to the line with my hands under the center, and that defensive middle guard staring me in the eye. He'll get me for sure before I can drop back out of here, I thought.

Melvin Didier was my first T formation center at L.S.U. It was a rather unique experience to become so well acquainted with a lineman. I did not see much of Melvin—only his rear end—for the next two years. But we were good friends just the same.

All of us were like ducks out of water that spring of 1945 and sometimes I feared Carl Brumbaugh would throw up his hands in despair and go back to Chicago.

My big problem right from the beginning was that I could not get set to throw. Dropping back from center threw me off balance. I found it difficult to plant my foot and get rid of the ball as I had done in the single wing. I was tripping and stumbling all over myself on the drop-back. And when I did get back there under control, which was seldom, I never knew where my receivers were or, worse yet, my blockers. In the single wing, it had all been right there in front of me, the line, the receivers, the blockers. I could see everything. In the T, I was moving one way and everyone else was going the opposite way. My entire perspective was changed.

Fortunately, Brumbaugh was a man of infinite patience.

"It will come, Y.A.," he used to say when he saw I was discouraged. "It will come. One of these days you will be a fine T quarterback."

"Not the way I am going now," I thought.

My first encounter with the T formation convinced me that dropping back from center is the single most important thing for a quarterback to master. Every passer must have the arm, of course. This is a must. But even with the arm, a quarterback is only as good as his drop-back. This one move must be worked on all the time to achieve speed, to learn to hit the spot with the right foot

99

and to be ready to throw. Drifting back to throw is wrong. The quarterback has to be ready to throw the ball right now. Timing is everything. He has only a second or two to hit that sideline pass or the turn-in or whatever he is going to throw. He must get back there in good shape and be set to pass the football. If my boy wanted to be a quarterback, this is the first thing I would teach him.

The T offense introduced by Brumbaugh at Baton Rouge was nothing like the T we run today in the pro league. In 1945 we used two tight ends. Everyone was shoulder to shoulder, packed in there like sardines. The only split man was the halfback who went in motion. Our first plays were straight-ahead dives and we thought we were pretty fancy. We were making shoulder fakes all over the place, trying to hide the ball. It was something to see.

But if the T formation was mystifying to us, it was even more so for our opponents that year. Except for Georgia, all the South-eastern Conference schools stayed in the single wing. And naturally, their defenses were geared to the single wing too. Alabama, with Harry Gilmer at tailback; Tennessee, Mississippi State, Tulane and Ole Miss were still running from the single wing.

I remember the first time we used the T in a conference game. I do not even recall who we played. That's not important. I sent Cason in motion to the left and nobody even went out to cover him! The defense did not know what the dickens to make of it. The next play I sent Coates in motion to the other side. Again nobody covered him. This was like shooting fish in a barrel. I just turned around and lobbed the ball to Cason or Coates, and away they went. The defense was dumbfounded. I kept thinking they would eventually adjust and pick up our halfbacks in motion. But they didn't. I must have completed 20 for 20 that day, or close to it.

And mind you, I was still stumbling and staggering back from the center. I was not a polished T quarterback by any means. My footwork did not remind anyone of Arthur Murray. My handoffs were hardly crisp, and often Coates and Knight went into the line trying to find the handle on the ball. I had practiced my steps and my pivots and my pass-drop faithfully. But I could not quite get the hang of it. Only my passing kept me in the lineup.

Although Bernie Moore's 4-F backfield was slightly less skilled in the T than the Chicago Bears, we surprised a lot of teams in 1945 and had ourselves a pretty good season. We finished with a 7–2 record, losing only to Alabama, which went to the Rose Bowl, and Georgia, which, being a T club itself, was not the least bit surprised by our new formation.

I averaged 54 minutes a game that year, as a quarterback on offense and a halfback on defense.

I got to know Melvin Didier better with every game although I did not meet him face to face until our annual awards dinner in January.

CHAPTER THIRTEEN

THE BELT–BUCKLE GAME

THE SUCCESS of the T formation, plus the end of World War II, brought a new era to Louisiana State, and to the rest of college football.

The guys coming back from the service were older and bigger and faster. Competition was tougher all around.

Even so, L.S.U., with its 4–F backfield, had a great football team in 1946. We won nine games and lost one to Georgia Tech in a real upset. We went to the Cotton Bowl where we played a score-less tie with Arkansas in the worst football weather I can recall. It was worse than December 29, 1962, when the Giants and Green Bay met at Yankee Stadium for the world championship. You expect bad weather in New York at that time of the year. But you don't expect snow, ice, sub-freezing temperatures in Dallas.

L.S.U. was a high-scoring T formation ball club in 1946 but we could not do a thing in the Cotton Bowl on New Year's Day. The field was a sheet of ice and the footing was treacherous. It was the same for both sides, of course, and Arkansas was no better off.

I was sitting in our dressing room that raw day trying to thaw out when a fellow walked up to me and said, "Y.A., I'm Creighton Miller of the Cleveland Browns. I'd like to talk to you."

"Sure," I said, "what about?"

"We have drafted you and we'd like you to sign with us," he said.

This came as a surprise. Here I was still a junior and the Browns had drafted me. I didn't understand.

"How can you sign me when I still have another year left?" I asked.

I was not familiar with the pro draft at all; in fact, I knew nothing about the way it worked. It seemed to me, though, that drafting a junior should be illegal.

Miller himself appeared puzzled.

"Well, maybe I'd better check into it," he said. "Anyway, you'll be hearing from us."

With that, he walked out of the locker room. That was the last I saw of him—or heard from the Cleveland Browns—until a year later when I became eligible for the pro draft.

Louisiana State should have had its greatest team in 1947, my senior year. But it did not. Why, I don't know. We had a wonderful backfield with Cason, Coates, Sandifer and Knight all at their best. We had a top offensive line with some great tackles in Ray Collins, Ed Champagne and Jeff Burkett. We had everything—but we lost three games out of ten and did not get a bowl invitation. It was a disappointing season, especially for Coach Bernie Moore.

Most of the guys who played with L.S.U. in 1947 wound up as pros. Ray Coates, the halfback, and Ray Collins, a tackle, played with the Giants later on. Cason went with the San Francisco Forty-Niners and Sandifer with Washington. Champagne was with Los Angeles, Burkett played for the Chicago Cardinals, and Hubert Shurtz was a tackle for Pittsburgh.

Two games from my senior year stand out in my memory, and neither of them was a winning effort for L.S.U. One was the famous "belt-buckle play" game which we lost to Mississippi, 20–18, and the other was my final appearance against Tulane, a game which ended in a 6–6 tie. Looking back, I had four terrific days against Tulane; I always seemed to be at my best against my brother Jack's old school. As a sophomore, I completed 11 of 12 passes for two touchdowns. The next season, I had eight of nine and two more scores. And in 1947, my swan song for L.S.U. at New Orleans, I completed 10 of 16 passes. Over the four years, I helped whip Tulane three times and had one tie. I've often reminded Jack of a pretty fair record against his alma mater.

The 1947 loss to Ole Miss at Baton Rouge resulted in the most embarrassing incident of my entire career: I lost my pants in front of 40,000 fans, among them my fiancee, Minnette DeLoach.

This was about three games from the end of the season and this ball game was to decide whether L.S.U. or Ole Miss would get a bowl bid.

The story goes that I intercepted a pass thrown by Charlie Conerly, the Mississippi tailback and later my teammate with the Giants. This is not so. I did intercept a pass—late in the third period with Ole Miss leading, 20–18—but Charlie did not throw it; he wasn't even in the game then. The pass was thrown by the second-string tailback, and I don't remember his name. But I do know it wasn't Conerly.

Anyway, I was playing the left corner on defense and this Mississippian tried to throw a pass out there in the flat. It's the kind of pass that's always dangerous to throw because if a guy intercepts it he usually has a clear field down the sideline.

I timed the ball perfectly and cut right in front of the Mississippi receiver just as he was reaching for the ball. We both had our hands on it for a split second and there was a struggle. I snatched the ball away from him but he grabbed me around the middle as I started to run and tore loose my belt buckle.

Football pants we wore in 1947 were not the skin-tight stretch type we have now. They were sort of baggy and loose and did not cling to a guy's hide.

I had taken only a couple of steps en route to the winning touchdown when I was aware that I was about to lose my pants. I had no choice. We needed six points more than I needed my pants, even with 40,000 fans, and Minnette, looking on. So, I tucked the ball under my right arm and with my free left hand I took a firm grip on the pants, and off I went with no one between me and the Mississippi goal-line. I remember crossing the 50-yard line and then the 40. I was not going too fast, first because I am not too fast anyway, and second because it is hard to run while holding up one's britches.

At the Mississippi 20, I had slowed up considerably and a couple of Rebel defensive backs had a good angle on me since I was still hemmed in along the sideline.

As the nearest one made a grab for me, I tried to shift the ball from my right hand to my left so I could stiff arm him. In the process, I completely forgot that my left hand was all that stood between me and total embarrassment.

My pants slipped to half-mast. I managed to stagger a few more steps as they slid down around my knees. I fell flat on my face, 20 yards from the winning touchdown. None of the opposition laid a finger on me but, there I was, very effectively taken out by my own darn drawers.

I staggered to my feet, frantically trying to pull up my pants, but I fell again.

By this time, Tiger Stadium was in an uproar. Everyone was laughing. Coates and Cason and Knight were laughing too but at least they had the presence of mind to get around me while I hitched up my pants.

When I got back to the L.S.U. bench, Bernie Moore was laughing too. None of us laughed for long. We did not score after that and finally lost the ball game. The way it turned out, though, it didn't make much difference. We got beat Y.A. style by Alabama and Harry Gilmer the next week and were knocked out of the bowl picture.

Losing my pants was not funny to me. I was embarrassed and humiliated. And more than anything else, I was damned sore because I had failed to get the touchdown. Furthermore, we blew the ball game. That was the worst loss of the two.

A guy can want to win so bad—that it sometimes *is* bad. Desire to win almost ruined my career when I was a freshman at L.S.U. I've never mentioned this to anyone. But I will tell the story now because this is supposed to be an account of my football life, and it will not be complete unless I add this confession:

As a freshman, I tried out for the varsity baseball team at L.S.U., along with Cason. I was a pitcher, and I wanted to be the best pitcher on the squad. So the very first day, in batting practice, I started firing that ball with everything I had. The coach told me to "let 'em get a piece of it" but the hell with that. Any pitcher who wants to get hit isn't worth a damn. I hummed that ball as fast as I could. I didn't bother with any loosening up exercises. I was too impatient to start striking guys out. I wasn't worrying much about control, or curves, or change-ups or anything; I just wanted to fog it past them.

I heaved one pitch too many and I felt a sharp twinge in my right shoulder. The next pitch I threw bounced halfway to home plate. I knew something was wrong, really wrong.

That was what finished me as far as baseball was concerned. Later, I did play shortstop with a City League softball team—the club that Cason played first base for. My one aim was to throw the ball so hard I'd knock Jimmy off the bag.

When spring football practice started, I did not tell Bernie Moore about my bad shoulder, which now felt like it might be bursitis. I wanted to play and I was afraid he might bench me if he thought I couldn't throw. So, even though it hurt like the dickens, I went through the motions at quarterback. That was the year we installed the T formation, and I could not afford to miss a minute. If Coach Moore suspected, he never said anything.

Then one morning I woke up and I could hardly raise my right arm. The pain went from the shoulder to the wrist and I couldn't have thrown a football across my room in G Building.

This had me worried, so I went to a doctor in Baton Rouge. I was afraid to go to the L.S.U. team doctor for obvious reasons.

The doctor told me I had a growth on my clavicle. He said it was protruding so far out that he might have to go in there and whack it off.

"Would an operation like that affect my passing?" I inquired.

"It could," he said honestly. "You might have a stiff shoulder for a time."

Time was one thing I didn't have, not with the season coming up. I thanked him and left.

Another doctor told me deep X-ray treatment might help. This seemed like an easier way out, so I took the X-ray therapy once a week in Baton Rouge. It did not cure my shoulder trouble but at least I was able to play football and that's the only thing that mattered to me right then.

The shoulder hurt me all the way through L.S.U. but fortunately the real sharp pain, the numbing kind, never hit me on the day of a game. Sometimes it would hit me on Tuesday and Wednesday, and I'd have a devil of a time throwing in practice. But by Saturday it would be gone and I would be able to pass as good as ever. Other times I would have an uncomfortable twinge Friday night and, mysteriously, it would disappear before game time. That's the way it went, even during my first years as a pro with Baltimore. The pain was always there, kind of deep in my shoulder, and I wondered when it would strike next.

It scared me to death but I kept it to myself. All I wanted was to play football, to "put it in the air," and if playing with a painful shoulder was part of the game, then I was ready to pay the price.

Football had been my one and only love at Marshall High School and it was my only love at Louisiana State. It was Jimmy Cason's love too, and I suspect that is why we were such close friends all through college. I don't know who was the bad influence, me on him or him on me. We were both poor students. I was just going to school for the first two years, majoring in nothing in particular, until Bernie Moore knocked some sense into me. Cason was about the same and thus we kind of gravitated to each other.

The minute the football season ended at L.S.U., Cason and I organized a campus touch football league. We played right in Tiger Stadium every afternoon from January 2 until Bernie Moore called the first Spring practice. Every day we would hustle up a bunch of guys and play touch. As long as Jimmy and I were on the same side nobody could beat us. We were better than anyone else on the campus, and we also were the biggest cheaters. We had a very bad reputation around school and after a while we had to play on different teams or no one would have anything to do with us.

As close as Cason and I were, there was always trouble when we played against each other. Jimmy was a tough competitor, a real bulldog. I was a plain lousy loser.

It is not exaggerating at all to say that Cason and I had a fist fight every time we were opponents in those touch games at L.S.U. And I mean fights where we punched the tar out of each other until someone broke us up. But the bad feeling never lasted. Jim and I would patch things up and go to a show together the same night. The next day we would be punching and banging away again, and then we would go somewhere that evening like nothing ever happened.

Cason was a real hard-nose; he didn't know how to take a backward step. He always had that chip up there waiting for somebody to try and knock it off. But I wanted to win just as badly as he did and, when we weren't on the same side, I fought him right down in the dirt.

I guess this is why we had a healthy respect for each other. We were two guys who never did learn how to lose gracefully.

Touch football the way we played it was more than just touch. Blocking was legal and, man, it was worth your life to run with the ball.

Bernie Moore watched us one day and said, "I wish I could get you guys to hit that hard in September."

Socially acceptable or not, our touch football battles served a purpose for Moore and his assistant coaches. They were busy at that time scouting the top high school players in Louisiana and Texas. They would bring them to Baton Rouge to visit the campus, as they had done with me two years before, and of course they would ask us if we would get the kids into a little game so they could size them up.

We always agreed, of course, because after a while it was tough to recruit players from the campus and we usually were on the look-out for new blood.

I wouldn't be surprised if a lot of fine football players were lost to L.S.U. in those Spring touch games. The coaches often were so disappointed in what they saw that they shipped the kids back home the same day.

Sometimes when I look back on those incidents, my conscience bothers me. What we did really wasn't the right thing. But at the time, it was the way Cason and I saw things. We felt that if a high school kid couldn't hold his own in a touch game he didn't belong at L.S.U. anyway. And if one of them happened to be a quarterback or a halfback, well, it was either him or us—and most often it was him, because Cason and I were still there when it was all over.

As I have mentioned, my first two years at Louisiana State were scholastically unproductive. I was one of the boys in G Building and somehow I had the mistaken idea that my sole purpose in life was to throw passes for the L.S.U. football team. I attended summer classes to regain my scholastic eligibility but once the football season started, the books threw me for a loss.

This was my situation in the spring of 1946 when Bernie Moore called me into his office one day.

"Sit down, Y.A.," he said, pointing to a chair. "There is something I want to talk to you about."

From the tone of his voice, I knew he meant business. Usually, Bernie was warm and soft-spoken. But there was a hard look in his eyes this time.

"For the past two years, you've been wasting your time here at school," he said. "You have been a success as a football player; I admit that much. But otherwise you are failure to yourself and a disappointment to me."

Failure! The word pricked me like a needle. I did not want to be a failure at anything.

Moore continued.

"You might as well make up your mind right now, Y.A., that you can't play football forever. It's time to snap out of it and hit the books before it's too late. You've never loafed on the football field, so I know you are not lazy. It's just that you haven't applied yourself in class like you do in the huddle."

Moore paused, as if allowing me time to plead a defense. But he was absolutely right, and I knew it. There was nothing I could say.

"This is the first and last time I will bring this up. But for your own sake, Y.A., get to work while you still have a chance to graduate."

Moore's talk hit me hard, especially the part about being a failure. No one was going to call Y.A. Tittle a failure.

I enrolled in summer school and loaded up on my courses. I even passed up the daily touch games at Tiger Stadium and Cason had to fight with someone else for a change. I worked hard to overcome my first two years but I was still a half-year short when my class graduated in 1948. I went back the following spring, though, after my rookie year with Baltimore and got my degree. I was proud of finally making it, considering my poor start at Louisiana State.

Between football and classroom work, I didn't have much time for anything else in college. I never joined a fraternity, which did not seem important then and does not now. I didn't date many girls either. My girl was Minnette DeLoach from Marshall. She was one of the first dates I ever had. In Marshall we had those little dances for youngsters at the country club where the parents paired up the boys and girls beforehand. As I recall, this was somewhat of an ordeal for the guys in town because none of us felt our parents had the right dope when it came to selecting our dancing partners.

Anyway, there was this Christmas dance one year and Minnette and I were taken to the country club by our parents. We were paired up for the evening. This was one arrangement I did not object to because Minnette was a beautiful girl with black hair and dark eyes and everyone in the seventh grade at Marshall Junior High was in love with her.

Minnette did not live near me, although I guess you could say everyone lives near everyone else in a place like Marshall. She went to East End Grammar School and I went to West End, and we did not meet until we both got to the first year at Marshall Junior High.

Oddly, after that first Christmas dance I did not date Minnette much until our senior year at Marshall High.

When I left for Louisiana State—by way of Austin—Minnette enrolled at Texas State College for Women in Denton. We did not see much of one another then or later when she transferred to the University of Arkansas.

Neither of us considered the other a "steady" in college; she went with other fellows and I had my share of dates. But we had sort of an understanding just the same. Any time I went back to Marshall we just naturally went out together. Minnette was my first girl and she was to be my last one, too. But at the time neither of us was looking that far into the future.

CHAPTER FOURTEEN

YEAR OF THE QUARTERBACKS

My LAST ball game for L.S.U. was against Tulane at New Orleans and true to his word, Creighton Miller of the Cleveland Browns was there to sign me to a professional contract.

And when I say "there," I mean just that. After the final gun, he walked right onto the field to meet me.

Miller said he and some of the other people from Cleveland would like to see me.

"Where?" I asked, still surprised at his being in the middle of the football field.

"We'll be at the Roosevelt Hotel downtown," he answered. "Get there as soon as you can."

"Okay."

In the locker room I asked Bernie Moore for his advice. For all my interest in football, I was completely unfamiliar with the workings of the two pro leagues, the All-America Conference and the National Football League. I did not understand the player draft, nor did I have any idea why I was the property of the Cleveland Browns and not some other club.

I had been too embarrassed to ask Miller, but Bernie Moore had been like a father to me for four years, so I turned to him for advice.

"Should I meet them, Bernie?" I asked after I had dressed.

"Certainly, Y.A., go and hear what they have to say. But don't sign anything until you've talked to me again."

I felt better knowing I had Bernie Moore to guide me.

When I got to the Roosevelt Hotel, Miller offered no explanation of why he had tried to sign me for Cleveland the previous year when I was still a junior with a season of eligibility remaining. Indeed, he acted like it had never happened.

Miller got right to the point.

"Y.A., we think you are a great passer and that you can be a star in pro football. We are prepared to offer you a contract for eight thousand dollars."

Eight thousand bucks! A fortune!

"Well," said Miller, "how about it?"

Remembering Bernie Moore's warning not to do anything until I had spoken to him, I said, "I'd like some time to think it over, Mr. Miller."

"That's fair enough," he stated. "I'll call you tomorrow."

I saw my coach the next morning and told him about my meeting with Miller.

"Don't sign yet," Moore advised. "They'll go higher. You are worth more than eight thousand dollars."

When Miller phoned that afternoon, I told him I had not reached a decision. He said that was understandable, and then asked if I'd like to be the guest of the Browns at the AAC championship game against the Yankees in New York in December.

The prospect of seeing my first professional football game was intriguing, so I agreed.

I flew to New York in December and was introduced to Paul Brown, the Cleveland coach, on Saturday morning while the team was working out at Macombs Dam Park, a city park across from Yankee Stadium. I wondered why they weren't using the Stadium for practice. Later I learned that the Yankees had been locked out of Cleveland's Municipal Stadium earlier in the season, and this was their answer to Paul Brown.

The Cleveland coach impressed me as being cordial but not friendly. Of course, he had an important game coming up the next day, so I could hardly expect him to spend much time with me. Also at Macombs Dam Park that day was George Connor, a big tackle from Notre Dame who eventually wound up with the Chicago Bears. We were both properly awed by our first look at the great Otto Graham, Cleveland's quarterback, and Marion Motley, the best fullback in the business at that time.

The following day, Connors and I sat on the Cleveland bench at Yankee Stadium as the Browns whipped New York, 14–3, for the league championship.

It was not a particularly exciting ball game but it was quite a thrill. I came away with the impression that the pros were a lot bigger, faster and smarter than anyone I had ever played against. Graham was effective if not sensational that day, and Motley was everything they said he was. The Browns were a team that made few mistakes. Paul Brown was on everything they did. Buddy Young played halfback for the Yankees and Spec Sanders, a Texas boy, was the tailback; the Yanks were not running from the T, strangely enough. I had never seen anyone as fast as Young. Also in the New York lineup were Tom Landry, Otto Schnellbacker, Arnie Weinmeister, Bruce Alford, Jack Russell and Martin Ruby. I played against all of them, except Weinmeister, the next year.

I talked with Paul Brown after the ball game, and he raised the offer. He said they would give me $10,000 plus a $2,000 bonus to sign with Cleveland.

This was big money, and so I accepted. I am not sure but I have always suspected that Moore discussed my contract with the Cleveland people and got them to increase the offer and to add a bonus.

Maybe Bernie was hoping I'd pay back some of the money he had loaned me during my four years at L.S.U. But that still was to take a while.

With $2,000 bonus money in my pocket and a contract for $10,000, I returned to Baton Rouge to finish out the Spring semester. I was carrying a heavy scholastic program to try and catch up in my grades but now, with my pro career clearly outlined before me, I somehow found time for a resumption of our touch football battles at Tiger Stadium.

I was not the only "pro" on the Louisiana State campus that Spring. Cason, with whom I still battled occasionally was the property of the San Francisco Forty-Niners; Piggy Barnes had signed with the Philadelphia Eagles; Hubert Shurtz had a Pittsburgh Steeler contract, and Dan Sandifer had signed with the Washington Redskins.

The fact that our daily touch football skirmishes were no longer fought in the spirit of pure amateurism did not lessen our enthusiasm in the least.

As future pros, I think we all felt we had to rack everyone a little harder. Pity the poor sophomores and juniors who dared challenge our group in '48.

Despite the long morning of tedious classroom work and the afternoon bloodshed at Tiger Stadium, most of Bernie Moore's boys survived the semester and left Louisiana State in June.

On June 20, I married Minnette.

I was raised as a Methodist, but as is the custom Minnette and I were married in her family's Presbyterian Church in Marshall. Then we took a two-week honeymoon trip down toward the Gulf Coast and through Mississippi and stayed briefly at a Louisiana plantation owned by one of Minnette's aunts.

While we were honeymooning, my future was being re-shaped by a series of events in the All-America Football Conference.

Admiral Jonas Ingram, commissioner of the Conference, announced that the league was ready to take over the Baltimore franchise, which in 1947 had lost 11 of 13 games and $165,000. Before the takeover, however, Ingram gave Baltimore a last chance to raise enough money to retain the franchise. A "Save the Colts Committee" was formed and thanks to the support of Baltimore's business leaders, over $200,000 was pledged to bankroll the franchise for at least another year. Bob Rodenberg, the first Colts' president, was replaced by R.C. (Jake) Embry, a Baltimore radio executive.

But the Colts needed help more on the field than they did in the front office, so Ingram instituted a unique "help the weak" program and appointed Ben Lindheimer, owner of the Los Angeles team, and Paul Brown as its directors. They were told to study the Colts' player personnel problems and offer suggestions as to how to strengthen the Baltimore team with players from the other AAC teams.

The upshot of all this was that a list of prominent AAC stars was made available to the Colts. New York turned over Dick Barwegen, an all-league tackle, and end Ollie Poole. Los Angeles gave up tackle Pete Berezney and Lee Artoe, another fine tackle. Cleveland contributed Ernie Blandin, one of the AAC's best tackles, and halfback Mickey Mayne.

And, for good measure, Paul Brown threw in a rookie named Yelberton Abraham Tittle.

So, before I could get into one play as a professional quarterback, I had been dealt from the Cleveland Browns to the Baltimore Colts —from the best team in the AAC to the worst.

Although I was unaware of it at the time, I almost crossed paths again with Bobby Layne, my roommate at Mrs. Poole's boarding house.

A quarterback was Baltimore's chief need that season. They had struggled through 1947 with Bud Schwenk and Ernie Case, but Coach Cecil Isbell did not intend to tolerate that situation in 1948. Isbell liked Layne, who had finished a brilliant career at Texas, so our coach flew down to Austin and arranged a meeting with Bobby. He spread ten new $1,000 bills on a bed and said to Layne, "This is yours for just saying 'yes.' " Bobby later told me his eyes almost popped clean out of his head.

"And that's not all," said Isbell. "We will give you a three-year contract. You'll get twenty thousand the first year, twenty-two thousand the second year and twenty-five thousand the third year."

Layne could hardly restrain himself. He told Isbell he would sign the following day. But from the time he said "good night" until the following morning, Bobby had a change of heart. He talked to D. X. Bible, his coach, who advised him that he might do better with the Chicago Bears, who were an established team in the National Football League, than with the Colts, who were a shaky proposition in a shaky league.

The Bears already had the incomparable Sid Luckman and Johnny Lujack from Notre Dame but George Halas wanted Layne, too. Isbell made four other trips to Austin but could not persuade Bobby to sign with Baltimore.

Once again I must wonder what would have happened to me,

and to Layne, if Bobby had signed with the Colts instead of the Bears. It would have set us against each other as was almost the case at the University of Texas four years earlier. Again our careers might have taken entirely different turns. Layne and I were still battling each other 15 years later in 1962, he with Pittsburgh and me with the Giants, but it could have been a lot different had we been rivals for the same job in the beginning, either in Texas or Baltimore. Then, too, I often think of the fate that sent me from Cleveland to the Colts as a pro rookie. With the Browns I would have had to compete against Otto Graham in his prime and, who knows, that might have been the end of Y.A. Tittle. Nobody was about to beat Otto Graham out of a job in those years.

I was not greatly disappointed when I received a letter from the Browns notifying me that I had been transferred to the Colts. The ways of professional football still were strange to me, and I did not question the switch which had so suddenly and unexpectedly changed my status. All I wanted was an opportunity to play pro ball. If it couldn't be with Cleveland, then Baltimore would do. Besides, Cecil Isbell called me and gave me every assurance that I had a good chance to quarterback the Colts. Bud Schwenk was gone. Bobby Layne had cast his lot with the Chicago Bears of the NFL. My competition would come from Charlie O'Rourke, who had been bought from the Los Angeles Dons as part of Commissioner Jonas Ingram's "help the weak" movement.

The letter from Cleveland arrived at a time when I didn't have a nickel to my name. Most of my $2,000 bonus from the Browns had gone for a new car. The rest of my savings, such as they were, had been depleted on our honeymoon trip. I still had a contract calling for $10,000 but that was only a piece of paper, and it wasn't negotiable at the corner grocery store. I was broke, and the sooner I reported to Baltimore, the better. I kissed Minnette goodbye—as I have been doing every July since—and boarded a plane for Chicago. There I intercepted a train from the East Coast which was en route to Sun Valley, Idaho, where the Colts had their training camp.

Now if a fellow has to train for pro football, there's no better place to do it than Sun Valley, at least from a player's viewpoint.

Those of us who reported to Coach Isbell that July of '48 have been spoiled ever since. It's tough to top a training camp where you live in Swiss chalets, eat at barbecue parties and get served by beautiful young waitresses.

After the first day, my new roommate, Windell Williams from Rice, looked around incredulously and asked, "How long has this been going on?"

Indeed, all of us felt the same way. Sun Valley was more of a vacation playland than a training camp. And the Baltimore Colts were the headlined tourist attraction that summer. Guests from the lodge flocked to our practice sessions every morning and afternoon. We were the center of interest and we all felt very important. Sometimes it was hard to remember we were there to play football.

Not all the surprises at Sun Valley were as pleasant.

I had not expected to find training camp loaded with quarterbacks. But, by golly, there were four of us there. Besides O'Rourke and myself, there was Dick Working from Virginia and Rex Olson from Brigham Young. Olson had been the No. 3 passer in the country the year before.

"What is Isbell going to do with all the quarterbacks?" I asked Sanborne one day.

"He's going to cut most of 'em," was John's answer.

It never had dawned on me when I was drafted by the pros that I would be involved in a competitive situation such as this. There never had been any question but that I was the quarterback for four years at L.S.U., and somehow I imagined it would be that way in professional ball, too. I thought, for instance, that at Cleveland it would be Graham and me, nobody else. And after my talks with Isbell, I naturally assumed that O'Rourke and myself constituted the entire Baltimore quarterback corps.

So the joke was on me that first morning when I had to wait in line for my turn to throw a few passes in practice.

But 1948 was a great year for quarterbacks all around pro football. Bobby Layne came out of Texas and went with the Bears. So did Johnny Lujack, the Notre Dame All-American. Charlie Conerly finished his career at Mississippi and signed with the Giants. Harry Gilmer of Alabama joined Sammy Baugh at Washington.

All of these fellows were in the Chicago College All-Star game that August, and my one regret is that I was unable to play with them although I had been selected. I pulled a leg muscle the opening day in camp at Sun Valley, the first one I'd ever had, and that put me on the shelf. In those days, we reported to camp first and then went to the All-Star game; today, the college players report directly to Chicago and then join their respective pro clubs.

It hurt to miss the All-Star game, and it also hurt to have to return the $200 expense money which had been forwarded to me in advance. I was still flat busted but fortunately we ate pretty good at the Sun Valley barbecues.

As the pre-season schedule went by you could see that O'Rourke and I were the two quarterbacks. I was playing quite a bit but Charlie was still No. 1 and Isbell made no secret of this fact. O'Rourke and I were good friends but there was a keen rivalry between us.

On this subject, I might say that I have always considered myself to be a friend of other quarterbacks with whom I have played. It was that way with O'Rourke and Adrian Burk and Sam Vacanti at Baltimore. It was that way with Frankie Albert and Earl Morrall at San Francisco later on. And it was that way with Charlie Conerly at New York.

All were rivals; all were my close friends. But when you are a professional athlete, it has to be every man for himself. Neither teams nor coaches want shrinking violets.

My friendship never went so far that I enjoyed sitting there on the bench while the other guy threw touchdown passes in my place. I want my ball club to win, of course, but secretly I am always hoping when I am not on the field we score on a run or an interception or something like that rather than on a touchdown pass.

Despite the diversions offered at Sun Valley, the 1948 Baltimore Colts were a good football team. Most of us were rookies; there were only a few veterans on the whole club. Those fellows who weren't rookies were new players brought in from other teams. It was an odd mixture, but it was a good football team just the same.

Windell Williams, Johnny North from Vanderbilt and Hub

Bechtol from Texas were the ends, and they could all catch the ball. The offensive line was terrific, thanks to the addition of Ernie Blandin from Cleveland and Dick Barwegen from New York. Barry French from Purdue and the late Al Klug from Marquette were fine guards. In the backfield we had Lamar (Race Horse) Davis, Bus Mertes, Mickey Mayne from the Browns, Billy Hillenbrand from Indiana and a skinny little guy, Aubrey Fowler, from Arkansas. Aubrey, at 28, was the oldest rookie in camp and, at 153 pounds, the lightest. He used every trick in the book to survive among the bigger pros, and most of the time someone on the other club was gunning for him. Whenever this happened, Fowler always stuck close to Barwegen, a bruising 260-pounder, and thus escaped the opposition's retaliatory measures.

Davis was one of the first receivers I threw to in pro ball, and boy, he could fly. No wonder they called him "Race Horse" Davis. I would be remiss too, if I did not add something about Billy Hillenbrand. I have heard it said over the years that Billy, an All-American at Indiana, never cut the mustard as a pro halfback. But let me say this: Billy Hillenbrand was one of the greatest halfbacks I have ever seen, and I have seen fifteen years' worth. He had more moves, or at least as many, as Hugh McElhenny and to my way of thinking, McElhenny in his prime was the finest running back in the history of the game.

Hillenbrand was not as fast as McElhenny. But he could pick them up and put them down; he had a wonderful "feel" for running. Billy was a great screen pass man; he was so slow he couldn't catch up with the linemen who were blocking for him, and this is perfect for a screen pass. He would just fall in there behind them and follow them right down the field. Hillenbrand was a smart ballplayer, too. He rarely made a wrong move when he was running with the football. I don't know what they expected of Billy, but in 1948 he was a great player for the Baltimore Colts.

My first ball game for the Colts stands out in my memory for something I said rather than for anything I did.

We flew up to Portland, Oregon, to play the Los Angeles Dons in a pre-season game. The Dons had Glen Dobbs, the great Tulsa tailback, and Jarrin' John Kimbrough from Texas A&M, and with a couple of minutes left in the game they were ahead of us by 19–7.

I was sitting next to Windell Williams on the bench. We were roommates, so naturally we were always kidding each other. I looked at the scoreboard clock.

"Dammit, Windell," I said, "if they don't get me in there soon, we're going to lose this thing."

I was joking, as I might with Del Shofner, my present Giant roommate.

Another few seconds went by and I said to Williams, "I tell you, Windell, Isbell is going to blow this thing unless he puts me in there."

With that, Isbell waved me off the bench. "Get in there for O'Rourke," he said. I doubt that Cecil had heard my wisecrack to Williams. It was more a case of his wanting me to get a few plays under my belt before the final whistle.

Sometimes everything falls into place for a quarterback in pro football, and that's what happened for me that night at Portland. We took the ball and—boom!—we go in for a score. As I recall, I threw a touchdown pass to Davis. We stopped the Dons after the kickoff and down the field we went again. I was calling time outs and throwing sideline passes in an effort to stall the clock. We were all the way to the Los Angeles 20 when the game ended. We almost pulled it out but Los Angeles beat us, 19–14.

But after the game was over, Windell goes around telling everybody, "Well, that's what Y.A. told me. He said we'd lose if Isbell didn't use him sooner. Old Y.A. almost did it, too, but Isbell put him in a minute too late."

This of course was overheard by a couple of sportswriters and the next day the papers played it up pretty good. I was greatly embarrassed, and I cautioned Williams to keep our private jokes to himself.

If Isbell was concerned by all this, he never showed it. But I decided to watch my lip anyway.

But the following week after we were beaten by San Francisco, 31–17, in a very poor ball game, all of us got a sample of Cecil Isbell's temper. He was so mad, he packed us right into the airplane and we flew all night, landing in Toledo around daybreak. Then we boarded a bus for the long drive to Adrian College in Adrian, Michigan, where we would be training for a spell. Isbell was so incensed he didn't even let us put up our bags at the college. Instead he ordered the bus driver to take us straight to the practice field.

"Now you are going to run," he snapped and with that, he blew his whistle to start wind sprints.

We sprinted ten and jogged ten, sprinted ten, jogged ten. It was hot and humid and we were dead tired from the game and from the long trip. But Isbell kept blasting away on that damned whistle and we kept sprinting and jogging, sprinting and jogging. It was a killer!

When Isbell finally let up on us, we just sank down on the dusty field, too exhausted to head for the showers. We were tired and we were mad.

"So, we lost a ball game! Does that mean this guy Isbell has to kill us off under a hot sun?"

One rookie walked into the locker room and smashed his fist through a thick glass door. The blood spurted out like a gusher. He just stood there, mumbling, ". . . the hell with it, the hell with the whole damned world."

If we thought the long, hard wind sprints marked the end of our ordeal, we were sadly mistaken. Isbell was not through with us yet.

The next day, still fuming over our San Francisco performance, he ordered full gear for our morning practice session, a most unusual procedure less than two days after a ball game.

"What's this for?" Williams asked as he pulled on his shoulder guards.

"It ain't for picture day, that's for sure," grunted Barwegen, who had a better idea than any of the rookies as to what lay ahead.

Isbell scrimmaged us for six full quarters that day. He had us banging away until we were ready to drop in our tracks. There wasn't a guy on the field who didn't ache from head to toe. We were getting new bruises on top of the lumps the Forty-Niners had given us.

Isbell finally called a halt to the scrimmage and we crawled back to the dorm. Most of us wouldn't have cared if we never saw a football field—or Isbell—again.

I don't know how they arranged the schedules in those days but anyway we played the Cleveland Browns, the AAC champions, on Wednesday in Toledo, and we beat them, 21–17. None of us thought we could get out of bed that morning, and yet we upset the best team in football in our final pre-season game of 1948.

I guess this fellow Cecil Isbell knew what he was doing at that.

CHAPTER FIFTEEN

"A BIG GREEN BAY"

BALTIMORE is something special as a pro football town. I discovered this in August of 1948 when Cecil Isbell brought the Colts home after our surprise victory over the Cleveland Browns in Toledo.

Thousands of fans were at the airport to meet us. They were shouting and hollering and waving all sorts of signs. There was a big parade up the main street of the town. I had never seen anything like it. We had only won a pre-season game, a game that did not even count, and the place was going wild.

"You'd think we won the championship or something," cracked Windell Williams as we sat in our open car during the parade.

"After this kind of reception, we had better win it," I said.

"Naw," said Hub Bechtol, "Baltimore fans are always like this . . . even when we get beat. They are really something."

Hub was right. The Colt fans were wonderful. They made us feel like champions. The whole town was behind the football team. Charles McCormack, one of the club's directors, organized a group called Colts' Associates, and they staged kickoff dinners, found jobs for the players and even sold tickets. You were a celebrity in Baltimore if you played football for the Colts.

This was surprising in a way. Baltimore had always been a baseball town. The Orioles just about owned the city in the beginning. Long before the Colts had their first football hero, Wee Willie Keeler, Hughie Jennings and John McGraw were the names best known along Chesapeake Bay.

But things had changed. In August of 1948, the Colts were the darlings of Baltimore. It was a wild football town. Even a rookie like me felt pretty important.

The best description of Baltimore as a football town was voiced by Tarzan White, an assistant coach with the Colts in 1947. Looking around him during one of the frequent outbursts of fan enthusiasm, Tarzan said, "This place is like a big Green Bay."

Anyone who has ever been caught up in the Packer frenzy in Green Bay knows what he meant!

Baltimore fans are among the most loyal in all of football. When the Colt franchise was disbanded in 1951, almost a thousand fans came to Philadelphia to see me play with the San Francisco Forty-Niners against the Eagles. They bought seats right behind the Forty-Niner bench and they cheered like hell everytime I did something. It gave me a warm feeling to think they had not forgotten me.

Soon after I arrived in Baltimore, Minnette drove up from Marshall with her father to join me. Our first chore was to find an apartment, which was not easy. This was right after the war, and locating a place to live was no simple matter. Everything was frozen.

We were unsuccessful at first. But one day Ollie Poole, Windell Williams and I got a lead on an apartment on the other side of town.

"Wait here, honey," I instructed Minnette. "I'm going to drive over with those fellows and see what it looks like."

The apartment was nice. It was also small. That meant only one of us could take it. But which one?

"Let's flip a coin," said Williams. "That's as good a way as any to settle this thing."

So we flipped and I won. The apartment was mine. I could hardly wait to tell Minnette. We moved our stuff in the same day. After we finished unpacking, Minnette said, "I think I'll take a shower."

"That's fine."

"Where is it?"

"Where is what?"

125

"The shower, of course."

I stopped to think for a minute. In our haste to move in, I hadn't noticed the shower. But there had to be one.

"Have you tried the bathroom?" I asked, hoping I didn't sound facetious.

"Yes," she answered.

"And?"

"No shower. Not even a bathtub."

By golly, that's strange, I thought. An apartment without a shower or a tub.

We checked every room in the place. No shower. In desperation, I called the landlady, who lived upstairs. She told me the shower was in the basement behind the hot water boiler.

"That's a fine place for a shower," I said, not trying to hide my annoyance. "Why didn't you tell us the shower was in the basement?"

"You didn't ask," she answered.

As I said, apartments were hard to come by in 1948, so Minnette and I resigned ourselves to using the basement shower. It wasn't too bad, except when it got real cold outside. Then it took nerve to go down there. It was like a refrigerator.

The 1948 season was my introduction to professional football, and Baltimore has always had a special place in my affections—even with the shower behind the boiler! We were in pro ball, the major leagues, and we were in a big town. We were all young and all of a sudden we started to win. This was an exciting experience. Baltimore was a great sports town, and we were swept up in the enthusiasm. Most of the guys on the roster had been married less than six months, and we had our own bunch. We ate together and did things together and we had a lot of fun. Everything was new and entertaining. We were winning at first, and we did not know the pain of losing.

A couple of days before the opening game against the New York Yankees, who had been the eastern champions the year before, Isbell told the newspapers that I would start at quarterback for the Colts. This stirred up quite a fuss, of course, because Charlie O'Rourke had done more than me in the pre-season games and besides he was an experienced hand. There was some criticism of

Isbell's choice but he stuck to his guns. It took courage for him to go with a green, untried rookie quarterback in the league opener. He had stuck his neck out, and I only hoped I could justify his faith in me.

Even Isbell in his most optimistic moment did not foresee what happened on September 5th at Memorial Stadium. Nor did I. It was something I will never forget. Every pro has a day here and a day there that are kind of special in his memory, and this was one of those days for me. We defeated the Yankees, 45–28, and I broke four All-America Conference passing records in the bargain. It was a game where everything fell into place. I had a similar day fourteen years later when I threw seven touchdown passes and gained 505 yards against the Washington Redskins for the Giants. In 1948, though, I had not expected anything like what happened. I completed 11 of 20 passes for 346 yards and had a total yardage figure of 354. I averaged 3.5 yards on my completions and 16.5 yards for every pass attempt. I accounted for five touchdowns myself and handed off to Billy Hillenbrand for the sixth.

I got all the ink that day, naturally, but the Colts' victory was really a wonderful team effort. Our defense gang-tackled savagely all afternoon. They knocked Buddy Young, the Yankees' great little halfback, out of commission and battered Spec Sanders to a standstill. The offensive line gave me great protection against Arnie Weinmeister and the other New York pass rushers. It was a combined effort all the way. And it was a tribute to the coaching job done by Isbell.

Two weeks later we went to New York and whipped the Yankees again, 27–14, to prove our opening victory was no accident. On the same road trip we added a win over Brooklyn. Going into October the Baltimore team that had won only three games in 1947 and had almost lost its franchise was leading the eastern division by a full game.

Then came the Cleveland Browns, and this was one of the toughest, hardest ball games I ever played in. We met them on a Tuesday night and it had been raining for two solid days. There was some talk of postponing the game but they finally decided to go through with it. The wind and rain kept the fans away. But the Browns were there. They had been eager to get back at us since the night we upset them in Toledo that summer. We welcomed the chance too. We were on a hot streak and we figured we could go all the way if we got past the Browns. It was a chance to bust the eastern race wide open.

Truthfully, I do not know how we ever played the game. The field was completely flooded. The wind was blowing so hard you could not see three feet in front of you.

"Points are going to be hard to get tonight," Isbell warned me before the kickoff. "The club that scores first will be in the driver's seat."

That is the way I felt too, even without Isbell telling me. Conditions would get worse as the game progressed. The field would be muddier and the ball would be harder to handle. The time to go for it was right in the beginning. Get a touchdown in the bank and then make them play our game.

On the third play of the game with the ball on the Baltimore 22, I called a screen pass right to Hillenbrand. Billy got out there in the flat and I lobbed the ball to him through the rain. He picked up his two screen blockers and went all the way for a touchdown. Rex Grossman kicked the conversion and we were up by seven big ones with less than two minutes gone.

Cleveland slopped back through the mud to tie the score later in the period on a run by Edgar (Special Delivery) Jones. But then Grossman somehow boomed a 40-yard field goal against the wind to put us back in the lead, 10–7.

And that is the way the score stood most of the night. We slugged it out in the mud and neither side could do much. Three points was not a big lead to be sitting on but the weather was on our side. In that wind and rain it was going to be tough for the Browns to get on the scoreboard again. We had another upset in the making and, boy, we fought like madmen to hold onto it.

Then we made our one bad play. The Browns turned it to their advantage, which all great teams have the knack of doing.

O'Rourke got off a poor punt with the slippery ball. From our ten he kicked it up to the 27. The Browns were knocking on the door with only two minutes left. Otto Graham passed once, to Mac Speedie for 21 yards, and then again, to Dub Jones for the touchdown.

That was it. We lost, 14–10. Even the fact that Cleveland coach Paul Brown called it, "one of the hardest wins of my whole career," did not help ease our disappointment.

The Cleveland game, however, proved that the Baltimore Colts were a ball club to be reckoned with. We had at least regained a degree of respectability after the terrible 1947 season.

From there, we went on to score victories over Los Angeles, Chicago, Brooklyn and Buffalo. The Bills were beaten, 33–15, in the last game of the season. This set up a playoff for the eastern division since both Baltimore and Buffalo had 7–7 records. The winner of the playoff would meet Cleveland, which had again won the western title.

The playoff generated tremendous interest among Colt fans. They were talking championship long before we returned to Baltimore.

But five days before the showdown with Buffalo, I was called to a player meeting after practice. Something was in the wind, and it wasn't good.

It didn't take me long to find out what. Some of the veterans on the squad thought that since there was no provision in our contracts to cover the possibility of a playoff, we should be cut in for a share of the gate receipts. There was a lot of arguing back and forth. Finally, Ernie Blandin and Dick Barwegen were appointed to carry the team's demands to Jake Embry and Walter Driskill.

Embry, the Colts' president, and Driskill, the general manager, listened to Blandin and Barwegen, who said the Colt players wanted more than just a one-game salary share for playing against Buffalo.

"If we don't get it," said Blandin, "there may not be a game this Sunday."

Embry explained the front office position. "We feel a divisional playoff is part of a player's regular contract. Also, we are having a difficult time staying in the black. This extra game could put us on solid ground. We would appreciate the players' understanding in this matter."

Blandin and Barwegen reported back to the squad, but there was an element that insisted on a strike unless the demands were met.

Word of the strike threat got back to Embry and he fought fire with fire. He told the team that ". . . if you don't want to play the game, we will announce to the public that the title has been forfeited to Buffalo.

"We will consider the season over, and we will all go home."

Another player meeting was called and a final vote was taken after we had agreed that we would go along with the majority no matter what our views. Personally, I wanted to play, money or no money. The opportunity to get into the championship was the only thing that motivated me.

Anyway, it was close. The "yeas" barely won out. There was bitter resentment after the vote. Even though we had agreed to stick together, the "money or strike" element did not accept the decision gracefully.

That was the second time I had been involved in a player dispute with management. The first was in 1946 before the Cotton Bowl game between L.S.U. and Arkansas. As was customary, the L.S.U. players had been offered $200 in expense money by the Cotton Bowl officials. This seemed like a pretty fair arrangement to most of us. I know that $200 was a lot of money to me. But there were some guys who wanted more.

We would be sitting around G Building at Baton Rouge and somebody would start it by saying, "We ought to get at least three hundred dollars!"

Then another guy would chime in. "Yeah, that's right. In fact, we should ask for four hundred."

"Right! Let's take a vote on four hundred."

Things really got out of hand. Fellows who only a few minutes before had been satisfied with $200 were shouting and yelling for more money. They took a vote and decided to compromise: they would ask for $300 instead of $400.

A delegation, which did not include Y.A. Tittle, was sent to talk with L.S.U. officials. The university brass turned them down in no uncertain terms.

So we went down to Tiger Stadium for practice that afternoon and we asked Bernie Moore if we could talk to him. He said okay, and we took him behind the scoreboard and told him we wanted $300 to play in the Cotton Bowl.

"You won't get it," said Moore. "And besides, you'll get your-selves into a lot of trouble if you pursue this thing any further."

But by this time the ringleaders were hot under the collar. They stomped off to one corner of the field and called for a vote. They voted to strike, not to play in the Cotton Bowl unless their demands were met. They took off their helmets, threw them on the ground and walked off the field. Bernie Moore looked on unbelievingly.

I do not intend to make myself a big man but I was one of those who voted to play. I just felt this wasn't the right thing to do. So you suffer the loss of a few dollars. In the long run, five years from now, I told myself, it won't be worth having a black mark against my name.

Naturally, there was hell to pay around L.S.U. when word of the walk-out reached university officials. For a time it appeared that all of us would be kicked out of school. But someone—maybe it was Bernie Moore, I don't know—interceded. Another meeting was held and it was agreed that we would get $250, or an extra $50, if we won the ball game against Arkansas. Of course, the Cotton Bowl ended in a scoreless tie, so all the trouble was for nothing.

Getting back to the 1948 playoff with Buffalo, this was a game between two ball clubs with real scoring power. We had Hillen-brand, Davis, John North, Mickey Mayne and Bus Mertes. Buffalo was quarterbacked by George Ratterman from Notre Dame, a real fine passer, and had Chet Mutryn, Zeke O'Connor and Alton Baldwin as runners and receivers. During the regular season, I had completed 161 passes in 289 tries for 2,522 yards and 16 touch-downs. That put me fourth among the AAC's passers, Ratterman was second to Otto Graham.

So the stage was set for a wide-open offensive battle when we met the Bills in Baltimore on December 12th.

We scored first on a field goal by Grossman, but Buffalo went ahead 7–3 on a pass from Ratterman to O'Connor. That's the way it stayed the rest of the first half.

The third period was all Baltimore. We scored on marches of 71 and 87 yards with Bus Mertes getting both touchdowns on runs of nine yards and one yard. Grossman contributed the extra points and we were in front, 17–7.

131

In the fourth quarter, Ratterman and Bill Gompers got together on a 66-yard scoring pass to cut our lead to three points, 17–14. The Bills got possession again late in the period and Ratterman started a race against the clock. After picking up two first downs, one via an off-side penalty on fourth down, he lobbed a short pass to Mutryn, who took three steps to his left and dropped the ball when he was hit hard by Sam Vacanti and Barwegen. John Mellus, our fine tackle, scooped up the loose ball and headed for the Buffalo end zone. The only thing that stopped him was head linesman Tommy Whelan's frantic whistling. Whelan ruled that Mutryn never had possession of the ball and therefore it was only an incomplete pass, not a fumble. That strange ruling enabled Buffalo to keep the ball. In six plays the Bills had the winning touchdown on a pass from Ratterman to Baldwin.

The clock showed two and a half minutes left, time enough for us to score again. But one of my passes intended for Davis was intercepted by Buffalo's Ed Hirsch and he ran it back for a touchdown. That made the final tally: Buffalo, 28; Baltimore, 17.

Colt fans were incensed by Whelan's call on Mutryn's fumble. They poured out of the stands at the final gun. Extra police were summoned to protect the officials from the crowd. The Buffalo and Colt players escorted Whelan to the dressing room through the hostile, bottle-throwing fans. When they finally got him there, he had a swollen eye and a cut mouth. His shirt was torn from his back. And he was scared half to death. I could not blame him, either.

Despite efforts of the police to break up the disorder, the crowd gathered outside the dressing room, yelling for Whelan's scalp.

"Let's Get Whelan . . . Let's Get Whelan."

It was the wildest scene I have ever witnessed in pro football. The fans started fist fights among themselves; they lit a fire in the stands; they charged here and there, knocking people down, waving, shouting. They stationed themselves outside the Stadium Administration Building. They refused to budge. They wouldn't move until Whelan came out. Meanwhile, Whelan and the others huddled inside the building and wondered how they could escape the mob. Finally, a plan was devised to smuggle them out among the Buffalo players. They got safely to the Bills' chartered bus, right under the noses of all those fist-shaking fans, and made their retreat from Baltimore.

The 1948 season started in tumult, with the sign-waving, cheering turnout at the airport in August, and it ended the same way, with angry, shouting mobs roaming the December twilight outside of Memorial Stadium.

It was a good season for me, a memorable season. I was named Rookie of the Year in the All-America Conference, and this was quite an honor.

But I had been deprived of my opportunity to win a championship. This was to become a familiar story in the years that lay ahead.

CHAPTER SIXTEEN

"THROW THE DAMNED BALL"

I owe my success as a forward passer to one man above all others. His name is Cecil Isbell.

Cecil Isbell made me a professional passer.

All of my coaches have had a hand in my development as a football player. Joe Magrill at Marshall High gave me confidence in my ability. Cracker Brown told me to "go ahead and throw the ball." Otis Mitchell taught me to be a winner. Bernie Moore convinced me to use my head as well as my arm. Later at San Francisco, Buck Shaw and Frankie Albert taught me that football can be fun. Allie Sherman, now my coach with the New York Giants, showed me how preparation and simplicity can win championships.

They all helped in their own way and at their own time.

But Cecil Isbell, my coach at Baltimore in 1948 and part of 1949, made the biggest contribution. "There is only one way to play this game," he told me, ". . . throw the damned ball!"

When Isbell said this, I listened. He knew what he was talking about. He had been one of pro football's greatest passers with the Green Bay Packers. He was the guy who threw all those touchdown passes to Don Hutson. In their time, and maybe even now, there wasn't a bettter combination in the league. When Isbell quit pro ball, his coach, Curly Lambeau, said of him, "Isbell was the master passer. He was the best of them all, better than Sid Luckman, better than Sammy Baugh. He could throw long or short, hard or soft. He had the touch for passing as few men have it."

Isbell was my kind of coach. I had always wanted to put the ball in the air, and he showed me how to do it!

The most important theory Isbell gave me was this: Depend on yourself to complete the pass!

This was his belief and it has since become mine. Depend on your own arm to get the ball to your man. Do not rely on pass patterns to miraculously work someone into the clear. Do not expect the defense to make a mistake. Completed passes do not just happen. They are made by the passer and by his receiver, man to man.

I do not want to depend on anybody but myself and my receiver. I mean I want Del Shofner to come into the huddle and tell me, "I can beat him on a down-and-in," or "I can take him on a square-out." And then I expect Del to beat his man, and when he does I depend on my own arm to get the ball out there to him. His job is to get open. That is what they pay him for. My job is to hit him between the eyes with the football. That is what I am paid to do.

Now, there are some passers who do not approach it this way. They hope a pattern will spring somebody loose. They are looking for help. Say a quarterback wants to hit an end on a slant pattern across the middle. Well, he circles a halfback to one side to pull the linebacker out of the way. He sends a flanker down deep to clear out the defensive halfback or safety. He puts his split end someplace else to open up the area. Now everything is set for the receiver. He slants into the zone that has been cleared out, and the quarterback hits him with the pass.

This is one way of doing it, and it may be okay, too. But it is not my way. Nor was it Cecil Isbell's way.

I would rather bounce back there and hit Frank Gifford on a quick square-out instead of waiting for a lot of other things to happpen. And if I can't beat them with Giff on a square-out, well, then I will beat them down-and-in. It is me and Gifford. I depend on Frank to whip his man out there in the secondary by a step or maybe by two steps if he is lucky, and then I depend on my right arm to hit him with the pass. I do not wish to be in the position of standing back there waiting for a pattern to get a guy nice and open so it is easy for me to drop the ball in his lap.

You have heard people state, "He's good at picking out his receiver."

The heck with picking out a receiver, I say.

I have just three seconds to get away from center, to set up and to throw the football. I am not that smart that I can go back seven yards and waste time looking around for someone to throw the ball to. I want somebody open right away, and if he is not open, I want a number two choice. If number two is covered, then I am going to throw the ball away, out of bounds, anyplace.

In the huddle, I might call Joe Walton, my tight end, on a square-out twelve yards deep. Gifford, my number two receiver, is going down and in, say, twenty yards. Now if Walton runs his pattern and beats his man, he is going to get that ball. I am going to pump it to him in a hurry. Gifford may be down there all by himself but he is not going to get the ball because Walton is my number one choice. If Joe runs his square-out and can't get free, then I will go to Gifford if he is open. If he is not open, I will try and throw it someplace.

My passing philosophy is "Number one, number two, or throw it away!"

Get number one open, have him beat his defensive man, and throw that ball to him in a hurry, inside of three or four seconds. Number two does not count if number one is in the clear. I do not care if Gifford is standing in the end zone all alone hollering his head off. He does not get the ball unless they have my number one covered.

I am not a quarterback who fades back there with the idea of looking at two or three different receivers and finally throwing to the one who is open. You can hit only one man on a pass, and you have to depend on your arm to get the ball out to him, not on a razzle-dazzle pass pattern suddenly springing a receiver into a hole in the secondary where nobody is covering him and where my mother-in-law could throw the ball to him.

This was Cecil Isbell's concept of forward passing, and it has been mine ever since I played for him as a rookie at Baltimore in 1948.

As far back as I can remember, I have always had a strong throwing arm. I was a good passer at Marshall High School and

I was maybe a little better at throwing the ball when Bernie Moore had me at L.S.U.

But Cecil Isbell taught me *how* to pass.

"Don't expect help from anyone but your receiver," he used to say. "It is you and him against the defense. He's got to beat his man. Then you have got to hit him with the pass. There are no magic tricks in passing. You make your own gains. And you do it by throwing the hell out of the football."

I consider myself fortunate to have come under Isbell's influence as a young professional. What he taught me about forward passing started me on the road to success.

Isbell was a fine coach and an even finer human being. He still is one of my greatest fans although it is sixteen years since I played for him. He will call me or write and say he saw the Giant game on television and he noticed that I was not taking a deep enough pass drop or that perhaps I was moving out of the pass pocket. When the Cleveland Browns gave me a rough afternoon at Yankee Stadium in 1963, Cecil called me and said, "Y.A., you are sending too many guys out of the backfield. You'd better keep a couple of those big backs in there and let them block for you. Remember, you only need one open receiver to complete the pass."

When I studied the films of that Cleveland game, I saw that Isbell had been right—as usual. I had been sending too many backs out as receivers, and the Browns were shooting through there to pressure me. The next time we met Cleveland, I kept my backs in and the Browns never laid a glove on me. We beat them, 33–6.

Unfortunately, Isbell was the scapegoat of the Colts' sudden and unexpected about-face in 1949.

When I came back to Baltimore for my second year, the coaches, the players and the front office exuded an enthusiasm which lulled everyone into a false sense of security. The Colts had come so close to winning the year before that anyone who even dared suggest we might not take the title in 1949 would have been tarred and feathered and tossed into Chesapeake Bay with the crabs. Walter Driskill, who had succeeded Jake Embry as president, got up at our Westminster, Md., training camp one day and said flatly, "Baltimore will win the All-America Conference championship this year!"

137

In the beginning, it seemed he might be correct. We opened the pre-season schedule against the Buffalo Bills and whipped them soundly, 28–12. That steamed the city of Baltimore to an even higher pitch; after the Bills were disposed of, there wasn't a man, woman or child who didn't agree with Driskill's prediction.

Then the bubble burst. We played our next four games on the road, and lost them all. None of the scores was even close—31–17 in San Francisco, 49–17 in Los Angeles, 21–0 in Cleveland, 35–7 in Chicago against the Hornets, a weak-sister team.

The day after the Chicago loss, the board of directors fired Isbell. And Driskill, the president and general manager, became our new coach.

As I recall, Driskill and Isbell were good friends and Walter did not want to succeed Isbell. He felt too deeply about Cecil being fired on the whim of some half-baked directors for something which was not his fault, namely the failure of the Colts' football team to live up to expectations.

"This is the last thing I ever wanted to do," Driskill said. But it was done. He was the new head coach. Isbell took his firing very hard. He was hurt to the point of withdrawing into a shell. He didn't want to be around people. He was a sensitive man, a man of great pride, and the firing cut him deeply.

To his credit, though, Isbell never held his dismissal against Driskill. They had nothing but the highest regard for each other, although things were understandably strained for the remainder of the 1949 season.

Driskill's overnight appearance as head coach of the Colts created new problems for me. Walter and I were not the best of friends; we had engaged in some heated contract discussions only a few weeks before. And now suddenly he turns up as my coach. One minute he is the general manager sitting in an office somewhere and not bothering with the ball club on the field, and the next minute he is standing in Isbell's shoes. It was a shock to the whole squad, and especially to me since I had been so close to Isbell. The adjustment was not easy to make. To me, Walter Driskill was the general manager, and Isbell was my coach.

This is the way we started after the fourth game of the season and I must admit there were no harmonious meeting of the minds

138

between Driskill and myself. He seemed irritated at me. I never have known why. Maybe Walter Driskill, general manager, told Walter Driskill, coach, what a tough bird Y.A. Tittle was to do business with.

Anyway, Sam Vacanti was at quarterback when we lost our first game under Driskill to the Cleveland Browns, 14–13.

Then came our only victory of the 1949 season, a 35–28 win over good old Buffalo, but after that we lost them all—24–21 to the Yanks, 17–7 to the Hornets, 21–14 to the Yanks again, 27–10 to San Francisco, 21–10 to the Dons and finally 38–14 to Buffalo.

During the last half of the 1949 season under Driskill, I somehow felt the team's failures were being pinpointed to me. I was completely frustrated. I wanted to please Walter Driskill but I didn't know how. The pressure built up week by week. I couldn't communicate with him. I worked hard to do the right things but it wasn't the same as it had been under Isbell. It got to the point where I was afraid to call a play because it might be the wrong play and Walter would be on top of me. I began trying to think like Walter Driskill would think. I was not me anymore; I was him. I got worse instead of better.

I do not want to say Driskill was "on" me all the time in 1949. But it sure seemed that way.

The squad would be sitting there in the dark watching a game film and all of a sudden Driskill would snap, "What play was that, Tittle?"

"Gee, I'm not sure, coach. Would you run it again?"

But he never did. Nor did he say anything. The projector kept grinding away. And I would slump down in my seat wondering what was coming next. I was only 22 years old and the pressure of this thing was getting to me. My confidence was going fast.

Whether it was Driskill or whether it was me, the Colts were a bad ball club that year. We should have been better because we had the same personnel as in 1948—Lamar, Davis, Ernie Blandin, Dick Barwegen, Barry French, Rex Grossman, Johnny North, Bob Nowaskey, Stormy Pfohl and Windell Williams, my roommate. We also had a lot of newcomers. One of them was Herman Wedemeyer, the flashy St. Mary's halfback whom Driskill got in an unusual deal with the Los Angeles Dons.

The Dons were loaded with fine backs, Glenn Dobbs, George Taliaferro, Hosea Rogers and some others, and Wedemeyer, a terrific open field runner and an exciting player to watch, was riding the bench. San Francisco wanted Wedemeyer since he had played his college ball in the Bay Area. But the Dons were bitter rivals of the Forty-Niners and they refused to trade Herman up north. Instead, they approached Baltimore.

"How much is he making?" inquired Driskill, fearful of inheriting a ballplayer with a top-heavy contract.

Driskill was informed that Wedemeyer had a contract calling for $12,000.

"That's too rich for me," he said.

But the Dons weren't to be shaken that easily. They wanted Baltimore to have Wedemeyer; they didn't want San Francisco to get him. So they told Driskill, "Okay, you pay him eight thousand, and we will make up the rest."

It was probably the only time in pro football history that one team paid another team to take an All-American halfback off its hands.

But even Squirmin' Herman, as they called Wedemeyer, was not enough to help the Colts in 1949. We finished with a record of one win and eleven losses. This poor showing was reflected at the box office, where Charles P. McCormick, chairman of the board, reported losses of almost $100,000 for the club that Driskill had predicted would win the league championship.

CHAPTER SEVENTEEN

"RUN, SHEEP, RUN"

THE ASSORTMENT of players who reported to the Baltimore Colts' training camp in the summer of 1950 may have constituted the worst professional football team in history.

And I was one of them!

Many things had changed between the end of the disastrous 1949 season and the bright beginning of 1950. For one, the All-America Conference had folded and Baltimore had been absorbed into the National Football League along with Cleveland and San Francisco. Walter Driskill had resigned in May, and the Colts found a new money man and president in Abraham (Shorty) Watner, who saved the Baltimore franchise when the board of directors was ready to throw in the sponge.

We also had a new coach when we reported to Westminster, Maryland, in July. He was Clem Crowe, who had coached at Buffalo the year before and who had been brought in to replace president-general manager, Walter Driskill.

Unfortunately, Crowe's record was no more distinguished than Driskill's had been in 1949. We played twelve games and lost eleven of them. And when the 1950 Colts lost, man, we really lost—70–27 to Los Angeles, 55–13 to the Cardinals, 55–20 to the Giants, 51–14 to the Yanks, 45–21 to the Lions, 38–14 to Washington, 31–0 to the Browns, and 24–14 to the Eagles.

I doubt if any of these lopsided defeats surprised Crowe. He probably saw the handwriting on the wall early in the pre-season schedule when we traveled to San Antonio not too far from Marshall and got whipped by the Rams, 70–21.

The dismal showing of the Colts that year was not Clem Crowe's fault. There were other factors.

The merging of the All-America Conference with the National Football League had left thirteen pro clubs in business, one too many for a balanced schedule. The NFL's only solution was to designate the thirteenth club as a "swing" team that would play each of the other twelve clubs once instead of meeting its rivals on a two-game home and home basis.

Baltimore was the "unlucky 13th."

Then, too, the Colts had been shortchanged when the National Football League distributed talent from the defunct New York Yankees and Buffalo Bills. The Giants received six players from the Yanks, among them Arnie Weinmeister, Tom Landry and Otto Schellbacher, while Cleveland skimmed the cream off the top of the Buffalo contingent, corraling John Kissel, Rex Bumgardner and Abe Gibron. This happened, mind you, before the other clubs had a chance to pick the surplus AAC players in an open draft. I never did understand this bit of maneuvering. The Colts needed help; so did the Green Bay Packers. We were the "have not" clubs but the Browns and the Giants got richer. We did get Chet Mutryn, a fine halfback, from the Bills but it would have taken a lot more than one player to make the Colts a contender in 1950.

Morale was low in training camp that summer. Crowe was faced with a difficult task of trying to build a collection of washed-up veterans, disgruntled rejects and inexperienced free agents into a ball club that could match the smooth power of Cleveland, Philadelphia, New York and the other NFL teams.

One of Clem's free agents advertised himself as a former West Virginia end, but subsequent investigation exposed him as a fellow who had been pumping gas since the eighth grade and had never even played high school football. I never blamed him for trying, but you don't build winning teams from this kind of material.

This is not to say the '50 Colts were entirely without talent.

A number of the good veterans from our 1948–49 teams were still on hand, fellows like Ernie Blandin, Barry French, Bob Nowaskey and Billy Stone. Gone were Billy Hillenbrand, Charlie O'Rourke, Windell Williams, Hub Bechtol, Lamar (Race Horse) Davis and Rex Grossman.

Adrian Burk, the fine Baylor quarterback arrived in 1950 as Baltimore's No. 1 draft choice, and I had myself another rival. Don Colo and Art Donovan came to Westminster, too, and of course they stayed around a long time as two of the game's top performers. Another addition that year was Hardy Brown, a tough-nut guy from Tulsa. I want to say some more about Hardy later.

I seem to remember that we had an awful lot of halfbacks from Notre Dame running around camp. There was Ernie Zalejski, Frank Spaniel, Bob Livingstone and Achille Maggioli. Herb Rich, a fine defensive back, joined us from Vanderbilt and I got myself a couple of good receivers in Harold Crisler from San Jose State and Jim Owens from Oklahoma.

Still, Clem Crowe was unable to find a winning combination. And we couldn't give him one.

Our first competition against a National League team was in a pre-season game with Pittsburgh and we made it close before losing, 30–27. From then on, things got worse. Cleveland trounced us by 34–17, the Chicago Bears by 21–17, San Francisco by 27–14 and then came that 70–21 beating by Los Angeles.

It was at this unpropitious time that Abe Watner made an incredible trade. He swapped Dick Barwegen to the Chicago Bears for five players!

Watner, a railroad man, justified his startling trade with the remark that "In my business, five for one has to be a good deal."

Good or bad, this transaction did not help the Colts in 1950. Barwegen stalled at first, not wanting to abandon his fish business in Baltimore, but finally reported to the Bears. The Colts acquired quarterback George Blanda, halfbacks Bob Perina and Ernie Zalejski, guard Tank Crawford and end Bob Jensen. We still lost eleven league games.

The Colts' troubles in 1950 can be simply put: we couldn't stop anybody. We didn't have a secondary. We gave up 462 points for the season. The National Football League book shows that most of the records for pass receiving, touchdown passes and passing yardage were set against Baltimore that year. Jim Hardy of the

Cardinals threw six touchdown passes against us on one game. Bob Shaw caught five of them. In the same game, Chicago set a record by scoring 48 points against us in one half. Cloyce Box of Detroit caught 12 passes in one afternoon and gained 302 yards all by himself, another all-time effort.

Once they got into our secondary, it was strictly "run, sheep, run."

I had my own troubles. Not necessarily in the order named they included: a sore arm, the appearance of George Blanda as a third quarterback, and a salary dispute with Abe Watner.

The sixth pre-season game was played against the New York Yanks at Shreveport near my old college and only 30 miles from Marshall. Quite according to our miserable form we lost, 42–17. It was doubly disappointing to me since most of my family and a lot of my old friends had come over for the game. Painful too, because I got cracked on my right arm when I was throwing a pass and had to leave the game. A knot the size of a tennis ball developed on my arm and it is still there. The doctor called it a spasm and said I would be unable to play against Green Bay the following week.

The spasm in my arm was painful but it didn't seem to me that it was acute enough to keep me out of the Green Bay game. I was bothered too because Blanda was challenging for my job pretty good. George had played one year with the Bears and was considered a fine all-around quarterback. He probably couldn't throw with me, but he could kick the hell out of the ball, which increased his value.

I was also aware, as we headed for a place called Egg Harbor, Wisconsin for a week's training that the Packer game was the last pre-season trial before the final player cuts. Even at that early stage of my professional career, I knew it wouldn't pay to be riding the bench when they were looking for excess guys to lop off the payroll.

There also was the matter of my contract. As I mentioned before, Abe Watner was a businessman-type and, although it is not always possible to apply business techniques to a sport like pro football, he was giving it one hell of a try. Abe had looked over the payroll and decided that $18,000 was an awful lot of money to be paying a quarterback who had been able to win only one game the year before.

Watner had been after me to sit down and talk terms with him but going into the Green Bay game, I still hadn't signed. The later it got, I reasoned, the better my chances. Even a novice like Watner wouldn't leave himself without his starting quarterback on the eve of the regular season.

But the arrival of a good one like Blanda changed my tactical situation drastically. With George and Adrian Burk in camp, I suddenly realized I might be expendable.

Worse yet, Abe Watner had reached the same conclusion. He called Clem Crowe in and told him to get me on the ball with my contract or else I might not be around.

Crowe could hardly believe his ears. But he knew Watner meant what he said.

On the eve of the Green Bay game, Crowe said to me, "Y.A., you'd better get together with Watner right away. He is talking about releasing you."

Watner's strategy was clear: if he was going to lose, he was going to lose cheap! I'm not saying he didn't have something there, but my spirits sank down to my cleats. Bad enough I had a lame arm and a discouraged coach with a team to match. Now, in the bargain, a hard-nosed owner wanted to cut my salary good or cut me out altogether.

We returned to Baltimore after losing to Green Bay, 16–14, and I put in four or five mighty bad days. Watner kept the pressure on me to talk contract or clear out. Crowe couldn't help me either; he had his own headaches—mainly in the form of a very bad football team.

I had no choice but to confer with Watner. I knew this meeting would cost me money. I no longer was in a strong bargaining position, not with a bad arm and two fine quarterbacks, waiting in the wings.

Watner was not a man to waste time in conversation.

"I can't afford to pay you eighteen thousand dollars a year," he said flatly, as our one-sided negotiations got under way.

"We are going to lose a lot of ball games and I'm going to lose a lot of money. I've got to cut down somewhere. I'm starting with you."

I was only 23 years old at the time and I hadn't much experience in money—especially this kind of money. Abe caught me by surprise. I couldn't even think of a good reason why I should retain my original salary.

"I want to be fair," he said, "so here's what I'll do. I will pay you a base salary of twelve thousand dollars. If we win five ball games, I will throw in a three thousand dollar bonus."

"Can I have some time to think it over?" I stuttered.

"Only until tomorrow," he snapped. "We open the season Sunday, and I want everything settled before then. You've got twenty-four hours, Tittle."

That night I called Cecil Isbell, who was then an assistant coach with the Chicago Cardinals. I told him of my meeting with Watner.

Isbell said the Cardinals would love to have me if Baltimore gave me my release. "But," he added, "I don't think you can get more than thirteen thousand."

So now I was faced with a real dilemma. There was nothing I would have liked better than playing for Isbell again. Things had not gone so good for me since the day he left Baltimore. On the other hand, Minnette was living in Baltimore and we had little Diane, and were pretty well settled. If I went to Chicago, I really wouldn't be making any more money than Watner had offered me, counting moving expenses and such. I decided to accept Watner's terms. On that proposition, Abe won all the way. We did not win five games. Nor did we win four games or three games or even two games. The 1950 Colts won just once, 41 to 21, over the Packers, who were almost but not quite as bad as we were. So I had to take the full six-thousand dollar slice. I really had no choice. But I resented the treatment because I didn't think any other ballplayer was so badly roughed up in Watner's economy drive.

Nothing Watner did in the front office, on the sidelines or we tried on the field helped Baltimore that year.

By the time we somehow defeated Green Bay in mid-season, we had lost 19 straight ball games, a humiliating series of failures that stretched back into 1949.

We were a poor ball club, and there was no getting away from it. Even the most zealous Baltimore rooters were beginning to lose faith.

Clem Crowe deserved a better fate. He was a fine man and a good football coach. But he was the victim of circumstances in 1950. Nobody, Knute Rockne, George Halas, Paul Brown, could have won with that ball team.

In the process of losing eleven games in 1950, Baltimore set a record for allowing points in a single half. It happened at Chicago's Comiskey Park on October 2, and it is indicative of the kind of season we had that this episode is one of the few I can remember that is worth telling. Oddly enough, we led the Cardinals by 13–7 that night and we trooped happily (I say "happily" because it was a rare day when we led at any point) into the dressing room, with not the slightest premonition that we were about to contribute to NFL history.

Starting right after the kickoff in the third period, the Cardinals ripped our secondary for 48 points—the biggest one-half scoring spree in league history. That was the night that Jim Hardy threw six touchdown passes, five of them to Bob Shaw. The final score was 55–13.

It was really "run, sheep, run" in Comiskey Park.

During this ball game, Clem Crowe, looking around for substitutes, found several Colt players hiding under a blanket. They apparently were not interested in playing. And since it wasn't that cold, I guess they did not want to witness the massacre.

Although I was the starting quarterback in most of our games that season, splitting the job with Adrian Burk, I did not throw my first NFL touchdown pass until our sixth game on October 29th against San Francisco at Kezar Stadium. I had come off the bench to replace Burk halfway through the second period. I remember the situation vividly. It was second down and 15. I threw an incompletion, and had a 13-yard completion nullified by an offside penalty. Then I threw 31 yards for a touchdown to Harold Crisler, the Colts' split end, who ran a post pattern, down and in. We eventually lost the game, 17–14, but I had a pretty good day with 18 completions in less than a half for two touchdowns and 230 yards.

147

Days like this were few and far between, however, and most of my memories of 1950 are unpleasant.

The end of the season also signalled the end of the Baltimore Colts, at least temporarily.

Abe Watner went to the NFL owners' meeting the following January and pleaded for player help. But he was soon to learn that football, like railroading, is a competitive business. The owners did not knock each other over in a stampede to bail Abe out of his troubles. In fact, no one volunteered the slightest assistance.

"If that's the way it is," Watner told them, "I want out."

So they paid him $50,000 for his assets, such as they were. The Colts were out of business. All Baltimore players went into the hopper for the 1951 draft; twenty-eight, including myself, were picked by NFL teams. The others became free agents.

None of us were particularly pained at the passing of the 1950 Colts.

Everyone has to start somewhere. Age: one year. Place: Marshall, Texas. Time: October, 1927.

A kid was a celebrity in Marshall if he wore a Maverick uniform. Football was the biggest thing in town, and it still is.

It was no simple matter for an old single wing tailback to learn the ways of the T formation at Louisiana State University in 1945. Everything seemed backwards in the beginning.

The 1946 season brought a Cotton Bowl bid to Louisiana State and all-Southeastern Conference honors for the Tigers' 4-F quarterback.

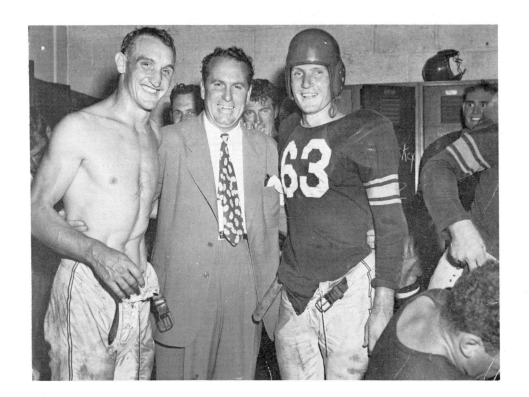

September 5, 1948: Colts 45, New York Yanks 28. Billy Hillenbrand (left) and Baltimore coach Cecil Isbell were part of the joyous post-game celebration. Colts had a great team that year but lost division playoff to Buffalo.

Frankie Albert (right) was the guiding spirit of the San Francisco Forty-Niner teams in the early 1950's. A southpaw, Frankie couldn't throw with the great quarterbacks of today, but he knew how to win — and that's what counts in the pro league.

They don't make them any tougher than Leo Nomellini, a great tackle for the San Francisco Forty-Niners for a lot of years. Big Leo was a good guy to have on your side. He scared some guys just by scowling at them.

A moment of decision. Giant coach Allie Sherman (center) and line coach Ed Kolman weigh key move against Green Bay Packers. There's no room for second-guessing on third and one. You get one shot — that's all.

No coach in the business can top Allie Sherman at spotting a flaw in the enemy's defenses during a ball game. Allie makes a **quarterback's** job a lot easier.

The wear and tear of fourteen years as a professional quarterback are etched in Charlie Conerly's face in this 1961 photo. Playing with a great competitor like old No. 42 was a rich experience.

A pro quarterback plays the game on his toes. He can't stand around flat-footed. It takes timing, balance and "feel" to make connections with those big backs crashing into the line. A split second often can make the difference between a 10-yard gain and a fumble.

Drop to seven yards. Step into the pocket. Plant that left foot. Pick out your man. And then "put it in the air."

The secret to successful passing is waiting until the last possible second before throwing the football—even when it means getting flattened by a big defensive end.

Del Shofner is the kind of pass receiver who makes the quarterback look good. The Giants' all-pro end has the speed to go deep for the "home run" ball — and that's the best way to get those points up there on the scoreboard.

A quarterback gets advice from everyone — even the small-fry. Pat Tittle, age 11, offers pop some post-game suggestions in Yankee Stadium dressing room.

No quarterback could ask for a better all-around receiver than Kyle Rote (left), the former Giants' end. Kyle wasn't fast and he wasn't big but he had the knack of getting open in that secondary. Boy, he had all the moves.

Mike Tittle (left) and brother Pat check pop's battle wounds after a particularly tough afternoon against the Dallas Cowboys.

When the Giants need the big play or the key first down, Joe Morrison is usually the man who gets the call. The ex-Cincinnati star does everything there is to do on a football field, and he does it well.

Pro football has undergone such vast and rapid changes that a youngster like Glynn Griffing has a tougher, more complex job on his hands than quarterbacks who came into the league a decade ago.

A professional quarterback feels the pressure all the time. It is part of him every minute of the game — even when he's on the sideline. There's no escaping it. He can't afford to relax or to interrupt his concentration. The gridiron is the battleground and he is the general.

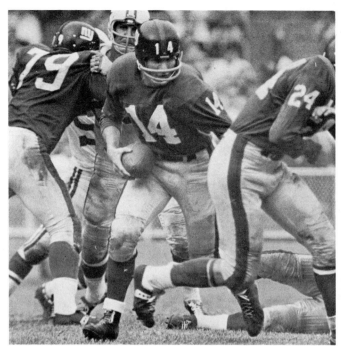

Hide the ball. Fool the defense. Freeze those line-backers for a split-second — and then throw the hell out of it.

Phil King (No. 24) is a real asset to the Giants. He's a 6-4 220-pounder who can pick up that tough yardage on third down. And he's a fellow who can protect the passer from those red-dogging linebackers.

The Tittle clan is happiest away from the thunder of football and the roar of the crowd. In this domestic scene are (left to right) daughter Diane, sons Pat and Mike, pop and Mrs. Minnette Tittle.

Allie Sherman, the Giants' coach, was a happy guy after win over Pittsburgh Steelers in final game gave New York its third straight eastern division title in 1963.

Professional football takes its toll of a man, especially a 37-year-old quarterback. The bruises heal slower. The aches last longer. You can still feel Sunday's game on Thursday. It gets harder all the time to prepare yourself physically and mentally for the next week.

Even in a crowded stadium, the quarterback is a lonely man. He's part of the battle, and yet he's detached from it. The responsibility for winning rests more on him than on any other player. His job is unique in professional sports.

CHAPTER EIGHTEEN

BUCK SHAW:
GENTLEMAN COACH

I BECAME a San Francisco Forty-Niner on the flip of a coin.

After Baltimore folded, I found myself exactly where I had been three years before as a green-eared kid out of L.S.U.—in the player draft, waiting to be plucked like a Christmas turkey.

The New York Giants had the bonus pick in 1951, a practice since discontinued, and they naturally selected Kyle Rote, an All-American halfback at Southern Methodist and probably the best college player in the nation. Long before the National Football League draft meeting, it was common knowledge that Rote would be the first man grabbed by the pros.

The Chicago Bears picked next and they went for Bob Williams, the Notre Dame quarterback.

Two down and old Y.A., the Christmas turkey, is still sitting there.

Since San Francisco, Green Bay and Washington had finished with identically unhappy records of 3–9 the year before, they were involved in the flip of a coin to determine which club would have the privilege of picking next.

The coin was tossed into the air and San Francisco general manager Lou (Lucky Lou) Spadia called "Heads!"

Heads it was, too, and San Francisco stepped up to make its selection.

"We'll take Y.A. Tittle," said Spadia.

I read about it the following day in the newspaper in Austin where I was living and working in the insurance business. As I recall, the news did not strike me with great impact. I had thought some club would take me and I told Minnette, "It might as well be the Forty-Niners as anyone else."

Not long after, I received a telephone call from Tony Morabito. He said he wanted to talk to me and would fly down to Dallas.

Morabito, who died of a heart attack during a San Francisco-Chicago Bears game at Kezar Stadium in 1957, was one of the finest men I ever met. He was hard-headed but warm-hearted. He was firm but soft-spoken. He had a great love for pro football.

Tony was the son of an Italian immigrant and he grew up in the same part of San Francisco that bred Joe DiMaggio and other great baseball players. But football was always Tony's true love. He drove a truck for a while after graduating from Santa Clara University and gradually became a pro fan, mainly because a Santa Clara fullback named Nello Falaschi was playing for the New York Giants. By 1941, enthusiastic Tony had enough cold cash to approach the National Football League and request a franchise for San Francisco. He was turned down on two counts: travel to the West Coast was too expensive, and the San Francisco area, with five major college teams, already had more football than it could handle. He tried again a few years later, guaranteeing to put a team into operation within three months after the end of World War II but he was still turned down by the NFL.

Morabito was not a guy who easily could be discouraged. When he learned that Arch Ward, a Chicago sports editor, was organizing the All-America Conference, Tony applied to the new league and San Francisco became a charter member.

"I expect to lose money," Tony said frankly. "It will take time before pro football catches on in San Francisco. But I believe this is a great sports town and I am willing to gamble."

Several years later, Morabito had occasion to demonstrate that faith. In 1949 he and his brother Vic bought out their two partners. To consummate this deal and to insure capital for operating the team that season, Tony mortgaged his home and borrowed $100,000.

Nor did Tony let his personal difficulties affect his generosity toward his players. Frankie Albert's 1949 contract was for $20,000, a record salary for the time.

I liked Morabito the first time I met him. He was a smart business-man and he was fair. I trusted him. Tony did not have to use a hard-sell on me in Dallas. I agreed verbally to a contract for $13,500, more than I had made the year before with the Colts. But money wasn't the whole reason. I was anxious to play football in a new atmosphere after the dismal 1949 campaign in Baltimore, and I was particularly anxious to play for Tony and his Forty-Niners.

When I got back to Austin I got a call from my old L.S.U. side-kick Jim Cason, who had been with the Forty-Niners during my time with Baltimore. He was tickled at the prospect of playing with me again, and I felt the same way.

"You'll like it with us," Jimmy said. "Buck Shaw is a fine coach, and we've got a good ball club."

"Will I get a chance to play out there?" I asked. Frankie Albert was a San Francisco hero and, frankly, I was concerned about how much quarterbacking I would do.

"Sure," he replied encouragingly. "This is a great opportunity for you. Albert's getting old, he can't go on forever."

San Francisco trained at Menlo Junior College in Menlo Park which is now my home. When I got to camp in July I discovered that Cason was not the only familiar face. There were Ray Collins, the big tackle from L.S.U. and Hardy Brown, who played with me for a year at Baltimore.

The Forty-Niners had rounded up a pretty fair bunch of rookies for the 1951 season. Joe Arenas and Billy Wilson came in with me that year, and so did Pete Schabarum, Rex Berry, Jim Mona-chino, Bill Jessup and a whole lot of other top ball players. Some say it was the finest draft in the team's history.

Camp routine under Buck Shaw differed greatly from anything I had experienced as a pro. The Colts of 1949 and 1950 were a dis-organized bunch of losers. Now suddenly, I was in another world. With the exception of 1950, when they had a 3–9 record, the San

Francisco Forty-Niners had been winners. True, they had never won a league championship, but they were always up there behind those great Cleveland teams. The Forty-Niners had a winning spirit. Shaw gave them confidence and Frankie Albert translated this confidence into victories.

Buck Shaw was unique as coaches go, or so he seemed to me at the time. He coached his ball club with kid gloves. He was a gentleman—dapper, polished, soft-spoken. In rare moments of displeasure, his roughest language was, "Darn it to hell!" When Buck made such an outburst, however, many a lagging player displayed immediate movement.

Shaw's approach to coaching seemed almost casual. He was a good organizer and he commanded respect despite the fact that he never resorted to the driving, sweating, cursing tactics that some used. He had the knack of getting his ballplayers to rise to the occasion without painful tongue-lashings, punishing wind sprints or annoying bed checks. He created an atmosphere of relaxation. But nobody took advantage of Buck. The players liked him too much to dog it on him. Shaw's teams did not always have the best personnel in the league but he achieved maximum results with the material he did have. No coach can be asked to do more.

I believe I was a better quarterback, a more effective football player, under Buck Shaw between 1951 and 1954, even though I was younger and less experienced, than I was later on in 1955–56–57 when Shaw left and San Francisco's coaching became rigid, disciplined, controlled and less relaxed.

It had been fun playing football under Buck Shaw those first few years. When he left, it was not.

Which is the right approach and which is wrong is not for me to say. A coach has to run his ball club the way he sees it. Paul Brown, a strong, stern personality, was a winning coach at Cleveland. Buck Shaw was a far different type of man—and coach. But he was a winner too, first at Santa Clara, where his teams won in the Sugar Bowl, then in San Francisco and later in Philadelphia.

Buck turned in a masterful coaching job with the Eagles in 1961. He had a quarterback named Norm Van Brocklin and not much else, but he won the Eastern title and beat Green Bay by 17–13 for the world championship.

If Cecil Isbell exerted a lasting influence on my passing that first year at Baltimore, Buck Shaw did as much for my mental approach to football after I joined the Forty-Niners. I liked Buck immediately. He put me at ease. He treated me as a man, as a pro, and there was nothing I wanted more to do than to win for him.

CHAPTER NINETEEN

OFF–THE–CUFF WITH ALBERT

No PLAYER typified the San Francisco Forty-Niners more than their quarterback, Frankie Albert.

The success of the team in those early years was founded on Tony Morabito's dollars and faith; on Buck Shaw's organizational ability and, perhaps more than anything else, on Frankie Albert's electrifying play and crowd appeal.

Some men are born to be set apart from others. Frankie Albert was one of these. He was a leader, an inspiration to all of us.

My own career became intertwined with Albert's from the day I reported to the San Francisco training camp.

Albert had a tremendous influence on me, almost as much as Cecil Isbell, but in a different way. Isbell taught me to have confidence in my passing arm and to "throw that damned ball." Frankie influenced my mental approach to quarterbacking. He may not have done so intentionally. After all, he was San Francisco's quarterback, a great favorite in his home town. I was a guy from Baltimore who was after his job. I never have known whether or not Albert resented my arrival in San Francisco. I do know one thing: in those early years we were not buddy-buddy. Albert had his own friends, a small tight group. I don't believe any of them ever succeeded in knowing him intimately. Oddly enough, my old L.S.U. buddy Jim Cason was one of those closest to Frankie, but I definitely was not.

Frankie Albert could have been called a "loner." When you met him at breakfast, it was "Hello" or maybe "Good morning." Never much more.

My first impression of Albert in 1951 was that he was far more polished than the rest of the ballplayers I had known. He was several years older for one thing, and he was much more mature and confident. On the airplanes, Frankie would sit and talk with the writers and the coaches, while the rest of us played cards and stuck together like a bunch of rookies. He was poised and articulate. The difference between this man-of-the-world and the rest of us was marked.

I encountered a similar situation years later when I was traded to New York. While the Giants were renowned for their togetherness, it was obvious to me from the beginning that Charlie Conerly and Alex Webster and Kyle Rote were more poised than the rest of the fellows.

This is how it was with Frankie Albert.

Frank may not actually have resented me in 1951 but neither did he go out of his way to hasten my development as a professional quarterback. He never conducted seminars. Most of what I gained from Albert was learned by studying him and observing him in action. This was just his way. Perhaps this is the way I have become. A quarterback can get very protective of his job.

One day at Menlo Park, I went up to Frankie and asked him about some minor point on a play. He made a face and said:

"Hey, Tittle, don't you know that you're after my job?"

Then he laughed like he had just been pulling my leg. I walked away wondering if he really had been kidding. I'm still not sure.

Today we are great friends. We live near each other in California and we play golf all the time. Our wives are friends too. The competitive angle is gone now. But it was there in 1951 and I suppose I felt it more than the Forty-Niners' established star.

What struck me most about Albert was his off-the-cuff approach to football. He had fun playing the game. He made it fun for us too. Frankie could always be expected to do the unexpected, so practice was never a chore when he was running the show for Buck Shaw. In many respects Albert and Shaw were alike. Buck coached in an offhand manner. Frankie quarterbacked the same way.

You've got to get your work done in practice. Albert always did. But he enjoyed it. I mean, Frankie might just keep that ball on a bootleg when everyone expected him to do something else. He would fool everybody and hand the ball to a lineman or maybe a fellow who was just standing there watching the play.

I do the same thing sometimes myself because it breaks up the drudgery. This is the first thing I learned from Frankie Albert: How to enjoy being a professional football player.

There was no monotony attached to practice for Frankie. When he wasn't working in the huddle, he would be punting the ball to a bunch of kids or maybe throwing them passes.

Buck Shaw smoked cigarettes during practice and he had a habit of flipping the cigarette over his shoulder when he was through. Albert would sneak up behind him, take a couple of forbidden puffs, drop the cigarette, and hop back into the huddle.

He was always clowning around but he was careful never to be disrespectful to our coach. Frankie knew where to draw the line.

Socially, whenever you got too close to Frankie Albert, he backed off. He was a good guy and all that, but he wasn't a laughing boy in the locker room. He never let us feel that he was one of us.

One of Frankie's traits that rubbed off on me was his manner of handling a ball club in the huddle. When he came into a huddle, he wasn't a routine signal-caller. It was never just, "Slant thirty-four . . . on two!" He would stick his head in there and look at everybody and say something like, "Slant thirty-four . . . count on two. Okay, let's run it, you guys!"

I can't really explain it that easily. But Frankie broke up the sameness of a huddle. He never let his club drift into monotony. Everyone listened carefully because you never knew what he might say next. And that's precisely what he wanted to achieve; he always had his players on their toes.

I can remember some of the great times he used to have with Leo Nomellini, the big Forty-Niner tackle. Nomellini was a University of Minnesota man and his hero was Bronko Nagurski, one of the game's all-time great fullbacks. Leo was an all-pro tackle but in his heart he always wished he had been another Nagurski. Albert knew this, as did the rest of us. In practice and in some of our scrimmages, Frankie would come into the huddle and say, "Well, okay, let's run a thirty-one wedge. Nomo, you get back here and play fullback."

Nomellini would drop back from his tackle spot and Albert would put John Stryzkalski up there in the line to fill the hole. Leo got a great kick out of the switch but I'm not so sure that Stryzkalski shared his enthusiasm.

Anyway, Leo at fullback was like a big elephant and Albert would hand him the ball. Leo would run up there through the middle on a 31-wedge. They would kick the hell out of him, but Nomo loved it. So did the rest of us.

Frankie did this in regular league games, too. Whenever we had a lead like 35–14 in the last period, he would use a play he called "Thirty-one, Nomo." Nomellini would come back just like a big old bull. He would prance his legs up and down and snort a few times. Then Albert called signals, "Hut-one . . . hut-two" and there would go Leo with the ball under his arm like a loaf of bread.

Everybody would holler, "Attaboy, Leo, you killed 'em that time."

Most times Nomellini got only a yard or two but the rest of our guys made it sound like he was tearing the opposition apart.

Back in the huddle, Albert would look at him and say, "Damn! you're really cracking that line today, Leo. I tell you what we're going to do, Leo. We're going to pound you in there a few more times to soften them up. Then we'll shoot Cason or Stryzkalski to the outside." Old Leo ate it up.

It was great fun and "Thirty-one, Nomo" was a great play. It didn't gain much yardage, and Leo usually got the stuffing belted out of him carrying the ball. But it made the San Francisco Forty-Niners a better team just the same—at least happier.

Albert had other ways of keeping everyone guessing. One of them was throwing passes for extra points. This mind you, when all the time we have Gordy Soltau, one of the best place kickers in pro ball. That didn't faze Frankie. He would get down there to hold for Soltau on the conversion try. Then he'd straighten up and lob the ball to a defensive end or somebody and the guy would run it in for the point after touchdown.

157

It never made much sense. Soltau was a sure thing for the extra point. The defensive end wasn't a good risk to catch the ball. Still, this was Albert's way of having fun and making us enjoy football.

There was a method to Frankie's showmanship too. Those little lob passes for the extra point rubbed salt into the wounded pride of the other ball team. It was bad enough getting scored against, but to have this little lefthander toss the ball in for the extra point was kind of humiliating. Albert was aware of this, and he used his trickery to full advantage.

I have been called a good bootlegger. But I couldn't carry Albert's helmet when it came to bootlegging the football. He was truly a master. Albert taught me the psychological effectiveness of the play.

The yardage isn't always important but the effect the play creates is. Maybe I run a bootleg and I fool them and I get nine or ten yards. It might have been a lot easier to hand the ball to Phil King or Alex Webster and let them make the ten yards. But here all of a sudden old bald-headed Y.A. has fooled them for a first down. Everyone feels like, "Now we've got them going. We're crossing them up. Y.A. has got them fooled."

Sometimes this is all it takes to get a ball club moving in the right direction.

Nobody could fool the defense like Frankie Albert. I remember him putting that ball on his hip and sliding around end for ten or twelve yards. He would dance out of bounds as soon as he made his first down, and then he would strut back to the Forty-Niner huddle like a little rooster while the other team did a slow burn. You could almost read their minds: "If we ever get that little runt out in the open again . . ."

The bootleg was a psychological weapon in Albert's arsenal. It got the fans "oohing" and "aahing."

"The little lefty's got those guys in his back pocket now. Let's go, Forty-Niners!"

This, as I have pointed out, is the real value of the bootleg. It's not the fact that you make five yards on the run, or that you complete a ten-yard pass to Joe Walton when you just as easily could have dropped back and hit him on the hook pattern without risking your neck running around with the ball on your hip. But if the quarterback can roll out and dump one over there and fool everybody, he can ruin an opposing team's morale. The other club sets its defenses to stop a run here or a pass there, and the quarterback shakes them up by running one way while everybody goes the other way.

Improvisation was Frankie Albert's middle name. He made up plays any time, any place. He pulled them out of the air. Most quarterbacks couldn't get away with this. But Albert did. He was an instinctive quarterback. He had a wonderful "feel" for the game and so he did things the rest of us couldn't.

In August, 1952, Hugh McElhenny made his pro debut in a pre-season game against the Chicago Cardinals. In the huddle, Albert turned to Hugh and said, "I'm going to fake to Perry up the middle. I want you to delay for one count and then start swinging around the end. I'll pitch it out to you."

"What play is that?" inquired McElhenny.

"It's no play," snapped Albert. "Just do what I tell you."

"Okay," said McElhenny.

Hugh took off for the right sideline as Albert made his fake to Perry. The Cardinal defenders were frozen for a split second as Perry crashed into the line. That instant was all Frankie needed; he turned and lateraled the ball to Mac in the flat, and Hugh went 60 yards for a touchdown. They never saw him.

During another game, against the Yankees, a group of photographers behind the end zone shouted to Albert that they had been unable to get any good close-up action shots.

"Stay right where you are fellows," Albert answered, not caring whether the Yankees heard him or not, "I'll pitch out to Stryzkalski and he'll come right at you."

The play developed just as Albert had described it. The San Francisco line opened up a hole, Stryzkalski went through for a touchdown and the photographers had their picture.

With this kind of a fellow as its leader, San Francisco was a tough team to beat.

Albert directed the Forty-Niners with a daring that was almost insulting to opponents. He was not a great forward passer—he threw a lefthanded ball that wobbled all over the place—but his razor-sharp imagination, great reflexes, his flair for the unexpected, his nerve—these made him a dangerous passer.

There never has been a better ball-handler in professional football than Albert. Maybe Eddie LeBaron came close but Frankie was still the best in my opinion. He could shuffle that ball in the backfield and make it disappear. I recall that even when looking at our game films in slow motion it was sometimes difficult to locate the ball when Albert was working his sleight-of-hand.

Whenever I stop to consider my present status in professional football, I can't help but think that Cecil Isbell and Frankie Albert, each in his own way, made the most important contributions to my early development. Isbell gave me the confidence in my ability to throw the football, to pick my man and to hit him between the eyes. The impression Albert made on me was more subtle. From Frankie I learned the nuances and the refinements of quarterbacking—and also the bootleg play!

CHAPTER TWENTY

"I CAME TO PLAY"

I HAVE always come to play, and I came to play at San Francisco in 1951.

Of course, Frankie Albert was still No. 1 with the Forty-Niners, and that's as it should have been. Frankie was older and he was in his sixth season. It was going to take a lot to move Albert out of his position, and I would have to bide my time. I was a better passer. Albert, though, was a superior quarterback in every other respect including the one most important to a professional football team—he knew how to win.

When I signed with Tony Morabito I told him I was coming to San Francisco to play, not to ride the bench until Albert got so old he had to retire.

"You'll get your chance," Tony had said, and his word was good enough for me.

Training at Menlo Park was quite an experience. The atmosphere was one of total relaxation, not at all like the pro camps I had been in during my three years. Buck Shaw believed in informality. The first day at practice, he walked onto the field and said, "Okay, boys, you all start running some plays."

Heck, we hadn't even learned any plays at that point.

Then he says, "You older guys show these new fellows some plays."

Next thing we knew, Albert and Norm Standlee, the fullback

and Stryzkalski and the rest of the guys get up there and start running plays. Albert sort of ran the show by himself after Shaw got things under way. He made up the plays as he went along. Nobody had so much as seen a Forty-Niner playbook but I got the impression we didn't need one as long as Frankie was in charge of things. He never had any trouble. If he couldn't remember a play, he simply invented one. And oddly enough, the veterans were so used to his off-the-cuff improvising that they fell right into line.

Albert would stick his head in there and say, "Everybody zone, and we'll pitch out to you Stryzkalski." And around they would come like they had practiced the play a thousand times. It was really something.

Again, I don't want this to be interpreted as meaning that Buck Shaw was not well organized. He was. His record attests to that. He was a winning coach with the knack of getting his teams ready his own way. His approach may have been different—but it was successful.

Football in 1951 was not like it is today. Shaw could afford to coach the way he did because the game was so different. We did not study two sets of films before each game. We did not take frequencies on the red-dog—Sam, Wanda, Tango and all of this defensive stunting—as we do in the modern era. We never studied automatics; we didn't even have automatics. The game was so vastly different then. There was none of the preparation we know today. The study, the intense study, that a rookie like Glynn Griffing of the Giants has to go through is unlike anything I experienced in my early years.

The quarterback's job was simpler then because the age of the specialist had not yet arrived. We did not have to face the great defensive stars who now play in the National Football League. In those days, the average life-span of a pro was two or three years; today, quarterbacks have to contend with defensive specialists who have seven, eight, nine years of experience.

A defensive corner back like Erich Barnes . . . a linebacker like Sam Huff . . . an end like Gino Marchetti, these fellows are experts at their jobs. They have size, speed and, most important, great experience. They are hard to beat. All we had in 1951 was a

5–3–2–1 defense, slant left, slant right, maybe a few red-dogs. That was it. There was no need to make detailed preparations for a ball game or to take frequencies or to sit there for hours and look at films.

Playing was simpler, and so was coaching.

Shaw ran a very informal camp, something that would be impossible today, and he got away with it because he had a fellow like Frankie Albert as the offensive leader.

All through the training period an Menlo Park that summer I looked better than Albert in practice. I guess this was because I was passing well and Frankie, as usual, was not. I was throwing the nice tight spirals, the kind that make the guys ooh and aah, and Frankie, well, he was flipping that lefthanded thing down there, sometimes end over end.

But even my passing couldn't shake his status as the San Francisco quarterback. I would still have to prove I could win before the Forty-Niners considered me anything more than a bald-headed guy from Baltimore.

My chance to prove this was delayed by a bad muscle pull the second week of camp that sidelined me while Frankie whipped Washington, 45–14, in the opening pre-season game. I missed the next game too, a loss to the Chicago Bears, but I was over my muscle pull and ready to make my Forty-Niner debut against the Pittsburgh Steelers the following week in Syracuse, New York.

At least I thought I was ready. We made the trip back to Syracuse by train. What a long haul! Somewhere along the line, probably because of the bouncing up and down in the sleeper car, my old bursitis hit me again. I had stabbing pains in my right shoulder. I couldn't even carry my suitcase off the train. Damn it, I thought. My muscle pull is cured and I have my shot at playing, but I can't even lift my right arm as high as my shoulder. How am I going to throw the ball tomorrow night?

I was concerned over whether or not I should tell Buck Shaw about my shoulder. The Forty-Niners did not know I had bursitis. I had just come off the injured list and I didn't want to go back on it, not with my first opportunity to play quarterback just a day away. How would I explain the bursitis? These fellows would begin to think I was some kind of a hypochondriac.

163

These thoughts were running through my mind when fate, in the form of a torrential rainstorm, interceded.

Syracuse was hit by the heaviest rains in its history that night. It rained and it rained and it rained some more. The streets were awash, power lines were down, the city was at a standstill. It was so bad they postponed the game, the first and only time I ever remember a football game being called on account of weather.

The cancellation was the break I needed. An extra day's rest might bring my arm around so I could play against the Steelers!

Instead of sitting around the hotel playing cards the next day, I went downtown to see the doctor who took care of the Syracuse International League baseball team. I don't recall how I even got his name. I could have gone to Pop Kleckner, the San Francisco trainer, but I didn't want them to know I had a bad shoulder. They had just cured me of a pulled leg muscle and I felt it would look like I was a chronic injury case. That's no way to start off with a ball club.

So I visited the Syracuse baseball doctor and he gave me diathermy treatment and an injection of cortisone. I went back the following day for another treatment and by game time my shoulder was at least good enough to get by with. I knew I wouldn't be able to throw the ball too well, but at the time I was only interested in getting into that game. Frankie started, naturally, but Shaw used me in the second half. I managed to bluff my way through with my sore shoulder and, due mainly to Albert, we beat the Steelers, 44–17.

San Francisco had come off a poor year in 1950, but in 1951 we had a good football team. A lot of new guys had come in, including Billy Wilson, one of the greatest ends I have ever seen, and we finished with a 7–6–1 record, a big improvement over 3–9.

When the regular season started, Frankie Albert was doing most of the quarterbacking, which was to be expected. I didn't get into the opening game, a 24–10 upset of Cleveland, but I didn't mind. I had resigned myself to a certain period of waiting. Albert had six years on me. More important, he had the confidence and the faith of the San Francisco players. I felt sure I would be a better quarterback than Frankie someday, but it would take time—and patience.

164

I must confess that I learned very little from Albert's style of play, I mean the mechanical aspects of his game. He was an individualist, an off-the-cuff quarterback, and I knew it would be a mistake to attempt to adapt my style of play to his. Besides, he was left-handed and he did everything backwards. But what I did gain from Albert in those early months was an appreciation of his approach to the game. He was daring, unafraid to take a chance. Pressure did not wilt Frankie Albert; he thrived on it. He had fun playing football and he made the game enjoyable for the rest of the team, even when it was for big money.

Everything was a laugh for Frankie Albert. Unfortunately, he did not coach that way later on.

Albert hurt his shoulder in the opening win over Cleveland and could barely lob the ball. But I was still trying to learn the Forty-Niner offense and Shaw did not have enough faith in me to let me run the show. So Frankie kept playing. But he couldn't throw, and we lost the next game to Philadelphia by 24–14, and we came home from a road trip three weeks later with a 2–2 record.

I was still riding the bench when San Francisco played Los Angeles in the fifth game of the season. The Rams of 1951 were one of the greatest pro teams ever assembled. They had speed, power and wonderful passers in Bob Waterfield and Norm Van Brocklin. They also had three of the game's finest receivers, Elroy Hirsch, Tom Fears and Bob Boyd. But we beat them by 44–17 that day. Albert was tremendous; he drove the Rams crazy. The San Francisco defense was hot too and it picked off six Ram passes. Visco Grgich and Leo Nomellini made life miserable for Waterfield and Van Brocklin. In fact the Dutchman got so hot that he finally blew his top and challenged Grgich to a fight after the game.

"Sorry," replied Grgich, "but I'm a coward."

Los Angeles came back and whipped us, 23–16, on three field goals by Waterfield a week later and so we had a 3–3 record when the New York Yanks came to Kezar Stadium.

I mention this game because it was a turning point in my career with the Forty-Niners.

The Yanks were a weak ball club but they jumped us and they were ahead by 14–12 when Shaw put me in the game in the fourth period. There was no alternative but to throw the ball and score in a hurry because time was running out.

In the huddle, I looked at Gordy Soltau, our left end, and asked, "Can you beat your man to the inside?"

"I'll try," he said.

"Okay, then, the snap number is on three. Let's pull this one out!"

I dropped back to throw but the Yanks had a defensive rush on and they broke through my blockers. It would have been suicide to stand my ground, so I scrambled out to the right. I got away from two tacklers and looked downfield for Soltau. There he was, cutting across the middle—and wide open, too! I reared back and threw a long pass, maybe thirty-five yards or more, toward Soltau, a beautiful pass. Just as I turned the ball loose, I got the hell knocked out of me. I was flipped clean over backwards. As I hit the ground, I heard the crowd cheering a San Francisco touchdown.

"Nice going, Gordy," I said as I got back to my feet.

But when I got to the sideline, everyone was congratulating Pete Schabarum, our flanker back, and shaking his hand.

"What's going on?" I asked Cason, who had been sitting on the bench.

"You just won the ball game for us, that's what," he answered.

"Yeah, I know, but why is everyone congratulating Schabarum?"

"He caught your pass," said Jimmy.

Then it dawned on me—I had missed Soltau, had thrown the ball a good two yards over his head, and Schabarum had caught it. He had caught it on his fingertips on the dead run, and he had kept right on going into the end zone!

Of course, after the game the writers said it was the prettiest pass ever thrown in Kezar Stadium. I was embarrassed, but not embarrassed enough to tell them I had really been aiming for Soltau and not Schabarum. In all truth, I hadn't even known where Pete was when I threw the ball.

This was not my first touchdown pass for the San Francisco Forty-Niners but it was my biggest. It won the game for us, and that's what I had been anxious to do for the team. I wanted to win for them as Albert had won for the past six years.

My lucky shot to Schabarum also stirred up some controversy in the newspapers. Several writers asked, "Why doesn't Buck Shaw use Tittle more?"

Around town, the fans divided into Tittle and Albert camps and all of a sudden it was a great big issue with everyone.

Frankie never mentioned whether it bothered him or not. As a matter of fact, he and I still were not close friends and we did not have much to say to one another.

But the Tittle-Albert controversy did upset Buck Shaw. He told one of the San Francisco writers, "I knew that inevitably we were going to get into this squeeze. It's the same thing in Los Angeles where they have Waterfield and Van Brocklin. One or the other is always on the pan with the fans and the press. That, or the coaches are."

The Yanks also provided another memorable afternoon in 1951, but this time the consequences were not as pleasant as the day I threw my accidental touchdown pass to Schabarum.

Two weeks after our win over the Yanks at Kezar, we flew east to meet them in New York. Again Shaw sent me in for Albert, this time with the score tied at 10-all and two minutes left on the clock. We marched down the field and, it seemed like we were going in for a score. I completed a pass to Soltau on the Yanks' 15-yard line, which would have been good range for a field goal try. But Gordy lateraled the ball to Stryzkalski as he was being tackled and Strike couldn't hold onto it. He fumbled. The Yanks recovered and ran out the clock before we could get another scoring shot.

In the Yankee Stadium dressing room after the game, I flung my helmet on the floor and slumped down on a stool. I was disappointed at having to settle for a tie with a ball club we could have beaten. If you look back at the western division standings for that year, you will see the Forty-Niners had a good chance to win the title. At least we did until the Yanks tied us in New York. The field goal Soltau lateraled away would have done it for us.

Anyway, I was sitting there, cursing to myself and thinking about the lost field goal, when a writer from the San Francisco Chronicle walked up.

"Well, Y.A.," he sympathized, "you almost did it—again."

Now this was immediately after the game. We didn't have the ten-minute cooling off period that is in effect today. I was still hot under the collar. I was angry with everything in general because I am not a fellow who always takes losing, or even tying, gracefully.

"Well, dammit," I snorted, "I can't do it every week with two minutes to go!"

The minute the words left my lips, I knew I shouldn't have said them. They were uttered under emotional stress. But it was too late.

That's all there was to it at the moment. The writer walked away and left me sitting there, still fuming. We had another week on the road, so I was unaware of the repercussions my untimely statement created back in San Francisco.

The headlines read: "Tittle Criticizes Shaw for Lack of Play!" And they were set in the largest type the Chronicle could find.

The story under the headline was even more inflammatory. It quoted me as saying, ". . . this is a passing game and not a running game," inferring that I was criticizing Buck Shaw's game plan and Frankie Albert's field strategy. They put other words in my mouth too, words I never said. The only thing I had said, regrettably, was "Well, I can't win every week with two minutes to go."

I learned the hard way to weigh my words carefully with members of the press.

The next week we went out to Detroit and I came back again and won the ball game for San Francisco, 20–10. I don't like saying, "I won the ball game" because naturally I did not win it alone. The rest of the Forty-Niners had a hand in it, too. But I did play more and my passing got us the winning points in the second half.

It was becoming evident that I figured more prominently in San Francisco plans. I was winning ball games for them, and that's how the pros evaluate a quarterback. Does he win or doesn't he?

Frankie Albert remained the No. 1 man, of course, and Buck Shaw never led me to believe any differently. But I knew I was making headway.

When we returned to San Francisco, I was still unaware of the sensational headlines my Yankee Stadium outburst had caused at

168

home. But Shaw soon heard about it and one day at practice he called me into his office.

"Sit down, Y.A.," he said, "there's something we've got to talk about."

I sensed from the tone of his voice and the look on his face that whatever he was about to say wasn't going to be good. Buck was normally a kind, soft-spoken man. But now there was a hard look in his eyes, or maybe it was a hurt look. I wasn't sure then, and I'm not sure to this day.

"Did you see this article?" he asked, holding a copy of The Chronicle in front of me.

"No," I replied.

Then he asked, "Did you make this statement?"

I hastily read the beginning of the story and said, "Well, yes, Buck but I didn't make these other statements . . . about 'this is a passing game' . . . and 'I believe you should throw the ball more' . . . that 'you can't play pro teams and score ten points and expect to win.' I never said any of those things."

Shaw's expression remained unchanged.

"You know, Y.A.," he said finally, "this makes me look awful bad, and it's not good for our ball club, either."

Shaw was right, of course. And I had been wrong. That much was clear. I apologized, even though I felt then, as I do now, that the Chronicle story was unfair and inaccurate. I felt deeply embarrassed, and I was sorry for Buck Shaw. He had always treated me fairly and I had not meant to put him on the spot.

Sportswriters have to write copy; that's their job. I appreciate their problems but I want them to appreciate mine too. Since that day at Yankee Stadium in 1951 I have been on my guard with writers. Most of them are fine fellows but the occasional one who isn't can wreck a ballplayer's career. I have been called uncommunicative and un-cooperative by the press. All I can offer in defense of this attitude is that I learned my lesson early—and I haven't forgotten it.

Shaw was a wonderful man. He never again mentioned the incident as long as he was my coach. The minute we walked out the door, it was a closed issue.

I put it out of my mind, too, and concentrated on our last two games against Green Bay and Detroit.

Frankie Albert and I split the quarterbacking against the Packers and we won the ball game, 31–19.

Detroit came to Kezar Stadium needing only a victory over us to clinch the N.F.L. western division title. The Lions were 7–3–1 and the Rams were 7–4. Our record was 6–4–1 going into the final game of the campaign.

Albert opened against Detroit, but Shaw got me in there sooner than usual and I played most of the game. With four minutes left, the Lions had us down, 17–14. But Joe Arenas took a Detroit punt on the dead run and raced 51 yards to the nine-yard line. That gave us our chance, and I scored the winning touchdown in the last minute on a bootleg play. I can still recall that play: I faked to Joe Perry over the middle and then to John Stryzkalski on a slant. The Detroit linebackers took the second fake. They didn't even see me hide the ball on my hip and go into the end zone standing up.

As I walked off the field, Hunchy Hoernschemeyer, the Lions' halfback, said something nasty to me, called me a dirty name. He was boiling mad because we didn't have a chance to win it, and yet we had upset Detroit and cost Hunchy and his teammates a lot of playoff money.

While the 1951 San Francisco team did not finish first it was a fine football club with great spirit. Our backfield of Perry, Stryzkalski and Arenas was as good as any in the league.

And speaking of Arenas, he was the fighting spirit of the 1951 Forty-Niners. He typified the hustle and aggressiveness of the entire squad. Here was a little boy who came out of Omaha as an unheralded draft choice and wasn't given much chance of winning the left halfback job from the likes of Sam Cathcart and my pal Jim Cason, not to mention several promising rookies. But Joe Arenas hadn't come all the way to San Francisco to be sent home again. We found this out the first day in training camp.

Albert called the squad together and said, "Let's line up out there and run some plays."

Well, Norm Standlee steps in at fullback and Stryzkalski at halfback, or maybe it was Perry. Bill Johnson takes the center spot and Bruno Banducci and some of the other veterans fill in along the line.

But before anyone else can make a move, Arenas hops in at left halfback. Rookies aren't supposed to take such liberties, but there he is, big as life. Everyone looks at everyone else in amazement. The same question is going through our minds: "Who the hell does this little guy think he is, stepping in there when we are going to run some plays?"

I must say that Joe wasn't too popular in the beginning. There were some Forty-Niners who hated his guts. They had him figured as a brash, cocky kid. He may have been, too, but he was a hard-nose with a tough attitude. They never did get him out of the left halfback spot after that first day in camp. He stayed there, and his fighting spirit soon infected the rest of the squad.

Albert and Arenas! They were some pair in 1951!

CHAPTER TWENTY-ONE

THE OLD THUMPER

POUND FOR POUND . . . inch for inch, the toughest football player I ever met was Hardy Brown, my roommate with the Forty-Niners.

He was so tough, he was damned near illegal!

Hardy was a linebacker. Maybe he was not the best linebacker in the business, but I doubt if any ballplayer ever persued his trade with more enthusiasm. No one could match him for instilling cold fear in rival ball-carriers.

Brown's favorite weapon was a numbing shoulder tackle, usually aimed at the head, and when Hardy hit them, they stayed hit.

I don't believe Hardy could have played in the National Football League today. At six feet and 185 pounds he was too small for a modern middle linebacker. He was also too slow. And nobody ever mistook him for a Rhodes Scholar. But from 1951 through 1955 Hardy Brown was the scourge of pro ball. Naturally, some exaggeration has crept into the re-telling of Brown's exploits. But I played with him for five years and I saw him do some things that were almost unbelievable.

One day in 1951 he knocked out the entire starting backfield of the Washington Redskins, leaving only Harry Gilmer, the quarterback, in one piece. And when I say "knocked out," I mean just that. Hardy laid them out stiff with his shoulder tackle and they were carted off on stretchers.

Against the Los Angeles Rams the same year, Hardy caught Glenn Davis coming through a hole in the line and hit him so hard in the head that the ligaments were torn in Glenn's knees. Now, you've got to belt a man pretty damned good in the head to tear up his knees, but that's what Hardy did. Davis was never the same again and shortly thereafter he quit pro ball.

Hardy always seemed to be at his toughest against Los Angeles. On the last play of a Rams–Forty-Niners game at the Coliseum, Dick Hoerner carried for the Rams and he met Brown head-on at the line of scrimmage. The gun sounded as they went to the ground, and both teams trotted off the field. When the Rams got around to counting noses in the dressing room, they discovered one man was missing—Dick Hoerner. They went outside to the field, and there was Dick just getting to his feet. He had been knocked cold for at least fifteen minutes. Hardy had left him for dead right on the 3-yard line!

I guess at one time or another everybody in the National Football League was after Hardy Brown, especially the Los Angeles Rams. It was said the Rams had a pool set up to pay the fine of any man who caught up with Hardy and put him out of commission.

They never did.

The only time I ever saw Brown get hurt was one day when he slammed into a Detroit runner and put him down so hard that the fellow ricocheted off the ground, catching Hardy under the chin on the rebound. The cut required six stitches but he was back in there in a matter of minutes.

Hardy could dish it out but he could take it too. He never missed a game while I knew him.

Brown's shoulder tackle was something to see, believe me. Just thinking about it makes me appreciate the fact that he was on my side in Baltimore and San Francisco—and not against me. If all defensive players were like Hardy, I would have quit this game a long time ago. He never used his arms to tackle. He got down in a crouch, like a panther waiting to spring on his prey, and when the runner got close enough, Hardy would come up under him and drive his shoulder toward the ball-carrier's head. His timing was beautiful. When he connected with that shoulder, their heads would snap back and they would drop in their tracks. I never saw a football player who could stop a man as convincingly as Hardy Brown.

One tackle he made stands out in my memory. San Francisco was playing Pittsburgh at Kezar Stadium in 1951, and the Steelers had a tough little halfback named Joe Geri, a fire-plug kind of fellow and hard as nails. He and Hardy were a great match up; they were banging away at each other all afternoon. But in the fourth period, Brown put an end to the contest. He threw that shoulder of his into Geri so hard that he popped Joe's eyeball clean out of the socket! I mean it was hanging right out there.

I have heard of guys losing their contact lenses during a game. But that day, Geri damned near lost his real lens.

Naturally, Brown's tactics made him a stormy petrel around the league. Most teams insisted he was hitting with his elbows, deliberately trying to injure or maim someone. On more than one occasion, rival clubs sent officials into the San Francisco dressing room to check Hardy's shoulder pads; they didn't believe he could do so much damage with regulation gear. They never found anything, though, and this made them even angrier.

In his time, Hardy was called everything from "dirty player" to "hatchet man." These slurs never seemed to disturb him. In fact, I always felt he thoroughly enjoyed his bad guy role.

"Hardy," I said to him one day, "I think you'd pop that shoulder into your own mother."

"Not unless she had a football under her arm Y.A."

Somehow, I felt he wasn't kidding.

Legal or not, Hardy Brown gave the 1951 San Francisco team a great lift. And, while maybe it wasn't good to be inspired by his kind of play, a lot of the Forty-Niners were trying to imitate Hardy. Nobody could throw that shoulder like him, of course, but at least they were socking.

He gave them some record to shoot at that year. He knocked out twenty-one opposing players!

Hardy's very appearance on the football field was enough to stir us up.

"Here comes the old thumper!"

That's all it took to get everyone in a hitting mood.

Fortunately for me, Brown's violence was restricted to the football field. As a roommate at Menlo Park, he was as quiet and as reserved a fellow as you'd want to meet. I used to look at him sitting there reading a book and wonder how he could be so tough in a pair of shoulder pads.

"There are times, Hardy," I kidded him once, "when I actually feel you are human."

"Just try and run past me with a football and you'll see how human I am," he shot back.

Again, I am sure he was joking, but just the same there was a glint in his blue eyes that gave me a chill. I do believe Hardy would have dropped me right there in the dormitory had I taken him up.

Hardy Brown was so tough that Buck Shaw refused to allow him to take part in the Forty-Niner scrimmage sessions and intrasquad games!

As a quarterback who might sometimes find himself across the line from Hardy, I heartily endorsed this ban. So did the rest of us. We all loved Hardy, but not enough to let him knock our heads off in practice.

Of course, Brown resented this arrangement. But there was nothing else to do. He did not know how to tackle a man properly. He couldn't lock his arms around the ball-carrier's legs in the accepted style of tackling. All he wanted to do was to throw that shoulder into somebody's face—and those were the days before we wore face masks!

Hardy wasn't too accurate. He might shoot at you five or six times, and never get you. But when he hit you, man, you were gone, right out of there.

Brown was an ideal middle linebacker in the San Francisco 5–3 defense because his duties were simple. His main job was plugging holes when a guard pulled or something like that. He made most of his tackles at point blank range in the middle of the line. When the 4–3 defense came along, he was through. He couldn't play the middle spot in the 4–3 because he had to pursue in the open field and make his tackles on the run, which was something he never had been required to do before. Actually, he was a poor tackler. He missed too often.

But I must repeat, when Hardy Brown hit someone, it hurt clear up in the last row of seats.

Brown and I had played together at Baltimore in 1950 and we were close friends with the Forty-Niners, so it was ironic that I was the one responsible for his being cut from the San Francisco squad later in his career. Well, maybe not entirely responsible but I feel I had a hand in it just the same. This was six years later, in 1956, and it was probably the only thing I've ever done out of order during my career. Sometimes I wish I hadn't done it . . . but I did, and so now I am going to confess.

In 1956, Hardy was on the threshold of being cut by Frankie Albert, who was then the head coach. Brown was not the ballplayer he once had been and financially he was in bad shape. He needed the job but he was about to lose it.

Nobody wanted to see Hardy go. He was still very popular with the ballplayers. The "old thumper" was well liked. But it looked very much like he was getting a final trial from Albert and his coaching staff. We were having a big scrimmage game on a Saturday afternoon and I felt bad. I knew this was the one that would make or break Hardy with the Forty-Niners. I decided to help him.

That morning I approached Hardy and suggested we make him look good in the scrimmage.

"How?" he asked.

"I've devised a set of signals that will tip you off where the play is going," I answered, not without a feeling of shame.

"That's not right," protested Hardy.

"I know, but it won't hurt anybody and it might make you look good in front of Albert. He's getting ready to drop you, Hardy."

Hardy was hesitant. This thing was against his nature. It was against mine too, but it was the only way to save his job.

Finally he said, "Okay, what do I do?"

"Just watch me when the offense comes out of the huddle."

Brown scratched his head. "What do I look for, Y.A.?"

"If it's going to be a pass, I'll rub my hands together."

I did not intend to throw the ball to Hardy but at least my tipoff would give him a chance to drop back and look good covering his pass zone. Pass coverage never had been one of his strong points, and the coaches would be watching him closely.

"Get it?" I asked. "If you see me rub my hands together you can start looking for a pass."

Hardy nodded.

"All right, now, if we are going to run the ball around right end, I'll come up to the line and raise my right arm. If the play is going left, I'll put my left arm up in the air. I will keep my hands together if the play goes up middle."

"Won't that be obvious?" asked Brown with a worried look.

"Maybe, but we can't worry about that now."

Everything worked to the letter early in the scrimmage. My tipoffs had Hardy looking great. He was slamming into the holes tackling ball-carriers, and he was dropping back expertly to cover on passes.

Of course, some of our halfbacks were not overjoyed to find Brown waiting for them at the line of scrimmage, but the way I looked at it, we all had a stake in keeping Hardy on the squad. If it meant a shoulder in the face now and then, well, greater love hath no man . . . etc.

Occasional glances toward the sideline indicated Albert and his coaches were very impressed by Brown's defensive play. His showing had come as a surprise. At this rate, it would be tough to cut him. He was the best linebacker on the field.

The trouble started when Albert sent Earl Morrall in to replace me at quarterback. I remember a look of panic on Hardy's face as I trotted off the field, taking my hand signals with me.

Morrall was not part of the plot to save Hardy, and Hardy knew it.

Fortunately (or unfortunately, as it developed for Brown) Frankie Albert decided to send the plays in from the sideline, as Paul Brown did at Cleveland, instead of having Morrall call his own game on the field.

So, Frankie got up there on the sideline, kneeling on one knee, with me right behind him. Albert has never known this; he probably thought I was just taking an interest in the scrimmage. Actually, I was eavesdropping on what he was saying to the guards who carried the plays into Morall. I had managed to get word to Hardy that I would do my best to flash my signals to him from the sideline and, man, was he watching me. Like a hawk!

Well, Albert would say to the guard something like, "Dive forty-nine!"

As soon as I heard this, I would hold my right arm in the air, tipping Brown that the next play would be a run to the right side.

If Albert said, "Dive twenty-eight!" I put up my left arm and Brown knew where to look for the ball-carrier.

It worked for a time and Hardy was looking great. Twice he threw the runner for big losses and two or three times he knocked down passes in the secondary. He seemed to be all over the field. Albert's amazement grew.

Then we ran into big trouble.

When I first began signaling from the sideline, the ball was on the 50-yard line and Hardy was looking at me. In other words, I was in front of him and he could glance across the line and see my wig-wagging. But all of a sudden Albert ordered the offense and defense to change sides and now Hardy had to turn and look back over his shoulder to see me. It didn't take me long to realize that the change in direction had confused Hardy. When I raised my right arm to tip off a play going right, he took a quick look at me—and ran to the left, clean away from the play. He didn't know whether right meant right, or right meant left. We hadn't had time to consider the possibility of the ball going in a different direction. It got worse and worse. Everytime they ran a play at Hardy's hole, he was chasing the other way. If the play went right, he went left. It was awful.

When the scrimmage was over, they cut him.

CHAPTER TWENTY-TWO

TO RUN OR PUNT?

THE SAN FRANCISCO quarterback situation had become a real headache for Buck Shaw by the start of the 1952 training season. He was under pressure from all sides.

Forty-Niner fans were divided into two loud factions, one insisting that Albert be retained as the No. 1 quarterback, the other that Shaw use Tittle more. The controversy raged in the newspapers and on radio and television. Thus camp opened under unfavorable conditions. Nobody seemed to know who was going to play where.

Shaw resolved the problem by putting in a rotation plan. Albert and I were to divide the quarterbacking on an equal footing. One week Frankie would start and play the first and third quarters, with me coming into the game in the second and fourth periods. The following week, that rotation was to be reversed.

"Win or lose," Buck said to us at Menlo Park, "that's the way it's going to be."

This arrangement, needless to say, was fine with me. It meant one thing: more playing time for old Y.A. and, selfish or not, that's the way I wanted it. I had come to play! I was a quarterback and my idea of football, professional or any other kind, was not riding the damned bench. But at the time, I felt that Frankie Albert was a better all-around quarterback, smarter, quicker, more cunning and, above all, a winner. This realization, however, did not prevent me from saying "Hot damn" to myself when Shaw told us of his rotation scheme. It looked like I was about to get a chance at my favorite pastime, throwing the football.

Albert still was not close to me, so I can't say whether or not he liked the half-and-half arrangement by which Buck figured to get the wolves off his back. Frankie never confided in me and I didn't ask him about such things. There remained a barrier of age and maturity between us and now the competitive angle complicated our relationship. I did hear from others, though, that he was opposed to the rotation.

I couldn't blame Albert. He probably saw the plan as a threat to his position as leader of the Forty-Niners. I know I would have under similar circumstances.

Whatever his personal feelings, however, Frankie Albert was a team man and the San Francisco Forty-Niners were his team. He never gave any sign that the situation bothered him. He was a brilliant quarterback during the early part of the season as we reeled off five straight victories, including two over the Detroit Lions, who eventually won the western division championship. In order, we defeated Detroit, 17–13; Dallas, 37–14; Detroit again, this time by 28–0 in one of the most memorable games I ever played in; Chicago, 40–16, and Dallas again, 48–21.

San Francisco was a happy football town when we returned from our road trip leading the N.F.L.'s western division with five wins and no losses.

Even the Albert-Tittle factions united in the common cause: a championship for the Bay Area—and for Tony and Vic Morabito, and Buck Shaw.

The Forty-Niners of 1952 were a sound, polished ball club. The offense, even with Albert and I trading places every fifteen minutes, could score; McElhenny was running wild. The defense, well, the defense had Hardy Brown in his prime, plus guys like Norm Standlee, then in the final year of a great career; Don Burke, both linebackers; Ed Henke and Charlie Powell at the ends and Jim Cason and Lowell Wagner in the secondary.

As I mentioned earlier, the most perfect game I ever played in—with the exception of the Giants' 33–6 win over Cleveland in 1963—was the 28–0 shutout of Detroit in the third game of the 1952 campaign. By perfect, I really mean a perfect defensive effort. I can't recall too many specifics but I remember that the Lions didn't get their initial first down until near the end of the fourth quarter. Powell, a rookie end who weighed only 215 pounds, got a starting job that day because injuries had trimmed our roster to 28 available men. During the warm-up, line coach Phil Bengston pulled Charlie aside and told him he would open at defensive end.

"You only have to remember one thing, Charlie," Bengston said, "Just drive in and rush Bobby Layne as hard and as often as you can."

"Which one is he?" asked Powell, a green kid of only nineteen.

"He'll be the guy throwing the ball," said Phil. "That's all you need to know. Go after him!"

And what a time Charlie gave Layne that day! He was draped around Bobby's neck on almost every play. Layne, one of the game's all-time great passers, didn't complete a pass until the last period. He was black and blue, and sore as hell, when Powell got through with him.

Detroit won the western championship that year with a 9–3 record, and two of those three losses were to San Francisco. In two games, they got just three points against our fine defense.

So things were looking pretty good when we met the Chicago Bears at Kezar Stadium on November 2. With a five-and-nothing record, the Forty-Niners could almost sew up the division title by beating the Bears for a second time.

But in this ball game our whole season turned on a single play.

In the fourth quarter we were leading the Bears, 17–10. We had lost some of our early-season sharpness but it seemed we still had enough to make it six in a row. With fourth down and two yards to go on the San Francisco 32, Albert dropped back to punt. Any kind of a punt by Frankie would have put the ball somewhere between the Chicago twenty or thirty yard line, where the Forty-Niner defense, which had held the Bears pretty much in check, could be expected to hold.

Albert saw daylight between a Bear tackle and the end, so instead of punting, Frankie made a run for it. It was the kind of gamble he had taken successfully many times. The hole he saw, or thought he had seen, closed abruptly. Chicago end Ed Sprinkle, who knew Frankie liked to run from punt formation smeared him short of the first down. I remember hearing a groan go up from our fans, as if they had just witnessed the wrecking of the Forty-Niners' title hopes—which indeed they had.

Chicago took the ball and drove to the tying touchdown almost immediately. Then the Bears came back with a minute left and won the game on George Blanda's 48-yard field goal. The final score: Chicago 20, San Francisco 17.

To his credit, Buck Shaw refused to criticize Albert's gamble in public.

Pressed by the writers for an explanation of Frankie's thinking on the weird play, Buck said only, "Frank has won a lot of games with this same kind of daring. He has gambled before—and won for us. That's all I have to say."

Although Shaw was noble in his defense of Albert after the heart-breaking loss to Chicago, a loss that put us on the skids for the rest of the 1952 season, I believe Buck actually was seething inside. This incident put an almost unendurable strain on our internal relations. There is little doubt in my mind that it had much bearing on Albert's decision to retire at the end of the year.

Frankie's "Folly on Fourth Down," as San Francisco publicity director Dan McGuire later called it in a book on the Forty-Niners, capped a frustrating season for Albert. It had started badly for him with the disclosure that, for the first time in his career, he was to be a part-time quarterback. It ended badly for him when we lost four of our last six games and finished third in the western division. I had a hand in our failure, of course, but looking back, I think what irked Albert the most was playing only half the time and sitting on the bench while I did my share of the quarterbacking. It was something, I feel, which had never occurred to him. He had been the club's undisputed leader for six years and he had not expected to wind up his career in this fashion. He was a man of great pride, a fierce competitor, and his pride was damaged, first by my intrusion, and second, by criticism heaped on him after our defeat by the Bears.

I think Frankie's resentment was justified. Here was a fellow who had pulled miracles out of his helmet for the Forty-Niners for years. Then one daring gamble which went wrong brought everyone down on his neck. It seemed to me that Albert was entitled to a few mistakes. Anyone is. But when he made this one, they yelled for his scalp.

I can't say just how Albert felt after the Chicago game. We still were not close. We sat together at quarterback meetings, we talked strategy, we worked shoulder to shoulder. But once we walked off that field, Frankie went his own way—and he never asked me to come along.

Frankie Albert and I were entirely different quarterbacks in every respect. He was an off-the-cuff player, an instinctive player. I was more a student of the game. I had to be. I studied football and analyzed it. I followed the accepted pattern of quarterbacking. Frankie's way was carefree and casual. Preparation was not part of Albert's make-up. He didn't seem to need it and his way worked well—for Frankie Albert.

He played by instinct alone, and to hell with the book!

Once we were leading a club by something like 34–0 and Shaw sent me in for Frankie late in the game. As I passed Albert on the way to the huddle, I asked him, "What defense are these guys in?"

"How the hell should I know?" he replied.

And I really believe he did not know, or at least that he did not care a great deal. He had gotten 34 points, so it made no difference to Albert what defense they were in.

When the defense started pressuring Frankie, he would run a draw play. He didn't particularly care what the defensive set-up was; if they put the pressure on, he called the draw. He had an instinctive feel for it. Maybe he could not explain why he ran the draw, but he sure ran them at just the right time. Frankie did not take his plays from frequency lists as we do today. Everything he needed to call a game was in his head.

If the defense was up a little tighter on the line of scrimmage, Frankie did not always know precisely whether they were in a

183

zone or a safety zone, or if a red-dog was coming, but dammit, it looked like about time to throw the ball on top of somebody. If these guys were firing across there, he might space his line wider and trap them. When they pinched in on him, he sometimes called a dive play in the huddle and then would fool everyone, especially the Forty-Niner halfback who was supposed to get the handoff, by hiding it on his hip and bootlegging around the opposite end all by himself.

No one ever challenged Frankie in the huddle. If he called the play, it was good enough for the San Francisco Forty-Niners. His timing was flawless. When he ran a trap, it was a good time to run a trap—maybe third down and seven. It might be a passing situation and, bang!, he would trap the middle man and away the guy would go.

First down was the same as fourth down to Albert. He would call a run or a pass or a pitchout anytime and any place on the field.

Albert's tactics impressed me deeply, as did his flair for the unexpected, but it was obvious he was a born individualist and I was not. So, I did not make the mistake of trying to copy him. I was not the signal-caller Frankie was and I never could be. Nor could I run a ball game the way he ran a ball game. Even today, with sixteen years behind me, I don't believe I could call a game like Frankie Albert. Passing, then as now, was my strong suite, and I have often wondered how much better a quarterback I might have become had I been as loose, as daring, as Frankie. If Albert had been able to throw better, he might have been the greatest quarterback ever. He couldn't throw long, though, and today you need that long bomb. Frankie was a southpaw, and he would get that damned ball up there wobbling and shaking and you would wonder if it would ever get where it was supposed to go.

The question has been asked of me many times: Could Frankie Albert, with his unique approach to quarterbacking, be a star today?

I say yes. He could be a great quarterback in any era. But he's the only guy who could do it his way today.

To my way of thinking a professional quarterback's greatness is based on one thing—does he win?

Maybe there have been better passers than Frankie Albert, and better ball-handlers and smarter signal-callers. These categories are open to discussion. But outside of Otto Graham, who was perhaps the greatest of them all on the record, Frankie was tops. He was a winner.

SHAW, STRADER AND ALBERT

FRANKIE ALBERT had departed by 1953 and I was the San Francisco Forty-Niners' quarterback.

Coach Buck Shaw handed me the football the day training camp opened and said, "It's all yours, Y.A."

But I was soon to learn that while Albert was gone, he was far from forgotten. No sooner had Buck told me the quarterback job was mine than a writer from the San Francisco Chronicle walked up to me on the practice field and asked, "How does it feel to be trying to fill Albert's shoes?"

I felt this was a loaded question. Frankie was a tremendous favorite in the Bay Area, as well he should have been. It was inevitable that I should be compared with Albert. But still, it was early for me to be standing in his shadow, cast all the way from Canada, where he was then playing. Naturally, I did not want to say anything that would reflect on him or impair the morale of our ball club.

Still, I did not want to give the impression that I was awed by the prospect of taking over for Frankie or that I lacked confidence.

So no matter what I said, I knew I would probably put my foot in it with the San Francisco press again. I answered the question as best I could.

"I realize it's going to be tough to replace Frankie. He was a great quarterback. But I have faith in myself and I think I can get the job done for the Forty-Niners."

The next day, The Chronicle headlined the story: "TITTLE DEFIES GHOST OF ALBERT!"

This, of course, is not what I had said, or even implied. I wasn't defying any ghosts. All I had said was that I believed I could do the job. He was Albert and he was gone; I was Tittle and I was still there. I was glad to be on my own. A quarterback must have confidence. And he must command the respect of his ballplayers or he can't hope to win with them. A pro quarterback's attitude is contagious; it infects every man on the squad. If he is the least bit unsure of himself, this uncertainty is transmitted right down the line and the ball club dies. Newspaper statements can reflect a man's attitude. So I decided to try to put my best foot forward when talking to the sportswriters.

I realized the odds that faced me as Albert's successor. The Forty-Niners had been his team for six years. He was their guy, and now I was standing there in his place telling them what to do. If there was the slightest indication on my part that I felt I could not measure up, well, I would be licked right from the start. I couldn't make them forget Frankie but I sure would prove that he wasn't the only quarterback who could win for them.

I was confident I could gain the faith of the Forty-Niner ball club. This is exactly what I told The Chronicle writer. I do not like a man who is overly modest, who won't admit his ability and accept praise. But on the other hand, I have always tried to accept praise with dignity and humility.

But alas for my hopes: the "TITTLE DEFIES GHOST OF ALBERT" headline stirred up a big fuss at camp. Some people construed it as a knock at Frankie. There was resentment. I could sense it right from the start.

I promised myself that from then on I would tell the newspapermen to find their stories elsewhere. It was the second time my remarks had been misinterpreted and blown out of proportion.

Nineteen fifty-three was my first year as a regular quarterback in the National Football League. I had been Baltimore's starting quarterback in 1948 and 1949 but there was no comparison. Football was different from what it had been in the old All-America

187

Conference. Things were more organized. The players were better. The crowds were bigger.

Although Albert and Norm Standlee and Alyn Beals and a few of the other Forty-Niner veterans had retired, the 1953 San Francisco club was not short on talent. Hugh McElhenny was in his second season and Joe Perry was still a top runner. Now we had the game's two greatest backs, McElhenny and Perry, on the same ball club. Joe Arenas was still pluggin' away. Gordy Soltau was at his peak as a receiver and as a place-kicker. Billy Wilson, who had come up in 1951, was becoming a fine pass-catcher. My old Texas sidekick, Bill Johnson, was the solid center. And to add new blood, Buck Shaw kept fourteen rookies on the roster, among them Charlie Powell.

The Forty-Niners caught fire in the opener against the Philadelphia Eagles—right after a 20-minute free-for-all between Charlie Powell and Bobby Walston, Philadelphia's star receiver. It spread all over the field. Two of the Eagles singled out McElhenny and jumped him. Hugh swung his helmet with one hand and threw punches with the other. His situation was perilous until several members of the Forty-Niner band joined the battle, using clarinets as weapons.

The fight was a draw but we won the ball game, 31–21, and seemed to find a new team spirit that carried us to a 9–3 record. This was the best performance in San Francisco history but unfortunately Detroit was 10–2 that year. We had to settle for second place in the western division.

Rarely did a game go by that McElhenny did not perform some amazing feats of broken field running.

The week after our slugfest with Philadelphia, the Los Angeles Rams had us down, 30–28, with less than three minutes left in the game. We had the ball on our own twenty and I knew the Rams would be looking for the obvious, a long desperation pass.

On first down, I glanced at McElhenny in the huddle and said, "They're expecting a bomb. Let's go with a screen right."

"Okay," Mac said, and I could tell he was just itching to get loose with the football.

With the Ram secondary playing deep, it was simple to slip a short screen pass to McElhenny in the right flat. Leo Nomellini wiped out the nearest Ram defender with a smashing block and Mac was off to the races. He twisted down the sideline, eluding tacklers every step of the way, and finally was pushed out on the nine-yard line. He had gone 71 yards! I called three running plays to kill the clock and then Soltau booted a field goal that gave us a 31–30 victory.

That Hugh McElhenny! He was really something in his prime. There never has been an open-field runner like him.

In 1953 it seemed that Hugh went all the way practically every time I handed off or threw the ball to him.

Hugh once told me he always ran scared—not only because of San Francisco opponents but also because of the memory of a boyhood incident. When he was six years old, he talked his way into a pick-up game on a vacant lot in Los Angeles. The owner of the property arrived minutes later with a shotgun. He pulled the trigger and several pellets lodged into the McElhenny backside as he fled the scene.

"When I carry the ball," Hugh liked to say, "I think of that man and his shotgun. That makes me go faster."

No quarterback could ask for two better halfbacks than McElhenny and Joe Perry. They could go inside or outside. They could catch the ball. They could block. And no pro backs ever worked harder to maintain their skills than these fellows. I've heard stories that McElhenny was "hard to handle" and that he disliked practice. But let me say this: I never once saw Hugh "dog it." He practiced like he played—all out. Even in scrimmages he wanted to score every time he got his hands on the football.

I wish every quarterback could have two guys like McElhenny and Perry working with him. They made old Y.A. look pretty good for a lot of years, and I shall always appreciate what they did for me and the team.

The Sunday after McElhenny's great run set up our win over Los Angeles, I suffered the most serious injury of my pro career up to that time.

I fractured my cheek bone in three places!

Like most of my other injuries, and there have been a number of them, the fractured cheek occurred when I was running a bootleg play against the Detroit Lions. I started from the five and made it to the end zone before the Lions spotted me. Jack Christiansen grabbed my arm as I crossed the goal-line and buggy-whipped me in a circle. At the end of the whip, my face met Jim David's knee. I could hear the bones crunching in my cheek. It was the worst pain I have ever experienced. I had scored, which didn't really matter since we lost the game, 24–21, but they operated on me and took sixteen bone chips out of my face later at a Detroit hospital. Then they put a balloon in my face and blew it up to hold the cheek in shape. I was hospitalized for a week and I was still there when Jimmy Powers, one of the Forty-Niner defensive backs, quarterbacked the club to a 35–28 victory over the Chicago Bears.

The broken cheekbone in Detroit in 1953 was the start of a long string of injuries resulting from Frankie Albert's pet maneuver, the bootleg. This play has helped me greatly, but it has also hurt a-plenty.

Against Detroit I suffered a brain concussion going into the end zone on a bootleg in 1962. The same year, my face was badly cut in the Pittsburgh game when I rolled out and made a run for it. In the opening game of 1963, I scored a touchdown against Baltimore on the bootleg but was tackled so vigorously that one of my lungs was partially collapsed. Bootlegs against Green Bay and Dallas put me on the shelf with back injuries.

After my injury in Detroit in 1953, I had a special face mask made and I got into the next game with the Lions long enough to throw one pass, which was intercepted. We lost that one, too, 14–10, but the following week we beat the Rams again, 31–27, with over 90,000 fans in the Los Angeles Coliseum. L.A. had us down by 27–24 with about five minutes left. But we moved 85 yards against the clock and won the game when I hit Soltau with a 17-yard touchdown pass. There were 12 seconds left when Gordy caught the ball and fell in the end zone.

I recall those 1953 battles with the Rams as two of the most thrilling football games I ever played in. They had everything— touchdowns, long scoring plays, excitement, last-minute drama. They drew tremendous crowds. They established professional football on the West Coast. They fulfilled one of Tony Morabito's dreams. The other, a championship for San Francisco, has yet to be achieved.

The enthusiasm generated by the 1953 Forty-Niners carried over to 1954. We won seven straight pre-season games and were regarded as the hottest ball club in the league.

We now had not only McElhenny and Perry, but also John Henry Johnson. They called us the "Million Dollar Backfield." I don't know how much old Y.A. was worth. But the others were priceless running backs, possibly the three greatest ball-carriers ever to play in the same backfield. What a trio! Johnson had come down from Canada via a trade with Pittsburgh, and he gave us the strongest offense in professional football. Perry led the N.F.L. in rushing that year for the second straight time. Johnson was right behind him, and McElhenny finished in the top ten despite missing almost half the season with a broken shoulder. When Hugh was hurt against the Chicago Bears, he had carried 64 times for 515 yards, an amazing average of over eight yards a carry.

McElhenny wasn't the only Forty-Niner on the hospital list in 1954. Injuries wiped out virtually our whole ball club. I have never seen anything like it. It's a wonder we won at all, much less seven games. And we had had such high hopes. . . .

In the opening game we whipped Washington, 41–7, and Arnold Galiffa, our No. 2 quarterback, broke his hand. That was the start of it.

I broke my left hand the following week in a 24–24 tie with Los Angeles, and Johnson was injured at the same time. Before the season was half over, we lost our two best linebackers, Hardy Brown and Don Burke. We lost almost the entire secondary—Jim Cason, Rex Berry and John Williams. The Forty-Niners were a patchwork ball team the rest of the year. Bill Jessup, an offensive end, wound up playing defensive halfback; so did John Henry. That's how critical the situation became. Buck Shaw was forced to use the league's most feared ball-carrier on defense because he had no one else. Buck juggled guys back and forth every week and sometimes it was remarkable that he managed to field offensive and defensive teams on the same afternoon.

The Forty-Niners could score. I completed 170 passes and Perry and Johnson ran wild. We finished with 313 points. But we couldn't stop anybody. The Rams rolled up 42 points on us halfway through the schedule and next week Detroit put it to us, 48–7.

This latter score was the worst defeat ever inflicted on a Buck Shaw team. I think it marked the beginning of the end for him as a coach in San Francisco.

Tony Morabito was an understanding man. He always had been fair with his players and his coaches. But Tony wanted a championship in the worst way and he thought he had the club to win it for him in 1954. Even when the team was wiped out by injuries, Morabito continued to believe that Shaw would work enough miracles to bring the championship to San Francisco. Buck was a sound coach, a top football man. But he was not a miracle worker. He got seven wins out of the Forty-Niners in twelve games. Few could have done as well considering the bad luck that beset us from the very beginning.

I am certain Morabito weighed these factors, and that he was aware of the difficulties encountered by Shaw during the 1954 season. I am just as certain, though, that the disappointment of failing to win the championship influenced Morabito's reasoning more than any other consideration.

After the final game with Baltimore, Buck Shaw was notified that his contract as head coach would not be renewed. His dismissal kicked up quite a storm.

The pro-Shaw faction argued that he had done a remarkable job with an injured ball team and that the least Morabito could have done was to give him another shot in 1955. The anti-Shaw group insisted just as vigorously that Buck rightly was removed because, after nine years, he had failed to win a championship. His casual approach to coaching was also criticized.

"He's too easy with the players," was a familiar charge. "He won't discipline anyone for anything short of murder."

Personally, I was sorry to see Buck Shaw leave. To my mind he was a great coach and I had enjoyed playing for him. When you don't win, change is inevitable. Buck's easy-going methods had not produced a championship for San Francisco. Paul Brown's rigid, severe tactics had brought Cleveland several world titles. Perhaps the time had arrived to try it Brown's way.

Morabito's reasons for firing Shaw were known only to himself. But I have heard since that once, when the Forty-Niners were losing money, Tony had asked Buck to take a percentage of the club in lieu of part of his salary. Shaw refused, and the story was that Morabito never really forgave him.

The 1955 season was a nightmare; I will never forget it. The Forty-Niners lost eight games and finished next to last. Buck Shaw's successor, Red Strader, died at the end of the year after being fired by Morabito. I had 28 passes intercepted, the second worst showing by a quarterback in N.F.L. history.

Strader, who had coached briefly in the All-America Conference, was a stern, fast-talking man, quite the opposite of Shaw. The difference carried over into their coaching methods. Red believed in organizing down to the last detail. He was determined that under his regime the Forty-Niners would no longer be known as the "country club of the National Football League"—a tag hung on us by a rival owner.

Red's get-tough attitude was reflected in the selection of his assistants. One of them was Howard (Red) Hickey, a strict disciplinarian who had been with the Rams for fourteen years.

The only assistant who didn't fit the new picture was Frankie Albert, who had returned from Canada to rejoin the San Francisco operation. Frankie was the same as ever, easy-going, relaxed, smiling.

Making the adjustment from Buck Shaw's training camp at Menlo Park to Red Strader's base at St. Mary's College was not easy for the Forty-Niner veterans—myself included. Most of us wondered where we would fit in Strader's plans since he had publicly announced his intention of "taking any measures that will make the Forty-Niners a winning football team."

Strader came to St. Mary's College with the reputation of being an organizer. And, man, did he organize!

You came onto the practice field and you jogged. You left the field and you jogged. You never walked in Red Strader's camp because the organizational plan did not include walking. You wore your helmet at practice. You went by the clock at St. Mary's College that year. Red had everything laid out step by step, minute by minute. And he saw that things were done that way. He patrolled the halls of the dormitory every night from 10:30 to 11 o'clock, personally making sure everyone was in his room. If Red said breakfast was at 7:30 A.M., boy, you had better be there at 7:30 and not 7:45.

The new approach was not an immediate hit with those of us who had grown used to the Shaw policy. After a few weeks at St. Mary's, there was an undercurrent of grumbling, most of it by the veterans. When we lost a couple of pre-season games, it got worse. You know, a bunch of guys start talking, blaming people, saying things about the coaches and the management. This is true of most ball clubs but it was a serious matter with the Forty-Niners that year.

In the end, Red Strader was made the scapegoat for the Forty-Niners' failures.

As much as I hate to admit it, I was part of the general discontent that eventually led to Strader's dismissal. The rest of the squad was involved too. Here's how it happened: we came home from a losing road trip and got beat by Baltimore. After the game, Tony Morabito dropped into the San Francisco dressing room to cheer up the team. "I'm only going to stay a few minutes," he said when he walked in. But Tony was there for over two hours. Someone mentioned that a team couldn't win under Strader's strict regimentation and Morabito's reaction was one of surprise. He said he had been unaware that such deep resentment existed.

"Well, it does," said one of the veterans. "We are being led around by the hand like a bunch of schoolchildren."

I believe Morabito's surprise was genuine. The Forty-Niner management traditionally left the coaches on their own after training camp opened. It was not inconceivable that Tony knew nothing about the dissension until the day he walked into the dressing room after the Baltimore game.

Anyway, when the 1955 campaign was over and we had lost our eighth ball game, Strader met with the owners for a review of the disastrous season. He was asked if the 4–8 record was a true indication of Forty-Niner personnel.

194

"Absolutely," he replied. "In fact, I'd say we were lucky to win four games this year."

This answer was a stinging indictment of Morabito's draft program, and it was also Red Strader's Waterloo.

I have always regretted taking part in that clubhouse meeting with Morabito. But I could hardly have avoided it. I was not always in agreement with Strader's policies, but I admired him as a person and respected him as a football coach. Red was always for the ballplayers even though he was hard on them. He was the one who got us more meal money on the road. He was the one who got us better beds in training camp. Whenever there was a battle to be fought for the players, Strader fought it. Red was for the players although there were times when this was extremely difficult for us to believe.

Football under Buck Shaw had been fun. It was not fun under Red Strader. It was a business, a regimented business where you punched in every morning and kept your nose to the grindstone until Red blew the final whistle. There was no laughing, no skylarking, no clowning. Buck used to toss a ball out onto the field and say, "Let's run a few plays, fellows." But Strader had everything organized. We had to worry about technique, steps, position, the reason for this, the strategy for that. The players often influenced Buck Shaw; Strader ruled his ball club with an iron hand. He was fair, but tough as nails.

Red coached by example. He drove himself as mercilessly as he drove the players. He never asked us to do anything he wouldn't do himself. When Red had a day off, he didn't go home like the rest of us; he stayed in camp and worked.

Strader's dedicated approach might have been fine with a winning team. But with a loser, which the Forty-Niners were in 1955, it backfired. Practice became drudgery. The game lost its interest, its fun. The excitement was missing. And each defeat made it worse.

By the end of the season, Red was going in one direction and the squad in another.

It was one of those situations that always recur in football. When something is wrong, someone has to go. Sometimes it's the coach, sometimes the quarterback—but hardly ever the owner.

I was distressed to hear of Strader's death shortly after his dismissal. He had given it a good try, but his methods were incompatible with the Forty-Niners' habits. With another team, Red might have won a championship. I guess we never did make the transition from Shaw to Strader.

Nor was the transition to our next coach, Frankie Albert, any easier!

Although Frankie's coaching experience was limited to a couple of Spring practices at Stanford and the Naval Academy, plus his one year apprenticeship under Strader I was happy to hear of his appointment by Tony Morabito in 1956. Like the other veterans who remembered Albert as a happy-go-lucky quarterback, I thought this would be a return to the happy times of Buck Shaw.

But Albert the coach was a different man than Albert the quarterback.

We found this out the first day at training camp in 1956. So did the sports reporters, one of whom wrote:

"When Albert got the Forty-Niner job, even his friends feared his dislike of practice routine might be his undoing. Small details were not his style. Only grand strategy appealed to him. But the sun hadn't yet sunk behind the Moraga hills after the first practice when those who had him pegged as a 'no detail' man realized they were wrong. The place reeked with organization. Frankie had mapped specific, sensible work schedules months ago, and they were followed almost to the split second. Things went off like clockwork."

Albert's first move on assuming leadership of the Forty-Niners had been to retain Strader's entire coaching staff. I have always suspected that Frankie's rigid approach to coaching, which was in such sharp contrast to his style as a player, was inspired by Red Hickey. Under Strader, Hickey had been end coach. But Albert made him backfield coach and gave him greater latitude. Hickey thrived on authority. Albert was aware of this, and he delegated more and more responsibility to Red as the season wore on. Frankie was not an experienced coach and, to his credit, he realized it. He seemed grateful to have a veteran coach like Hickey to lean on.

Albert, who had been a bold gambler and a reckless quarterback was far more conservative as head coach of the Forty-Niners.

Many times when we had a short yardage situation at midfield, Frankie frantically signaled from the sideline for a punt. As a player, he would have run for the yard and damn the percentages.

Frankie's new-found conservatism did not bother me. His sudden and unexplainable decision to call the game from the sidelines did.

Paul Brown had won five straight divisional championships for Cleveland by sending in the plays to Otto Graham. But Frankie Albert was not Brown. I was not Graham. And the Forty-Niners definitely were not the Cleveland Browns. Graham and the Browns had grown up under the messenger-boy signal system and were oriented to it. They knew no other way to win games and they did not object to Brown's sideline quarterbacking as long as it proved successful.

But this was not my idea of how to play quarterback.

Here I am, a nine-year veteran, and all of a sudden I am standing out there in the huddle like a damned statue in the park. Albert is sending in the plays with our two ends, Clyde Connor and Gordy Soltau.

They run into the huddle and they say to me, "Frankie says run a thirty-seven slant."

So I repeat the play like a parrot, "Thirty-seven slant."

And that's all the quarterbacking I did.

To my way of thinking, a pro quarterback can't call a winning game if he does no more than parrot someone else's instructions. Graham did it, to be sure, because he was in a class by himself, and in a very special situation. But no one else has ever won a championship with the game being called from the sideline. I have to have the "feel" of a ball game to be effective. I have to match my brain against the defense. I have got to try to outsmart and outthink them. I want to set them up and then finish them off my own way.

"Establish" is one of the favorite words used by Allie Sherman, my present coach with the Giants, but establish is what a quarterback must do. And he must do it on his own. He has got to step in there and run that team and make it go. He must lead his ball club through his own strength, knowledge, skill and imagination.

With Albert sending in the plays—or maybe it was Red Hickey —I was sort of detached from the action. My brain was dulled and I lost my interest in the strategy of the game. All that was required of me was to listen to Conner or Soltau and then execute. I felt like a trained monkey.

In the early part of Albert's reign I was not a quarterback. I was not a leader. I was a puppet and my strings were pulled from the bench.

This was one of the most trying periods of my professional career. I could not adjust to it.

I have often wondered what Albert's reaction would have been if Buck Shaw called his plays for him when he was quarterbacking the San Francisco team. He probably would have quit.

I never felt exactly like quitting but it was mighty frustrating. I was not a good quarterback because I did not have control of my ball team. The Forty-Niners were not a good team, either, and we lost six of our first seven games in 1956.

Earl Morrall, a rookie from Michigan State, replaced me after the fifth game but by that time I did not really care. I was disappointed in Albert's insistence on sticking with the messenger system. I did my best, but for the first time in my long football career, my heart wasn't in the game. Morall split games with me but it didn't matter much. Let him parrot Albert's sideline strategy; I'd had my full share of it.

I don't recall exactly how it happened but my resentment finally broke out into the open. I said something about not liking the plays Albert was sending in. I shouldn't have opened my mouth, of course, because he was still the head coach and I was paid to listen to him. But my frustration was growing with each defeat and I guess I couldn't keep myself under full control.

Albert told me to see him in his office at Kezar Stadium the next day. When I arrived, Tony Morabito was there. For the first time I saw a different side of Frankie Albert, a tough, hard-bitten side. The smile was gone and so was the easy manner. His voice was cold and firm.

"Y.A.," he said, "I know you don't like me calling the plays. You said so the other day, and everybody heard you. But I'm the coach, damn it, and I'll call the plays and you'll do what I tell you. If you don't want to go along, well, maybe we'll make some changes."

I was stunned. I never realized Frankie's attitude could be so harsh. And I didn't think I had this much coming.

"Okay," I said, "but I still don't like it."

Tony Morabito never said a word. But it was obvious that he was the authority behind Albert's firm stand. He was present to let me know that he backed his coach to the hilt. Even in my frame of mind, I had to admire old Tony for this. He was a stand-up guy.

I sat out the next two ball games. Morrall did the quarterbacking and Albert did the signal-calling. We got whipped by Detroit, 17–13, and by Los Angeles, 30–6, and we were in last place.

The Tuesday following our loss to the Rams, Albert conceded that maybe he had been wrong about trying to call the game from the bench. He pulled me aside in the locker room and said, "It's all yours from now on, Y.A."

This must have been a tough thing for Frankie to do, I am sure. But six losses in seven games are enough to make any coach make changes. It was either change or have our season go all the way down the drain. Albert was stubborn but he was also smart enough to see that his plan wasn't working.

Now, I am inclined to think Frankie overlooked one vital fact when he decided to send in plays. He had been a great quarterback but his greatness was based on his ability to improvise, on his daring, on his knack of uniting his ball team with one electrifying pass or run. These personal attributes made him a winner on the field. But from the bench, Albert couldn't lift the team as he had done from the huddle.

With control back in my hands, we defeated Green Bay, 17–16, played a tie with Philadelphia and then ran out the season with successive wins over Baltimore, Green Bay and Baltimore again.

I do not for one minute want to create the impression that I alone was responsible for this sudden about-face at the end of the 1956 campaign. It remains, however, that the Forty-Niners responded better to a play called in the huddle than to one carried in from the bench. Everyone got the "feel" of the game better. We were loose and relaxed, and we played winning football.

As for Soltau and Conner, they told me later they were damned glad to be in the ball game for more than one play at a time. Albert had nearly run their legs off sending in plays.

So, the season ended and we finished third with a 5–6–1 record behind Chicago and Detroit. Albert gained in wisdom and in years, and we all got ready for the big title push in 1957.

CHAPTER TWENTY-FOUR

ALLEY-OOP

THE 1957 season was the year of the Alley-oop pass—and of San Francisco's defeat by Detroit in a playoff for the National Football League's western division title.

It also was the year Tony Morabito died.

Our owner had suffered a heart attack several years before and had been advised by his doctors to stay away from the pressure of pro football. But the game was Tony's life and a championship for the Forty-Niners was his dream. He disregarded orders and continued to run the San Francisco franchise. He worked around the clock. He made the road trips. He laughed with every win and cried a little with every loss.

Death finally overtook Tony during the first half of our game with the Chicago Bears at Kezar Stadium in October. In a moment of excitement, he slumped over in his box and was dead before he could be rushed to a hospital. We were trailing the Bears, 17–7, in the third period when Dr. Bill O'Grady came down on the field and told us the sad news.

We were all shocked. He was our friend as well as our boss. Through a series of coaching changes and player shake-ups, Tony had remained the one constant part of the Forty-Niners—solid, dependable, trustworthy. There wasn't a man on the field that awful day who didn't owe him something. Big Leo Nomellini cried unashamedly. So did Joe Perry. I fought back the tears and a lump rose in my throat.

After the initial shock wore off, we took our grief out on the Bears. Nomellini, tears streaming down his face, rushed Bear quarterback Ed Brown savagely, forcing him to throw hurriedly. The ball was picked off by Bill Kerchman, our big tackle, and he went 54 yards for a touchdown. Our defense kept Brown under pressure in the last quarter and Dick Moegle intercepted another Chicago pass. He twisted all the way to the Bears' 19-yard line. Joe Perry banged to the 11, and then I threw to Billy Wilson for the winning touchdown. There were twelve minutes left and Chicago had the ball for 25 plays, but the Forty-Niner defense swarmed all over Brown and Willie Galimore, and the game ended 21–17 in our favor when Moegle intercepted another pass to clinch it.

We never could give Tony his hoped-for championship. But he had a winner that bleak day in Kezar Stadium.

The Forty-Niners of 1957 were really something. We won eight games and lost four to tie Detroit for the western division championship. Every game was a photo finish, a cliff-hanger. In six of our eight victories, the final margin was a touchdown or less. We edged Los Angeles by 23–20, Chicago, 21–17, the Bears again by the same score the day Tony died; Detroit by 35–31, Baltimore by 17–13, and Green Bay, 27–20.

Most of our victories were achieved on fourth-period comebacks. We lost the same way in the western playoff when Detroit came from being down 27–7 and whipped us, 31–27.

Aside from Morabito's death and losing the divisional title, that season was the most rewarding one of my career. I completed sixty-three percent of my passes, the best I have ever done, and I was named N.F.L. Player of the Year. Only the 1963 campaign with the Giants, when I threw a record 36 touchdown passes, rivals 1957 for excitement, drama and good fun. It was the kind of year that sticks in a man's memory. The Forty-Niners had no license to even be in the title picture. We appeared to be just a so-so club. But we pulled out wins one after the other and suddenly found ourselves with a shot at the championship.

Looking back, I guess San Francisco wouldn't have come close except for R.C. Owens and the Alley-oop pass. Owens, a big kid out of College of Idaho, must have won three or four of those comeback games practically by himself.

The Alley-oop pass was born by accident one day when we were practicing for our second game of the season, against Los Angeles. We had been upset by the Chicago Cardinals, 20–10, in the opener and morale was low when we assembled at Redwood City to begin work for the Rams. The general feeling seemed to be, "How can we hope to take the Rams if we couldn't even handle the Cardinals, one of the weaker teams?"

The last part of the afternoon was devoted to a dummy pass scrimmage. But things did not go well. Our ends were dropping the ball all over the place. The defensive linemen were rushing through before I could pick out my receivers. Nobody was doing his job; it was a sloppy effort. Finding myself trapped on one particular play—and disgusted—I flung the ball high in the air, practically straight up, not even taking the trouble to aim it at anyone. Well, it went up and up and seemed to hang there, and then it floated down near Owens who was surrounded by three defensive backs. Suddenly, R.C., who had been a great basketball rebounder in college, leaped into the air and grabbed the ball as the defensive guys plain stood there.

No one was more surprised than me to see the pass caught.

Someone on the sideline, maybe it was Red Hickey, shouted, "Hey, that's our Alley-oop play!"

The name caught on, and so did the maneuver. For the rest of the week Owens and I worked on the Alley-oop pass after regular practice had ended.

There was nothing very fancy about the Alley-oop. The idea was for me to throw the ball as high and as far as I could. R.C. would amble down the field, wait for the ball to get about 14 feet from the ground, and then outjump everybody for it. And, boy, I want to tell you—he could jump. I never saw a fellow who could get as far off the ground in one leap. He was usually head and shoulders above the defensive backs at the top of his jump.

Nobody took the Alley-oop very seriously that first week. Albert and Red Hickey may have thought of it more as a tonic for the team's morale, because everyone was having so much fun watching it. And Owens and I had a lot of fun with it.

The newspapers, of course, played it up pretty big and by the time we kicked off to the Rams at Kezar that Sunday, everyone was looking for the Alley-oop. Everyone except the Rams, who obviously felt it was just a gimmick.

Maybe it was too. But I threw two Alley-oop passes to Owens that day and we beat Los Angeles, 23–20.

The first came near the end of the first half. The Forty-Niners held a 9–7 edge but we wanted more before we left the field. With the ball on the Rams' 46 and fifty seconds on the clock, I dropped back and aimed the ball at the corner of the end zone, throwing it as high as I could. Owens ran down there, with Don Burroughs covering him, and they both went up for the ball. R.C. went a little higher, though, and took the ball right out of Burroughs' hands for the touchdown.

The San Francisco fans picked it up and started chanting, "Alley-oop, alley-oop, alley-oop."

"Nice going, R.C.," I said as we trotted off the field.

"Just keep putting 'em up there, Y.A.," he grinned "I'll go up and get 'em for you."

He did too. The Rams came back in the second half and went ahead of us, 20–16. There was less than three minutes left when we got the ball for our last scoring shot. McElhenny and J. D. Smith took it down to the Los Angeles 11-yard line on some fine running.

On second down, I stepped into the huddle and said, "We'll go for the Alley-oop!"

That was the first time I ever actually called the play by name in a huddle. But everyone knew what to do, especially Owens.

R.C. jogged into the end zone and stood next to the Ram defensive halfback Jesse Castete. I dropped back, waited for a count or two, and then heaved the ball almost straight up in the air. I must have looked funny from the stands. Both teams were just standing there waiting for the damned thing to come down. Nobody was moving. I remember looking at Owens and laughing to myself. He didn't even appear concerned. But at just the right instant, R.C. uncoiled and went up that invisible ladder of his. Castete jumped with him but not high enough. R.C. came down with the football hugged to his chest and we had ourselves a 23–20 victory.

The Alley-oop was no longer considered a gimmick. It was now a legitimate weapon. The only defense against it was a defensive back who could out-leap R.C. Owens, and there was no such animal in the National Football League.

Owens was a great all-around receiver. He could catch the ball high, low or in between. He had wonderful speed for a six-three 200-pounder and big hands that could squeeze the football like an orange.

The week after we defeated Los Angeles with our two Alley-oop specials, Owens pulled another game out of the fire with an unbelievable catch against the Chicago Bears.

Chicago had gone in front by 17–14 with four minutes left in the game. The Bears had possession of the ball and were doing a good job of killing the clock. But Ed Henke and Charlie Powell checked them with some fine defensive play, and Ed Brown had to punt. Joe Arenas took the kick and fought his way out of bounds on the San Francisco 43-yard line, stopping the clock.

I went to our best percentage play, a screen to McElhenny, and it gained 26. Next, I threw to Clyde Conner for twelve yards. Then a pass to Billy Wilson picked up another twelve and we were on the Chicago seven.

As the ball was snapped, the Bear linebacker knocked Owens down on the line of scrimmage. He crawled into the end zone on his hands and knees and was in that position when I shot the ball, low and hard, toward the corner of the end zone. Somehow, R.C. managed to lunge and grab the ball with those big hands of his. That made it Forty-Niners 21, Bears 17 as the game ended.

"I call that one my 'prayer pass,'" R.C. said in the dressing room.

Against the Green Bay Packers a week later, I had an official say to me, "Hey, Y.A., when are you going to throw one of those big Alley-oops? I never have seen the thing."

"How about the next play?" I asked.

"Great, Y.A."

So, I told Owens to get on his horse and I threw that thing way up in the air. R.C. ran down the field and camped under the ball. Up he went. He batted it out of reach of the two Packers who were covering him, caught it on the rebound and fell over the goal-line for a touchdown.

The official walked over to me and said, "Thanks, Tittle. But don't try it again. The next time you'll be bringing down rain, and we've got a nice dry field here."

When I threw the Alley-oop to Owens we had been ahead by only three points, 17–14. His touchdown catch made the final score 24–14.

Nearly all of Owens' catches in 1957 were big ones. But none was as important—or as spectacular—as the one he made against the Detroit Lions. It was the greatest catch I have ever seen in football.

Detroit had gone ahead of us by 31–28 with a minute and twenty seconds to play, and the fans already had started filing out of Kezar Stadium. The Forty-Niners had received more than their share of miracles. But this was expecting too much.

There was only a minute remaining when Arenas ran the Lions' kickoff out to our 28-yard line. Our only hope, of course, was to throw short passes and get the ball out of bounds and stop the clock as often as possible. We knew it, and so did the Lions. I hit Gene Babb for one yard. Billy Wilson caught one for twelve yards and squirmed out of bounds. I lobbed a screen pass to McElhenny for ten yards and he got to the sideline. We were moving, but so was the second hand of the clock.

I called McElhenny on another screen and this time he picked up eight yards and got out of bounds. Then Hugh ran the ball and bulled his way out on the Detroit 41 to stop the clock with nineteen seconds left.

The fans stopped moving toward the exits. They were standing in the aisles.

We had only one play left: the Alley-oop. We knew it and so did Detroit. And it would be the last play of the game.

The Lions used a four-man rush, dropping everyone else into the secondary. But still they broke through my blockers, and I ran for my life back to the fifty and toward the sideline. Those big linemen were breathing down my neck every step of the way. For a second, I didn't think I would ever get the ball away. Owens was running down the right sideline, covered by the Lions' great defensive back, Jim David. They were shoulder to shoulder. Finally, I could wait no longer. I let fly. I threw the ball higher and farther than I ever had before—or since. As the ball climbed up there, I got knocked flat. I watched the rest of the play on the seat of my pants.

Owens had gotten down to the one-yard line. He was just standing there. Jim David was standing next to him. Jack Christiansen, who had come over to help David, was standing there. Carl Karilivacz was there. Everybody was there. They had old R.C. surrounded, outnumbered and practically buried.

But R.C. went up in the air with that great spring of his. The Lions jumped too, all over him, hacking away. But Owens made another of his tremendous kangaroo leaps and caught the ball. He fell into the end zone among those frustrated, teeth-gnarling Lions. It was a helluva shot; Boy, it was something!

Although the Alley-oop pass often looked like an accident, which it was originally, the play was carefully planned thereafter as a regular part of our pass offence.

It was really something when I called for the Alley-oop in the huddle.

In San Francisco we designated our left end as "port." The flanker back was "rip." I don't know why, but that's what they were called. The tight end was Y if he was on the right side, and X if he was on the left side. Our actual pass plays were given number designations like 51 and 61 and 77.

So when I called the Alley-oop play in the Forty-Niner huddle, it might have sounded like this:

"Fifty-one . . . Y right . . . rip . . . Alley-oop!"

That's the way we called it. R.C. Owens would be rip. He would go jogging down the sideline and Billy Wilson would square out on a sideline pattern. I always tried to run around back there a little on the Alley-oop because, even though I was no great shakes as a runner and everybody in the league knew it, this put some pressure on the defense. At least I scrambled them a bit and when the ball went way up in the air, Owens had a chance to position himself like a basketball rebound man and jump for it.

The Alley-oop got us off to a fast start in the western division playoff with Detroit. I tossed one into the clouds from the Lions' 34-yard line in the first period and Owens outjumped David and Christiansen to grab it for a touchdown. R.C.'s acrobatic catch upset the Lions and before they could settle down I had thrown a 47-yard touchdown pass to McElhenny and another to Gordy Soltau for a 21–0 lead. Soltau added a field goal in the second period and we walked off the field with a 24–7 advantage.

It looked like we couldn't miss making the N.F.L. championship game.

But professional football is a game of changing momentum. Early in the third period, McElhenny ran all the way to the Detroit nine. But they stopped us cold—even the Alley-oop, and we settled for another field goal by Soltau.

This great defensive stand seemed to instill the Lions with new hope.

They pushed us all over the field in the second half. Tobin Rote, their quarterback, had a hot hand. We lost our poise and our drive and they forced us into errors of commission and omission. In the end Detroit had 31 points and San Francisco had 27.

This game taught me a valuable lesson: no lead is ever really big enough. You can't let up in this game. When the other guy is down, you have to stomp on him and keep piling it on. There is no such thing as taking it easy because you have two or three touchdowns on the other ball club. That's asking for trouble.

"Bomb the hell out of them no matter what the score is." That's my philosophy.

In 1963 at Yankee Stadium, the Giants defeated San Francisco by 48–14, and after the game Jack Christiansen, the Forty-Niner coach, criticized Allie Sherman for leaving me in the game so long. He accused Sherman of "rolling up the score."

Christiansen should have known better. He was in the Detroit lineup that day in 1957 when the Lions wiped out our three-touchdown lead in less than a half to beat us for the division title.

The way I see it, the scales balance out over the long run. Sometimes you are going to wallop the other side, and sometimes you are going to get it yourself, maybe worse. I never asked anyone to let up on me in football, and I have no respect for anyone who expects me to hold the score down on them. I'll beat you as bad as I can whenever I get the chance. I'll throw for a touchdown on the first play of the game, and I'll throw for six points on the last play, too.

Winning is fine. Winning big is better and certainly a lot less worrisome.

I have been on the losing end of a lot of lopsided scores in my day, and one game in particular stands out in my memory. In 1958, the year after the Alley-oop pass, the Los Angeles Rams crushed San Francisco, 56–7, a galling defeat that probably started Frankie Albert on his way out as coach.

We were 3–3 going into the Coliseum that day and Albert still held out hope for another shot at the western division championship. But the Rams really put it to us—and before 95,000 fans. They scored early and often, and they made their last touchdown with one second left. If the clock hadn't run out, they would have continued piling up the score.

The following week, the story was almost the same. The Forty-Niners were beaten and demoralized even before Detroit trimmed us, 35–21.

It was after the Detroit game that Albert, showing the strain of coaching for the first time in three years and no longer the chipper, boyish looking ex-quarterback, went to Vic Morabito, Tony's brother, and told him he intended to resign.

"I just can't take it anymore," Frankie said. "I don't mind what they say about me, but my family has taken a lot of abuse lately. It's not worth it, Vic."

Morabito tried to calm Frankie.

"Think it over carefully, Frank. There still are four games to go."

"I have thought it over," replied Albert. "There's no other way. I'm through as soon as the season ends."

Albert had been under pressure right from the start of the 1958 campaign. I had played a poor pre-season schedule. Frankie benched me and made John Brodie the No. 1 quarterback. This caused quite a storm of protest in San Francisco. Just as they had in the Tittle-Albert controversy of 1952, the newspapers took sides. One article stated, "Tittle may not have been effective in the exhibition games, but he's had slumps before and always managed to snap out of them when the chips were down." The opposition countered with, "Tittle hasn't won it for the Forty-Niners. Now Brodie deserves a chance."

Looking back, it was an ironic situation for Albert to find himself in. In 1951, Buck Shaw had been pressured to bench Albert and make room for me. Now, six years later, the scene was being repeated, only this time Frankie had to choose between me and Brodie.

Frankie was openly criticized in some quarters for going with Brodie. I have always felt, however, that the decision to bench me and let John run the show was inspired by Red Hickey and not Albert. Frankie was the head coach. But Hickey called many of the shots. He exerted a great influence on Albert.

Hickey was a real football man, however, and a hard worker. I seldom saw eye to eye with him but I never questioned his dedication or sincerity.

Red never cared whether his players liked him or not.

"All I ask," he said the day he took over as Albert's successor in 1959, "is that my players give me one hundred percent on the field."

When I heard that Red had been named head coach, I felt perhaps I had outlived my usefulness in San Francisco. Hickey was not exactly my greatest fan, and I sensed that Brodie would soon be moved into quarterback, a move which had started the year before under Albert.

I recalled that in 1958, the season after I was named N.F.L. Player of the Year, Brodie had been the starting quarterback in our very first game. I never did understand this. At least I deserved a chance to hold my job until he proved he could take it from me. But Hickey, through Albert, did not operate this way. No one was indispensable to Red, as he proved to me despite my honors of the previous season.

Oddly enough, Red went with me through the first seven games of 1959. We won six of those seven games and Hickey, whether he wanted me at quarterback or not, was smart enough not to break up a winning combination. And I'm sure it was all very impersonal.

With the season half gone, the Forty-Niners had a 6–1 record and led the western division by a game. Twice before, in 1952 and 1957, however, we had led by the same margin and then faded in the stretch. Would the 1959 team collapse?

"This team won't panic," snapped Hickey when an interviewer put this question to him.

I don't believe Red was complimenting us or was merely confident of a Hickey-built team.

Despite the success of the Forty-Niners in the early part of 1959, I was not having a great season by any means. I completed less than 46 percent of my passes, and I was bothered by occasional dizzy spells. Doctors told me this was caused by Meniere's disease, a rare disturbance of the middle ear which affects one's balance. This was the damndest thing. All of a sudden, bang!, I wake up one morning and I am screwy. I could hardly get out of bed and when I did, I couldn't stand up.

Luckily, the dizzy spells usually occurred in the middle of the week and I was okay again by Sunday. But my passing still was poor. I couldn't help wondering if the inner ear business wasn't affecting my accuracy. Something was wrong. I was missing guys in the open, over-throwing them, under-throwing them.

Red Hickey must have wondered too, because he had Dr. Bill O'Grady put me through extensive tests to discover if my trouble really was Meniere's disease. The results of the tests were inconclusive and I was given a clean bill of health.

The dizzy spells persisted, however, and my passing got worse.

The turning point for the 1959 San Francisco team came on November 15 in Wrigley Field, Chicago, where we lost to the Bears, 14–3, and Hickey made his move from Tittle to Brodie.

Chicago scored first after taking the opening kickoff. On our first series, McElhenny ran into the clear for a pass, beating the Bear halfback by three yards, and I threw the ball twenty feet over his head. Wilson got free on the next play, and this time I threw the ball right to a Chicago defensive man for an interception.

I walked back to the bench shaking my head. In all my years, I had never missed two receivers the way I had just missed McElhenny and Wilson. It was puzzling. Maybe this Meniere's ailment was responsible for my bad throwing. I felt fine physically, but something was haywire.

Red Hickey was not the Laughing Boy type, but as I reached the sidelines, he now wore a disgusted look. He was not trying to hide his displeasure with me. That much was certain.

When the Bears punted to us a few minutes later I started back onto the field. I was pulled up short by Hickey's voice.

"Stay where you are, Y.A., Brodie is going in."

So there I sat while Brodie ran the ball club. Red sent me back in with only five minutes to play, but after several completions, I had another pass intercepted by Bill George, the Chicago middle linebacker. Out I came again.

I later heard that Hickey said he benched me because of my health. If this is so, the only thing I can say is that it was a helluva way to talk to a sick man. Red didn't seem particularly interested in my health when he sat me down that day.

Against Baltimore the following Sunday, we got bombed, 48–14, and I really did have a health problem. The Colts hit me from three sides on a pass play and down I went. My inner ear was fine, but the ligaments in my right knee were severely damaged. They carried me off on a stretcher and the doctors told me I was through for the season.

Now the way was cleared to use Brodie.

CHAPTER TWENTY-FIVE

"TEN, NINE, EIGHT"

THE SKY was dark above Yankee Stadium. But the scoreboard lights shone brightly against the December afternoon. From the Giants' bench across the field, I could see the count: Cleveland 7, New York 7.

I glanced from the score to the big clock. There were two minutes left.

Two minutes! The Giants were just 120 seconds away from winning the N.F.L. eastern division championship. We had gone into this final game of 1961 needing only a win or a tie against Cleveland to clinch the title. All we had to do was hang on for a while longer and the championship was ours. I had wanted to win it big, going away, but at that moment I was happy to have seven points in the bank. So were the rest of the Giants. Winning the championship was the important thing. How we won it would be forgotten the next day.

But it was not over yet. The Browns, with Bobby Mitchell at flanker, were a threat no matter how much time was left. Mitchell, one of the fastest men in pro football, could bust a game wide open in one shot. He had done it plenty of times before.

I was sitting on the bench next to Charlie Conerly. We had failed to make a first down on our last series and Allie Sherman had sent the punting team into the game. The ball was on the Giant 35 as Don Chandler dropped back to kick. This would be the big one. A long punt would push Cleveland back and make it tough for the Browns to go the distance in the last minute. If Chandler got off a poor kick . . . well, none of us even wanted to think about that possibility.

"Damn, I hope he puts this one out of here," I said to Conerly.

"If anyone can, it's Chandler," said Conerly. "He's the best pressure kicker in the league."

Just then, Chandler swung his leg. His foot exploded against the ball. It sounded like a cannon shot. The ball spiraled up and up, and for a moment it seemed to disappear against the black sky.

Mitchell was back there waiting for the ball on the 30. If Bobby ever got his hands on it, we were in for trouble. But he didn't. The kick sailed far over his head. He back-pedalled like crazy but it was no use. Chandler had gunned this one too far for anyone to catch. The ball flew over 70 yards and before Mitchell could pick it up on the bounce, Bob Simms, the Giants' fine rookie linebacker, flashed in front of him and downed it on the Cleveland seven.

Chandler's great punt had put the Browns in a hole, or maybe it was more like a grave. They couldn't dig their way out either. Mitchell was stopped by Sam Huff on a couple of end runs and then a long pass from Milt Plum to Mitchell fell short. Sam Baker punted and we took over. Sherman sent Conerly in to kill the clock and I just sat there trying to make the time go faster. There were fifteen seconds left when Charlie ran the ball into the line on a quarterback "keeper."

At that instant, I experienced one of the greatest thrills of my football career. When the clock showed ten seconds left, the big crowd in Yankee Stadium started to chant, "Ten . . . nine . . . eight . . ."

It got louder and louder and it echoed around the ballpark like thunder.

"Seven . . . six . . . five . . . four . . ."

In all my years I never had been a part of anything like this. I threw off my foul-weather cape, jumped to my feet and joined the fans as they tolled off the last few seconds:

". . . three . . . two . . . one!"

BANG! The game was over. A roar went up from the fans, and I jumped around like a silly schoolboy, shaking hands and slapping everyone on the back. It was my first time with a winner. I flung my helmet in the air, and then realized it could kill someone if it ever hit them on the head. But no one seemed to mind. The sideline near the Giants' bench was a bedlam.

It was a good half hour after the game before I could unwind. I did not realize how tired I was, mentally and physically, until I sat down in front of my locker and started to peel off my jersey.

Boy, it had been a long year. But looking back, the 1961 season with New York gave me my greatest thrill in football. It was not the finest season I ever had personally. I think I had better years with San Francisco in 1953 and 1957, and even as a rookie with Baltimore in the All-America Conference in 1948. But this was the most satisfying season because so many people, especially the Forty-Niners, had written me off as a pro quarterback after San Francisco traded me to the Giants. I must confess there were doubts in my mind, too. My injuries—the bad back and the pulled groin—had depressed me, made me uncertain as to whether I could take the physical punishment any longer. The problems of adjusting to a new way of life with the Giants, while not insurmountable, concerned me greatly in the beginning. Could I make the change at 35? I had asked myself that question a hundred times. I had confidence in my ability to throw the football when I reported to New York, but at the start I was not at all certain I could successfully adapt myself to a new team, a new coach and a new city.

Once when things were going poorly, I remember saying, "If I ever get back to San Francisco, I swear I'll never put these cleats on again."

These uncertainties had churned inside of me all season—from the day I reported to the club at Salem, Ore., to this late December afternoon in the Bronx. But everything changed when the fans started their dramatic countdown. Then it hit me—by golly, I was with a championship ball club. After thirteen years, I was a winner. I would be playing in the "big one" for the first time. This was my greatest thrill. Oh, I guess the 1962 and 1963 seasons were equally important to me from a personal standpoint; I set a lot of passing records and everything, and we won the division both years. But by then I was kind of used to winning. That's something you become accustomed to when you play with the New York Giants.

215

Hugh McElhenny, my old teammate from San Francisco, came to the Giants in 1963 and it also was his first time with a championship team after a lot of years. I watched him when the fans started the "Ten . . . nine . . . eight . . ." business in the last game against Pittsburgh, and I could see he was moved as much by this exciting moment as I had been three years before. It's an experience that gives even a hardened old pro like Mac a lump in the throat. If I didn't know better, I would swear I saw tears in his eyes that day. Must have been the wind . . .

I will remember 1961 for other reasons too. Aside from making me a winner, my association with the Giants brought me into contact with two of the finest men I have ever known in pro football—Allie Sherman, my coach, and Charlie Conerly, with whom I shared the quarterbacking that year.

The expression "real pro" wears kind of thin after a while, but Charlie Conerly was just that, a real pro.

What Charlie did in 1961 was not easy for a man of great pride and intensity. He stepped aside for the first time in fourteen years and gave his ball club to another quarterback. And make no mistake about it—the New York Giants *were* Charlie Conerly's club, as much as any football team can belong to one man. Charlie had led them for over a decade and he had won for them, which is the true measure of a pro quarterback.

My appearance in August created a ticklish situation for the three of us, for Sherman, for Conerly and for me.

Although Conerly was 40 years old, and maybe older, he was there to play in 1961. He had pride and he obviously did not want to end his career riding the bench as a second-string quarterback. Nor had I come to New York to sit down on the sideline and watch somebody else play. Thus, Sherman had a couple of hot potatoes dumped in his lap. But Allie handled the problem wisely. He managed to convince Conerly and me that we were both vital to the club's success and that he could not win if he did not have us working together.

"Any split between you two old guys" he said, "will crack this club right down the middle."

I do not believe anyone realized then, or indeed even now, what a tremendous job of psychological coaching Sherman turned in that year. He juggled Charlie and me all season, and made us both feel like starting quarterbacks. More important, he handled a sensitive situation without impairing the wonderful spirit of the Giant ball club. The team played as well for me as it did for Conerly—and we won the whole thing.

Conerly had some great clutch performances for the Giants in 1961. In the sixth game of the season, the Los Angeles Rams came into the Stadium and jumped ahead of us, 14–10, in the second half. I was awful that day and finally Sherman yanked me out of there and sent in Charlie. It was a hell of a spot to be thrown into. The Rams had the momentum and we couldn't do anything right. But Conerly seemed to thrive on pressure. He threw a couple of touchdown passes, one to Kyle Rote and the other to Del Shofner, and won the game for us, 24–14. He made it look easy.

The next week, Charlie was given the starting assignment against Dallas. In other years, this would have bothered me. I might have felt it was unfair of the coach to bench me because of one bad ball game. But Sherman handled things differently and I did not mind. I had not played well and that was it. Charlie deserved the start; he had earned it by bailing me out against the Rams.

"I'm starting Charlie because he played well last week, and *not* because you played poorly," Sherman told me the day before the Dallas game.

That was the positive approach and I was satisfied.

The season was half over now but I had not completely shaken my homesickness. Everything had been fine while Minnette was in New York. But when she left to go home, things fell into a lonely and monotonous routine. It was tough to be alone in a big city like New York. It was tough being at the Concourse Hotel, a dreary place. I had seen the sights with Minnette. We had been to dinner at the big restaurants, we had taken in some Broadway shows. It had been a new and fascinating experience. But now she was gone and I was sitting around that hotel by myself, eating by myself, watching television every night until it was time to go to bed. Shofner wasn't much help because his fiancee was in town and he was with her most of the time. One night I went to a neighborhood movie. I sat in the back row. It was the first time in my life I ever had gone to a movie by myself. After a half hour or so, I got up

217

and walked out. I could not enjoy the show knowing I was there alone.

So, this was a difficult time for me. It did not help either that my quarterbacking had been poor against the Rams and a week later when I replaced Conerly in the Dallas game.

The turning point for me, and for the Giants, I think, came in the second meeting with Washington. I completed 15 of 28 passes and threw for three touchdowns, and we murdered the Redskins, 53–0. That started us on a great four-game winning streak. We whipped Philadelphia, 38–21; Pittsburgh, 42–21; Cleveland, 37–21. In four games we got our offense rolling and we scored 170 points.

That hot string boosted our record to 9–2 and all of a sudden everybody was talking about an eastern championship. But the Eagles were still up there with us, and I had been disappointed too many times with San Francisco to even allow myself to think about a championship. If we won it, fine. But I sure as heck wasn't going to spend the playoff money with three games still ahead of us. I had seen the Forty-Niners blow too many "sure things" to get fooled again. Besides two of our last three ball games were with Green Bay and Philadelphia.

As it was, the Packers beat us, 20–17, the next week in Milwaukee, and so everything was riding on the Eagle game in the next-to-last week of the season. We went into Philadelphia with only a half-game lead over the Eagles. If they beat us, they would be a half game up with one to go. There were no ands, ifs or buts about it. We had to win!

This was the day Charlie Conerly made his greatest contribution to the Giants.

I started at quarterback against Philadelphia and threw a long touchdown pass to Shofner on the fourth play of the game. It was almost too easy. Games that start easily often do not finish up that way. This was something else I had learned over the years. Sure enough, the Eagles caught us and then went ahead, 10–7. Unexplainably, I lost control of the game. My passes were off target. I called the wrong plays. The more I pressed, the worse things got. It was the same thing that had happened to me against Los Angeles earlier in the season.

With six minutes left in the second quarter, I felt a tap on my shoulder as I started to call a play in the huddle. I didn't have to look around. I knew it was Conerly. Sherman had gone with me as long as he dared. This was not my day. Allie couldn't afford to fool around with a cold-armed quarterback.

But Charlie certainly wasn't cold. He was red hot. He had been watching the Philadelphia pass defense from the bench and the minute he got into the game he called a play that went all the way. The Eagles had been doubling on Shofner and Rote in passing situations, leaving Joe Walton, the tight end, under single coverage. So Conerly sent Shofner deep to clean out the left side, and then crossed Walton into that area and hit him with a touchdown pass. Boy, you couldn't beat an old pro like Charlie. Pressure was his middle name.

I was through for the day. That much I knew when Conerly tossed that touchdown pass to Walton. I was angry with myself for letting down in the key game. But if I had been in Sherman's shoes I would have gone with Charlie too.

Charlie was the whole show in the second half. He tossed two more scoring passes and we knocked off the Eagles, 28–24. That sent us into the final game against Cleveland needing only a tie, which we got, to take the eastern championship.

As I said, no one was more valuable to the Giants in 1961 than Charlie Conerly. He won the big games coming off the bench, which is the toughest way to win them. You get in there and you are cold. You don't have the feel of the ball game. It takes time to gauge the speed of your receivers, the wind and the condition of the field. Meanwhile, the defense knows you are not warmed up and they come at you like all hell. It is like pinch-hitting with two out in the ninth. The pressure is terrific.

I started most of the games at quarterback for the Giants that season and, while no one came right out and said it, I guess Charlie was considered the No. 2 man. But if this secondary role affected him, he at least managed to conceal his disappointment. I admired him for this. In his place, I doubt if I could have carried on as well. I am a person of strong emotions and, unlike Charlie, I can't hide my anger or my disappointment. He was strong and silent, and his expression was unchanging. Charlie's thoughts were his private property and he seldom shared them with others. Even his closest friend, Frank Gifford, did not always know what was on Conerly's mind.

Both Charlie and I owed a lot to Allie Sherman for his handling of a delicate and potentially explosive situation. Two old warhorses like us, both wanting to play, could have created a real problem. But except for one touchy moment in the Washington game when Conerly thought Sherman had yanked him because one of his passes was intercepted, there never was a speck of trouble. Allie pulled the strings at the right time. He kept Charlie and me working together as an entry. Meanwhile, the Giants were winning.

New York City was a wonderland for me after we won the eastern championship in 1961. All the Giants were heroes. Each day brought some new reward. I had never seen anything like it. I won a Chrysler automobile. I was named to the Associated Press and United Press International All-Pro teams. I was given the Jim Thorpe Award as the most valuable player in professional football, an award voted on by the players themselves. And then one day my phone rang and Arthur Poretz, a public relations man, told me I had won the Howard Clothes award as the most popular Giant. Poretz said over half a million New York fans had voted in the contest.

"I'm honored, Art," I said. "What is the award?"

"A yacht."

I couldn't believe my ears. "A what?" I asked.

Poretz laughed. "It's a thirty-foot cabin cruiser, Y.A."

"But I'm not a yachtsman," I protested.

"You are now."

I had been worrying about getting my new car back to the West Coast, and now I had a cabin cruiser on my hands as well.

"Don't worry about it," said Art. "We are having it sent to California. It will be there when you get home after beating Green Bay in the championship game next week."

I would have traded the car, the yacht and every other honor that year to have beaten the Packers for the title. This was my first championship game and maybe it would be my last. After fourteen years I had my shot. And, boy, I wanted it bad. But we ran into a great football team in Green Bay that year. They kicked the heck out of us, 37–0, and probably would have beaten us three out of four in a series. Not by 37 points, but they were the better football team and there was no denying it.

The championship game was not nearly so close as our 20–17 loss to Green Bay three weeks earlier. We could have won that one; we were in the game right to the end. But in Green Bay on December 30th we just didn't have the offensive opportunities. Paul Hornung, who set a championship game scoring record with 19 points, went in for a touchdown on the first play of the second quarter, and then Bart Starr passed to Boyd Dowler for another score a few minutes after Ray Nitschke intercepted one of my throws. So, it was 14–0 right quick.

If we had any hopes of catching up, they were stamped out on the next series of downs. On the first play from our 32, I had Rote and Shofner wide open on a deep pass pattern. But before I could get rid of the ball, Willie Davis, the big Packer defensive end, crashed into me from the blind side and dumped me for a loss. There's no telling what might have happened if I had been able to get that pass off. On the next play, I tried a screen pass to Alex Webster. It was a good call; the Packers were fooled. But he could not get open, though, so I had to go to my second man, Joe Walton. The pass was incomplete. On third down, Rote beat Hank Gremminger on a deep route, but I under-threw Kyle badly and the ball went right to the Packer defensive back.

Green Bay rolled right in for another touchdown after Gremminger's "interception" and we were finished. The game became a rout.

I was incensed at myself. Here I was in my first championship game, and I went and threw the football right into Green Bay's hands. I practically gave them two of their first three touchdowns. Damn, it made me sore. Of all the times to miss my man!

Conerly tried later but he didn't fare much better. Neither of us could move the Giants. Our defense played well early in the game but it finally broke down when the offense couldn't hold onto the football. It was a bad day.

The dressing room was an awful scene. The Giants were a team of great pride and to have been crushed like this was a terrible blow. Everyone except Conerly showed the emotional strain of the embarrassing defeat. As always, his expression gave no clue as to his inner feelings.

No one felt the loss more deeply than Allie Sherman. His eyes were moist and he was flushed with anger and humiliation. But he wasn't sulking. Nor was he about to let his ball club sulk. He jumped up on a table in the middle of the crowded room and hollered for attention.

"Now I know how tough this thing is," he said, and the bitterness of the moment hung on his words.

"But let me tell you this. You are Giants, and when you walk out that door, you're going to walk out with your heads held high. You're going to look them in the eye. You are not going to look ashamed or beaten."

Rosey Grier, the 300-pound defensive tackle, growled, "Damn right, Allie."

Then Sherman said, "We have been whipped before, and we'll get whipped again. But don't let this one get you down. We will be back again. We have had a great season and I am proud to have been your coach. We are all men, so square those shoulders and walk tall. Goodbye, and thank you."

Although I took the defeat in Green Bay as hard as the next guy, I have always believed there is nothing deader than last year's football games. I never think about statistics and standings once I hang up my gear. As far as I am concerned, a ball game is a ball game. I play as hard as I can. I do my best. But once it is over, I try and put it out of my mind. It doesn't do any good to live with a thing like that 37–0 affair in Green Bay. The score is in the books now. Worrying isn't going to change anything.

What makes it difficult sometimes is that people won't let you forget a game, especially a championship game. Wherever I went in the months following the Packer game, the question was thrown at me, "What happened in Green Bay?"

Now, how in the hell can a guy answer that one? I can't say, "I don't know," because I was the quarterback and I guess they figured I should know. The reasons why we lost are unimportant now. What matters is that we lost. The Packers beat us, 37–0, but the outcome would have been the same had the score been 7–6.

I had had my shot at the championship. And I had blown it. As my plane headed west from Chicago the night of the championship game, I wondered if I would get another chance. I wondered too if I would be back with the New York Giants in 1962.

CHAPTER TWENTY-SIX

"WE ALWAYS WIN"

MY RETURN to San Francisco in 1962 as a Giant was something less than triumphant.

We flew to the West Coast from Fairfield University in August to play the Forty-Niners in our first exhibition game. Naturally, I was mighty excited at the prospect of playing in Kezar Stadium against my old ball club.

I had left San Francisco a year before as a washed-up old quarterback. Now I was coming back as the N.F.L.'s Most Valuable Player and a member of the team that had won the eastern division championship in 1961.

What a difference a year had made!

Naturally, I was anxious to play well in front of my old fans. But it did not turn out that way. I was awful and the Giants were awful, and the Forty-Niners damned near ran us out of the ballpark. The score was 42–10. It was quite embarrassing to me. Here we were the eastern division champions and had come in holding our heads high. Then we went out there, showed nothing and were just plain humiliated.

It was only an exhibition game but I took the loss hard. It had been a bitter experience to play so poorly in my old ballpark. I had wanted desperately to help win this one for the Giants. It was important to me for personal reasons, too. Red Hickey had traded me because he thought I was through as a good quarterback. I had wanted to prove him wrong.

It was a full twenty minutes after the game before I started to take off my jersey and pads. I just sat, too disappointed in myself to do anything or say anything. Finally, I got up and walked over to where Frank Gifford was dressing.

"By golly, Frank, I do not see how we can win this thing again. Look what these guys did to us out there today. They murdered us."

"Oh, we are going to win, Y.A., don't worry about that," Gifford replied confidently.

But I still was not satisfied.

"How are we going to win it?" I asked. "Rote has retired. Conerly has retired. Pat Summerall is gone. Livingston has been traded.

"And how about you, Frank?" I asked. "You are trying to make a comeback and you have been hurting ever since you got to camp. How the hell are you going to do it?"

"Listen, Y.A.," he said firmly, "we will win this thing because we always win!"

"But how?" I asked, wanting more reassurance.

"I don't know how," he replied, "but just mark my words. We are going to win."

Gifford reflected the Giants' general attitude. This confidence in their own ability, their own destiny, made them different from any team I had ever played with. They always went into a season with the idea of winning everything in sight. There never was any doubt. Gifford knew they would win. Huff knew they would win. Webster knew they would win. True, they figured on a long, hard struggle but "we will win it" was the consensus.

The struggle started sooner than any of us expected. We lost two of our first five games. Cleveland beat us in the opener, 17–7, and then Pittsburgh took us by 20–17. That put us at 3–2 going into our game with the Detroit Lions at Yankee Stadium.

If the 1962 season had a turning point it was October 21st against Detroit. A loss to the Lions would have dropped us to .500. There's no telling what direction we might have taken from there. This was a "must" game. And I want to tell you, that Detroit club was tough. They had those big strong guys up front on defense, Sam Williams and Darris McCord at end and Roger Brown and Alex Karras at tackle. The linebackers, with Joe Schmidt in the middle, were just great. This defense was the best in the business in 1962. Nobody had been able to gain a yard through the Lions on the ground.

Despite all this power, Allie Sherman told us, "We will run on them, and we will pass on them."

Sherman's battle plan was simple:

"Nobody runs straight at Karras and Brown and the rest of those big boys. They are always trying to run slants and sweeps with fancy angle blocking. But that is not the way. You've got to beat those front four guys head to head. You can't pussyfoot around them. That is what we will do Sunday. We will take the ball and run it straight at them. We will not look for the easy way. We will beat them right up front, man to man, and we will win the game."

This was Sherman's theory for the rest of the season. Go at their big men. Break them down. Run through them. Open them up for the forward pass.

It worked against Detroit. We won the ball game, 17–14.

This was a real battle. Our offensive line slugged it out with the Detroit defense every yard of the way. Rosey Brown, at 260 pounds, had a great duel with the Lions' end, Sam Williams, six-five and 250. Giant guard Darrell Dess, a squat six-footer, banged heads with six-five 300-pound Roger Brown and moved the Lion tackle out of there when he had to. Boy, it was really something to see! Those big babies were knocking the hell out of each other right down in the dirt. Every yard gained that day was earned.

I stuck closely to Sherman's pre-game plan. Phil King and Alex Webster ran the ball straight at the Lions on quick traps and dive plays. They ground out the yards the hard way. Then, when we had Detroit run-conscious, we threw the ball. Not long, but effectively, just enough to keep them honest.

The Lions scored early on a 48-yard pass from Milt Plum to Gail Cogdill. But we took the kickoff and controlled the ball for almost eight minutes, moving down to the Lions' four-yard line. With a first down, I figured they would be expecting a power play into the line; we had been having success with King and Webster inside the tackles. So I faked Webster left, and bootlegged the ball around right end for a touchdown. As I crossed the goal-line, Dick (Night Train) Lane, the Lion halfback, hit me a pretty solid shot in the helmet. I went down hard. I was shaken up but I was able to walk off the field under my own power.

On the sideline, Sherman asked me if I was okay and I said, "Yes."

I had been knocked dizzy in ball games before and I was not concerned over this incident. But then a funny thing happened. Sherman called me off the bench. He wanted to discuss a defense the Lions were using.

"When they go into that set-up, Y.A.," he said, "your best automatic call would be a thirty-four."

"A thirty-four?" I asked. "You know we do not have a 34-automatic, Allie."

Sherman's eyes popped open. The 34-automatic was one of our standard plays. I had been using it for two years, and here I was standing in front of him telling him we had no such play.

"Are you sure you are all right?" he inquired again.

"What makes you ask?"

"Well," he said, "you got a pretty stiff shot in the head on that touchdown. Maybe it shook you up more than you think."

I told Sherman I was feeling fine. But all of a sudden things got fuzzy. Little wheels started spinning in my head. I couldn't remember a thing—not a single play, not a single pass call. I did not even know how to set a formation. I felt great but my mind was a complete blank.

They sat me down on the bench and Doc Sweeny came over and asked me what my name was.

"Y.A. Tittle," I said. "You know damned well what my name is, Doc."

"Sure I do, Y.A.," he said, "but I wanted to see if you did."

Then Doc asked me, "Who are we playing today?"

"Detroit."

It is strange. I could have told Doc the score and the down and everything else that was going on. But I could not remember a single Giant play or formation.

227

I sat there the whole first half not knowing what had happened to me. They took me into the dressing room at half-time and all of a sudden my head cleared. I could remember again. Boy, was I relieved. I ran over to Sherman and yelled, "You're right, Allie, we do have a thirty-four automatic. Great play, too."

I got back into the game in the second half and we beat the Lions. King scored a touchdown in the third period from a yard out to tie the score at 14–14. Then Don Chandler kicked a nine-yard field goal for the winning points.

This was one of the most satisfying victories I ever took part in. We had to win the game and, by gosh, we did win it. We beat our opposition where it was toughest—along the front line. The Lions were a great football team. But on that particular day the Giants had more desire.

Our win over Detroit started the big push. It gave us confidence, made us aware of our capabilities. Inspired, we continued the push. We won nine straight and clinched the eastern division title with two games left on the schedule.

But that temporary amnesia was not the only evil that befell me against Detroit. Somewhere along the line I injured my right elbow. It was bruised and bled freely. The next morning, my arm was swollen and stiff. I took diathermy treatments for the rest of the week. But my elbow did not respond. It did not look like I would be able to play against the incoming Washington Redskins. Ralph Guglielmi, who had come to New York in a trade after Conerly retired, got most of the pre-game work at quarterback. Sherman told me if the arm did not improve by Friday he would go with Ralph against Washington.

I cursed my bad luck. Here the Giants were just catching afire, everything was beginning to click, and I had to come up with a bad throwing arm!

But miraculously the stiffness left my arm and on Saturday I was able to throw the ball in practice.

"Think you can make it, Y.A.?" Sherman asked me after practice.

"Damned right, Al. I am ready," I answered.

"You'd better be," he said. "These guys haven't been beaten yet, you know."

Sherman did not have to remind me. Washington was on a hot streak of its own, thanks to Norm Snead's passing and the catching of Bobby Mitchell, who had come from Cleveland in a trade. The Skins came to town leading the eastern division with four wins, two ties and no losses. They shaped up as another tough one.

Sunday, October 28, 1962, turned out to be the greatest day I ever had in pro football.

I threw seven touchdown passes to tie the National League record shared by Sid Luckman of the Chicago Bears and Adrian Burk, my former Baltimore teammate. I completed 27 of 39 for 505 yards. I figured in every score in the Giants' 49–34 victory over the Redskins.

This was a day when everything fell into place. What made it different from other days and other games I cannot say. Perhaps it was the kind of day that happens once in every quarterback's life. My receivers made flawless moves against the defenders. Our offensive line gave me great protection. Every pass pattern worked precisely as Allie Sherman had drawn it on the blackboard.

Still, the Redskins were not impressed. Especially since Snead had a hot hand, too. He got his team off to a 7–0 lead with a long bomb to Mitchell, who veered to the inside, got a step on Erich Barnes and took Norm's pass in full stride.

This was a passing day. It was easy to see that. But that is the way I like it—putting the football in the air.

Not long after Mitchell's touchdown in the first period, I moved the Giants to the Washington 22. Shofner cut downfield from his flanker position and drew halfback Claude Crabb with him. Too late, Crabb realized he had been fooled. Morrison broke into the unprotected zone, made a great fake and raced into the clear. I hit him and he went in for the touchdown.

Washington marched upfield with the start of the second period but Barnes intercepted one of Snead's passes and returned it to the Redskin 20. Three plays later I threw my second touchdown pass, a five-yard shot to Walton in the end zone. Joe was almost over the end line but he made a great diving catch for the score. That is what I meant when I said this was a once-in-a-lifetime game. Catches like the one by Walton do not happen to a quarterback very often.

Snead came right back with a touchdown toss to Fred Dugan, but Washington missed the extra point and so we still held the lead, 14–13.

Just before the half, we drove down to the Redskin two-yard line. On third down, I started a bootleg run around right end. Jim Steffen, the Redskins' left halfback, came up to stop the run. I tossed the ball over his head to Morrison, who was free and clear in the end zone.

That made it 21–13. When we left the field at halftime, I had completed 13 passes in 21 attempts for 279 yards. Normally, that would have been a good days work for an entire ball game.

My fourth touchdown pass was a 32-yarder to Shofner. Del ran a beautiful down-and-in route, split the Redskin defensive backs and made a great catch.

Next I threw what we call a play-action pass. I faked a slant to Webster, which froze the Washington defense long enough for Walton to get free on a sideline-and-down pattern. The deception was so effective that when I dropped back to throw, I found Joe standing all by himself in the end zone, not a man around him. I doubt if the Redskins knew he was there. Again, this kind of thing does not happen very often among professionals. It takes a lot of hard work to get a receiver open by as little as a step, and there was Walton with no one within twenty yards of him.

Number six was to Frank Gifford on a down-and-in. It was one of the best passes I have ever thrown. I led Frank perfectly. He caught the ball without having to break stride and kept right on going into the end zone. The play was good for 63 yards.

It was so easy that day, almost like playing pass and catch at a Tuesday practice.

All the while, of course, my pass protection was wonderful. You don't get off as many completions as we were throwing without Grade-A help from your line. Ray Wietecha at center and guards Darrell Dess and young Greg Larson closed off the middle to the Washington pass-rushers. Tackles Rosey Brown and Jack Stroud hand-fought the defensive ends. No Redskin laid a glove on me all afternoon.

With a 42–20 lead going into the fourth period, I was waiting for Sherman to wave me to the sideline and send in Guglielmi to finish up. But Allie had been notified from the press box that I was one touchdown pass away from the record. He decided to let me go for it.

Everyone on the ball club seemed eager for me to have a shot at No. 7. Webster did some great running and Shofner made a couple of spectacular catches to move the ball to the Washington five-yard line.

"Now throw the damned thing in there," growled Alex as we huddled back on the 12.

"We probably could run it in just as easy," I pointed out. "Everyone in the park is looking for a pass."

"We didn't bring you this far to have you run it," said Shofner. "Put it in the air, Yat. You may not get another chance."

My seventh touchdown came off another play-action call. I faked a handoff to Phil King over left guard. Meanwhile, Walton sifted out into the right flat. I got the ball away just as Redskin end John Paluck crashed into me. A fraction of a second later and it would have been a seven-yard loss instead of the touchdown pass to Walton that tied the N.F.L. record.

Joe Walton deserves special mention in any discussion of the Giants' passing game. Joe doesn't have Shofner's size or speed, nor does he have Gifford's moves. But pound for pound he is one of the finest offensive ends in pro football today. Walton is what I call a "guts" footfall player. He makes the big catch under pressure. Third down and ten, I look for little Joe. Fourth down on the one, Joe is my man. I can count on him fighting those linebackers and breaking into the clear just long enough for me to hit him. And Joe doesn't drop them, either.

The day I tied the record with seven touchdowns against Washington, Walton caught three—and two of them were from the five-yard line. And believe me, that's where the going gets tough. There is no room down close for a receiver to use speed or deception. He's just got to have the knack of slipping into that end zone and giving the passer a split-second target.

Later in the 1962 season, I threw six touchdown passes against Dallas. Again Joe Walton made the tough short-yardage grabs, one from ten yards, one from two yards and the last from the eight.

You won't find Walton's name on the annual all-pro teams. The fellows who pick those squads usually manage to overlook his contributions to the New York Giants. But without Joe Walton, Tittle wouldn't make the all-pro team either.

The Dallas game on December 16th, in which I set a league record with my 33rd touchdown pass of the year, was my second great thrill of 1962. But it was anti-climactic. The Giants had clinched the division title two weeks earlier with a 26–24 decision over the Chicago Bears. The Dallas victory and a 17–13 win over Cleveland were merely icing on the cake.

The season that had opened on such a disappointing note in San Francisco back in August ended in grand fashion.

As Gifford had hold me, "We always win."

CHAPTER TWENTY-SEVEN

"BEAT GREEN BAY"

DON CHANDLER, who kicked a lot of big field goals for the Giants in 1962, kicked the biggest one at ten minutes after four on December 2nd. It traveled sixteen yards, and it beat the Chicago Bears, 26–24.

It also made New York the N.F.L. eastern champion for the second straight year.

The minute Chandler's kick sailed through the uprights at Wrigley Field, every one of us automatically turned our thoughts to another showdown with the Green Bay Packers. The memory of the 37–0 beating they had given us the year before was still fresh. We had been hoping for another shot at them. And now we had it.

Green Bay, as I recall, had not yet won the western division title. But that was only a matter of time. No one, or hardly anyone, at least, was beating the Packers in 1962.

Allie Sherman's fears that we would let down in our last two games were unfounded. Even with the Packers on our minds, we got past Cleveland, 17–13, and Dallas, 41–31, finishing the season with a record of 12 wins and only two losses.

New York City was a football madhouse the week before the title game with Green Bay. People talked of little else. I have never seen a town so wrapped up in a football team. Championship fever was everywhere. Between periods at a Madison Square Garden hockey game, the fans started to chant, "Beat Green Bay . . . Beat Green Bay. . . . Beat Green Bay." This chorus was picked up all over town. Every time you turned on the radio, some disc jockey would be saying, "Beat Green Bay." Signs in store windows said the same thing. Fans would stop me on the street or come over to my table in a restaurant and say, "Let's go, Y.A., beat Green Bay."

Boy, it was something that last week in December.

Green Bay was the heavy favorite but I felt we had a better chance than in 1961. I wanted this one badly because now I was the Giants' only quarterback. The year before I had shared the job with Charlie Conerly. When the Packers beat us by 37–0 I was naturally disappointed but it was my first championship game and I was new to the team and, well, it just did not hit me as hard as I thought it would. Charlie and I had split a lot of work that year. Maybe when the responsibility is not all your own it does not effect you as much as when you are on the spot all alone. Previously, if Conerly and I both had a bad day, we would go have a cup of coffee somewhere after the game and console each other by saying, "Boy, we were awful out there today!" We shared the praise and we divided the blame. In 1962, though, Conerly was gone. I was it. Of course Ralph Guglielmi was there too but I did most of the playing during our long winning streak, and now it was up to me to beat Green Bay for the championship.

I thought we could do it. So did the rest of the Giants. There was an intensity about the team that week which I had not noticed before. The defense was really worked up. We could hear them in the next room at their meeting, kicking chairs, stomping around like a lot of bull elephants and growling at each other.

If the New York defense could have played offense on Sunday, December 30th, we might have won the championship. Andy Robustelli and his gang were superb. The defensive effort was one of the best I have ever seen. But, as in 1961, our offense could not move the ball. The Packers beat us again, 16–7. It was the hardest-hitting football game I ever played in, and it was played under weather conditions that were almost unimaginable.

It was a bitter cold day. And icy wind that swept through Yankee Stadium at better than 40 miles per hour made it seem even

234

colder than seventeen degrees. By the time I threw my second pass in the pre-game warm-up drill, my fingers were frozen stiff and I could hardly hold the football. The wind knifed through my uniform and stung my hide from head to toe.

"This is not our kind of day," I said to Sherman, who was bundled in a heavy parka with a hood over his head. "The wind is going to raise hell with our passing."

"I know," he said. "But there isn't much we can do about it. Don't throw long if you can help it."

Although the Giants were primarily a passing team in 1962, Sherman's game plan for Green Bay called for us to take the ball to them on the ground right at the outset. We wanted to establish our running game, as we had done against Detroit earlier in the year. We were going to take on their big boys up front, Willie Davis, Hawg Hanner, Henry Jordan and Bill Quinlan. We were going to run it down their throats, wear them out. Even if we made only two or three yards a shot in the beginning, we would at least be hitting them, pounding them, making them respect our running. We might have to give up the ball a few times and kick it out of there. But that was okay too. We felt our defense could get it back for us in a hurry. Defense is the key to winning football. If you don't have a sound defense, you can't afford to blast away and kick it to them and then come back and kick it to them again. You have to go for the long ball when you have the chance because if they get the ball, you might not get it back for a long time. But the Giant defense was solid in 1962 and so we had no reservations about taking it right to the Packers with our running game.

Besides, the day was better suited to running. The wind was blowing up a storm and it was worth a guy's life to put the ball in the air. This was all right with the Packers, I'm sure. They were basically a rushing team anyway. Green Bay fullback Jim Taylor had gained almost as much yardage by himself as the entire Giant backfield. In front of him was a great offensive line. The Packers were a grind-it-out ball club, a possession team. Their attack was made for a cold, windy afternoon.

I am not implying this is the reason the Packers beat us. They were the world champions and they might have beaten us on a good day. But I will always feel we would have had a much better shot on our kind of field, and on a day when I could have thrown the hell out of the ball. We will never know. But they were a fine football team and I don't mean to take anything away from their victory. It was well deserved. They scored 16 points and held us to seven. That was enough to do it.

Despite the adverse conditions, we still almost won the game. Our defense did a tremendous job and, with a few breaks, things could have gone our way. What do I mean by breaks? I'll tell you. Sam Huff and Robustelli and the rest of our defensive guys hit Taylor and the Green Bay backs so hard that they fumbled five times. But five times the ball bounced right to some Packer who happened to be standing in the right place at the right time. We fumbled twice, Phil King on a run and Sam Horner on a punt, and Ray Nitschke recovered both our bobbles for the Packers. Now you can say Nitschke played an alert defensive game and deserved to get those loose balls. But a fair critic also would have to admit we deserved better than 0-for-5 after knocking Taylor, Paul Hornung and Tom Moore loose from the football with some of the hardest tackling I have ever seen.

The Giants' defense could not be faulted for the defeat. Robustelli and his boys were mean. And they were aggressive. They gave Taylor the same treatment they have given Cleveland's Jimmy Brown over the years—a maximum physical effort on every play. Three and four of them hit Taylor every time he came through or around the line. They drove into him and flattened him on the frozen ground. The Packer fullback was charged with three of the five fumbles.

After the game, Green Bay quarterback Bart Starr said, "It was terrible. The huddle would form and we would watch Taylor come back after Huff and Katcavage and the rest of them had hit him, and he would be bent over holding his insides together. I never saw a back get such a beating."

Taylor carried the ball 31 times that day and scored Green Bay's only touchdown. "It was the only play of the game they didn't touch me," he said later. "But they sure made up for it the rest of the time. It was the toughest game of my life. They really came to play."

The Giants *had* come to play. But we just did not have the

236

ball bouncing our way. Every time Don Chandler punted, the ball would trickle into the end zone and they would get it out on the 20. Every time they punted, the ball seemed to roll dead on the eight-yard line. It put us in one hole after another. What could a freezing quarterback do with the ball on his own eight and the field covered with ice? You have to get that ball up around mid-field once in a while. Then with a couple of bombs you are down to their ten and maybe you go in for a touchdown. Starting drives time and again against that tough defense down near our own goal-line was murder. They had us backed against a wall all after-noon.

The break that hurt us most, I feel, was Horner's fumble of a punt by Max McGee in the middle of the third period. The Packers were leading by 10–7 at the time. But we had our defense in high gear and we were going after them. With the ball on his own 33, Taylor tried a sweep and Rosey Grier decked him for a yard loss. Jim tried the left side next and Dick Modzelewski flattened him for another loss. Then Starr's pass to Ron Kramer was incomplete—thanks to a furious rush by Robustelli. So McGee had to punt on fourth down. It was a low kick and Horner almost had to kneel to catch it. But he fumbled the ball and Nitschke recovered for Green Bay. Instead of having a shot at scoring, we were back on defense. We lost our momentum and Green Bay gained it. Jerry Kramer kicked a field goal a few minutes later and it was 13–7. It also was the beginning of the end for us.

Nitschke was a pain in the neck all day. In the first half, I had Joe Walton wide open in the end zone but the Green Bay middle linebacker barely deflected the ball as it left my hand. It hung there for a second and it came straight down to Dan Currie, another line-backer, and he ran it up to the fifty. I can still see Walton all alone in the end zone waving at me to get the ball to him. It was a sure touchdown.

I guess I'm just looking at the thing from a loser's point of view. All losers can go back over a game and say if the breaks had gone this way or that way it would have been a different story. But I'm sure if you listened to Green Bay's version, they probably thought they had a lot of breaks going against them too, breaks I paid no attention to because I was looking at it from the other side of the fence. They won the ball game, and the championship, so they didn't have to talk about breaks.

The real bad break was the weather, and it was just as bad for both ball clubs. The difference was that I had to throw the football 41 times that day to Starr's 21.

I doubt if any quarterback could have thrown well in that wind. I sure couldn't. It was terrible. Wind is not a lot of fun to play in anyway, cold or warm. The ball is going to do a lot of things you don't want it to do. If you are going against the wind, a pass that is not perfect might flutter a little and the spiral breaks up, and then anything can happen. It's like a duck flying on one wing. When you are throwing into the wind, you've got to fire that damned ball with everything you have. You can't float it up there or it's liable to be blown back to you. Throwing with the wind, it is difficult to judge how much "lead" to give the receiver. Sometimes the wind takes the ball and you over-shoot him by 20 yards. Then you try and compensate for the tailwind and suddenly it dies down, and you find yourself under-throwing your man. A cross-wind is even worse. It makes the ball curve. I have seen the wind so bad that I had to aim the ball at the right sideline and let it blow back toward the middle of the field.

Against Green Bay in 1962, the wind became a mental as well as a physical problem. It shook my confidence. I kept telling myself, "Be careful, watch it," when I was dropping back to throw. I was afraid the wind would make the ball dip and flutter or hold it up there long enough for them to intercept. I couldn't pass under this handicap and worry about depth and footing and balance—and the fierce pass rush of Quinlan and Davis and Jordan, the Packer front men.

To be effective, a passer has to be loose and relaxed. He has to get back there in a hurry, pick out his man and let fly. The defense gives him four or five seconds to do this. He doesn't have time to calculate wind velocity and angle of drift.

The bitter, icy wind that swept Yankee Stadium in the 1962 championship game was the most formidable pass defense I have ever tried to throw against.

It has been said that I threw the ball too much for that kind of a day. But if you examine the course of the game, you will find that 28 of my 41 passes were thrown in the second half, and most of these in the final period when we were scrambling to avert defeat. The ball control business is okay, but when you are behind 16–7 in the last quarter, well, it is the long bomb or nothing. On a dry field maybe we could have stayed with the run because a fellow can get some good turf under him on a quick trap and go 50 or 60 yards for a touchdown. But it's tough to go the distance running over a frozen field. Wind or no wind, there was no other way for us but to pass against Green Bay late in the game.

They say a frozen field works to the advantage of a passing team. The receivers, knowing their routes, have the edge on the defensive backs. This may be true, but I say it depends on the situation—score, time, position of the ball. A frozen surface can hurt a passing attack more often than it helps it.

The 1961 title game against the Packers in Green Bay was an example of this. We got off to a poor start and the Packers scored two quick touchdowns. As soon as we fell behind, the icy field worked against us. They put the blitz on Conerly and me, but we could not throw the ball to get force out of it. Normally when a club red-dogs like the Packers did that day, it means there is single coverage in the secondary. With the linebackers committed to a rush, the halfbacks and safeties are back there alone. In this situation, the backs have to move up and play the receivers tighter. They can't afford to let you catch the short one in front of them. If they miss the tackle, you might go all the way. In most cases, this situation is a passer's dream. The defensive backs are in there tight and they are covering your receivers man-on-man. And nobody's going to play Del Shofner tight and prevent him from catching the football.

But it did not work this way in 1961. The Packers kept their secondary deep even while they were shooting the linebackers. And they got away with it because the field was frozen and our receivers were unable to get traction. The footing was so treacherous that when I threw a quick slant to Kyle Rote to beat the corner linebacker's blitz, Kyle could not turn up the field and go very far. He just skidded on the ice. The Packers could afford to play deep that day. They did not have to fear the home run ball. Nobody could run very far or very fast without slipping and falling. They gave us the short passes, knowing the frozen ground would keep Shofner and Rote from breaking loose when they caught the ball.

They blitzed every other play, and we couldn't do a damned thing but slip and slide around on the ice. It might have been different in a close ball game. Maybe then they couldn't have played their defensive backs way off the line like they did. But they had us over the barrel by three touchdowns and we had to throw the ball to catch up. We had to play the game their way.

Now usually when a defense puts the heat on you and shoots those linebackers in there, you call a quick trap. You drop down and you trap them and, boom! you zip a halfback through the line and away he goes. There are no linebackers to stop him. He might be good for 50 yards. But you can't run on a frozen field; you can't get that fast start. You can't catch those little flare passes that are so effective against the red-dog because the receiver has all he can do to keep his footing. He slips and skids and when he finally gets headed up the field, he runs into a defensive back. If he tries to cut past the halfback, he falls flat on his face. The defensive man doesn't even have to tackle him.

So that's how it was in my first two championship games as a Giant. In 1961 Green Bay whipped us on the ice. In 1962, they did it in the wind.

I had two shots at the "big one" and I came up empty-handed both times.

CHAPTER TWENTY-EIGHT

BE PREPARED—TO WIN!

IF I WERE asked to explain the success of the New York Giants, I could do it in one word—preparation.

This is where Allie Sherman and the Giants often have it over other clubs in the National Football League. This is why the Giants have won six eastern championships in the past eight seasons.

Personally, I think I have become a better football player and a smarter quarterback in the last three years because of the Giants' approach in this area. I always have had desire. And I always have been able to throw the hell out of the football. But I never knew what real preparation was until I came to New York in 1961.

The Giants do not only prepare to play a ball-game—they prepare to WIN IT!

This is the difference. This is the positive approach that sets the winners apart from the losers. It is an intangible thing but it is very real just the same. This is what Frank Gifford meant when he told me before the 1962 season, "We will win it, Y.A., because we always win it."

Gifford's attitude is typical of the Giants. After eleven years in professional football, Frank still approaches a ball game with the enthusiasm and desire of a rookie. He prepares, believe me. And he works hard. Regardless of Frank's outside activities in television and radio, from July to December he is a football player before everything else. In training camp he drives himself to the limit of

241

his physical and mental resources. There is no halfway with Frank. His greatness is no accident. He lays the groundwork all week. And every move is directed at a single purpose: "Win the game like we have always won the game!"

The Giants' defensive team prepares for a ball game with the same dedication, the same intensity. I never realized football players, especially defensive football players, studied so hard or at such length. Our guys study and prepare every minute. Tom Scott, the linebacker, reads his playbook endlessly. So do Sam Huff and Jim Katcavage and the others. They know the stuff forward and backward, but they never let up in their studying. And now I see the same thing in the younger fellows, like Jerry Hillebrand and Bill Winter. They are always studying, reading, firing questions at defensive coach Andy Robustelli: "If the tackle comes at me this way, what do I do?" Or maybe, "When they make this move, should I close down?"

An amazing thing happens to most young players when they join the Giants. They see Gifford constantly reading his playbook. They see Huff and Katcavage studying defenses after the squad meetings are over. They see this and they watch this, and suddenly it becomes contagious. Seeing the veterans working so hard makes the youngsters follow suit.

This was my first impression of the Giants—this dedicated approach by the defensive players. In my early discussions with Jim Patton and Dick Nolan I noticed right away that they continually talked football, at mealtime; when we were having a beer, and at night in the dorm. But not just general football. These fellows talked specifics. They aimed every remark at the club we would be playing that weekend. They talked about keys. "We will key the guard when they are strong right, and we will key the tackle if they change over." Every move seemed to be based on a definite key; nothing was left to chance. Patton and Nolan had it all figured way in advance.

I had never heard defensive football discussed like this, and it gave me a good insight into the Giants' organization and into the players who made New York a winning team. They won because they prepared to win. It was total mental and psychological preparation. Physically, the Giants were no better, no bigger, no faster

242

than other men I had played with. But they won because they were better prepared.

"You must always consider the possibility of losing," says Allie Sherman, "but it is much better to think in terms of winning. But you have to do more than think about winning. You must prepare to win."

Pre-game preparation by the Giants' offense is just as detailed, just as thorough as anything the defense goes through, maybe more so.

We don't just look at game films and study them; we memorize every single detail. We study three films for every game, two of the team we are playing and one of our own films. Of a total of, say, 175 plays we take frequencies so we know what they do on first and ten, what defenses they will be in on second and long, what defenses they prefer on third and long, what kind of red-dog moves we are likely to see on third down. This, of course, does not mean these frequencies will always hold up. But at least it gives us an idea. It might indicate to us that on first and ten we can expect ten percent red-dog. This, obviously, is not a big red-dog down for them, so we can use certain plays here that might not be as applicable on third down when our frequencies show we can expect seventy percent red-dogging.

Now, all professional teams take frequencies. But not every club approaches this phase of preparation to the extent Allie Sherman's teams do.

Nothing is overlooked. Nothing is left undone. We might get beat, but when we do it is because the other club beat us physically, and not because we went into the ball game unprepared. In this respect, Sherman is a master coach. He is a perfectionist when it comes to details. In setting up the passing attack, for example, we study the individual moves of each defensive back on the opposing club. How deep is their pass-drop? How many cross-over steps do they take before turning upfield to cover the deep receiver? Which ones favor the outside? The inside? When does Night Train Lane of the Lions cross his legs on a deep pass-drop? Maybe because he is so fast he can back-pedal quicker than another man and this means he crosses his legs at thirteen yards instead of sooner. Thirteen yards! Okay, that is where we will run our zig-in pattern, or that is when Shofner will make his break to the outside. We want to catch Lane with those legs crossed so he can't react to the move of the receiver. Maybe the next defensive back we see on the films is not as fast as Night Train. This one starts dropping back to cover on a pass and crosses his legs at eight yards so he can run with the deep receiver. Fine. That is when we will have Gifford square-out to the sideline.

This is what I mean by total preparation. A player can look at game films until his eyeballs drop out. But he needs a coach like Allie Sherman to direct him, to show him how to get the most out of what he is watching. This is how Gifford studies, even after eleven years as a great pro star. And this is how Shofner and Walton prepare. This is why they are great receivers. When they beat their man in a key situation on Sunday afternoon it is likely on a move that was carefully and meticulously plotted by Sherman and end coach Ken Kavanaugh in a dark room on Wednesday.

I might draw a parallel here with a story about the woodchopper who was told he had to cut down a big tree in twenty minutes or lose his job. He spent the first ten minutes sitting there sharpening his axe. His friends were concerned. They asked, "Why are you wasting your time? You have only ten minutes left?" The wood-chopper said nothing. But when his axe was sharpened, he went to work on the tree and whacked her down in no time at all. In some ways this is how we do it on the Giants. We spend all week sharp-ening and preparing for the job on Sunday. That film is run and re-run until the projectors get so hot you think they will blow out. Every man has his own area of responsibility. Glynn Griffing and I study the rival defense as a whole. Shofner, Gifford and our other receivers concentrate on the defensive backs and linebackers. Each lineman studies the guy who will be in front of him on Sunday until he knows everything about him.

Sherman is on top of everything. He is continually talking to these linemen, pointing out the opponent's strengths and weak-nesses. "He comes up with his arms, Darrell. You're going to have to get into him quicker." Then to Bookie Bolin. "This baby 'reads' a lot. Go after him . . . hard!" He stops the projector a minute later and says, "Watch this end, Rosey. See how he takes a drive-step inside and then slides to the outside? Stay with him."

Every pass block is explained and demonstrated by Sherman, whose first love is the pass offense. The blocking techniques often change from week to week depending on the team you are going against. In most cases, the blockers are told to take a step back and get ready to pop their man. But maybe the coaches notice something in the films and the technique is altered. Then the pass blockers are instructed to ". . . move out and get into your man quicker. Don't step back. Go after him sooner."

Allie Sherman coaches with youthful enthusiasm which he transmits to his ballplayers. He makes us like our work. Playing football for Sherman is fun, at least for me it is. It is like playing for Buck Shaw when I first went to San Francisco. I get tired physically, which is to be expected at my age, but I never lose my zest for the game.

I will not attempt to compare Allie Sherman to the other professional coaches I have played under—Shaw, Frankie Albert, Cecil Isbell, Red Strader or Red Hickey. Each coach has his own ideas, his individual philosophy. Some coaches win, like Sherman; others don't. However, it is not always the coach's fault when his club loses. Victory is not the only yardstick of a good coach. Unfortunately, it is often used as such. I have played for some fine men who seldom won. Allie Sherman is a fine coach who knows how to win. What the difference is, I can't really say. Maybe it's an intangible something that is inside a man.

Sherman's theories reflect the thinking of the rest of the Giants' organization, Jack and Well Mara, the owners; Ray Walsh, the general manager, and Jim Lee Howell, the former coach and now personnel director. The Giants select people like Tom Scott, like Sam Huff, and like Frank Gifford and Joe Morrison, who are successful men, not just big, strong football players. They are intelligent men. And I will make this point again: the one factor which should be considered by clubs when they choose players in the draft is to find fellows who are intelligent and capable of thinking on their feet, who can outsmart the other guy. Football is still a game of brawn and speed, it is true. I guess a premium always will be placed on the boys who are the biggest, can run the fastest, hit the hardest and catch the ball best. But then there is the one other area that has become so important—intelligence.

245

I never gave much thought to all this brain work until I was traded to the Giants. But now it is clear to me. Smart players stay in the league and as a result, they get smarter, harder to fool. Now, a defensive halfback who has been playing in the National Football League for nine or ten years knows twice as much about his job as his predecessor.

To be a great football player today, a man must have brains. Size and speed are no longer enough. Intelligent thinking has become a necessary part of the game.

Sherman's contribution to me has been his example of preparation, of total dedication. Other coaches have had this approach too, but the difference is that Allie has allowed me to become a part of it with the Giants. Prior to coming to New York I was only a player. I sat in the meetings just like the rest of the guys and watched the films, listened to my coaches, got some ideas . . . then hustled down with the guys to get a couple of beers. And the next day it was the same thing all over. I was a hired hand. I had no vote. I had no voice. Just a passing arm.

But with the Giants it has been different. Sherman has encouraged me to make suggestions, to talk about pass patterns and to tell him when he puts something up there on the blackboard, "Well, gee, Allie, I don't know whether I like that one or not. I don't think I can throw that pattern against this defense."

And then Sherman might say, "Well, Y.A., if you feel that way, let's throw it out. It isn't the only pass pattern we have."

Sherman has, in short, let me become a part of the planning, part of his preparation during the week. Not a coach, of course, because I am still a ballplayer, and that is the way I prefer it. But at least now I have the feeling that I am contributing more to the Giants than just my passing on Sunday afternoon. Not only is this Sherman's game, it is also part mine. If I do not like something, Sherman hesitates to put it into the offense.

Once Allie and I were discussing a certain play and we got into a little debate. We kicked it around, each of us trying to make his point and finally he said that he thought his way was better and that he should know because he was the coach. I did not press the argument much further. Noticing I had backed off, he asked,

"Y.A., don't you believe this would be better?" I answered, "I guess so. Maybe you are right, Al."

"Wait a minute," he said. "Wait just one minute, Y.A. I would rather you be completely sold on what you do, even though I may not think it is a hundred percent right, than to have you do something you don't believe in."

That is how Sherman coaches. He wants his players to believe in what they are doing. He wants them to have complete faith in the preparations he makes for them. He convinces you, and if he can't convince you, he is not so inflexible that he won't listen and maybe try another way. That is why the Giant players are so much a part of every ball game. They have contributed to the pre-game planning. They feel they have a stake in the thing.

Sherman is a coach who believes the keynote to success in football is simplicity. I have always believed this too, but it took Allie to show me how this approach could win ball games. In the Giants' system, everything is simplified to the point where perfection, or at least a high degree of execution, are most easily achieved. Involvements are kept to a minimum. Sherman would rather have his team master a few fundamental plays and have the confidence to execute them than to have a large number of complex plays which can't be perfected.

Sherman's entire philosophy is based on one major precept:

"Let's play OUR game. Let's not beat ourselves."

I remember one of the first talks I had with Allie. It was at Willamette University in Salem, and he was trying to explain the Giants' approach to football.

"If they beat us and kick the hell out of us," he said, "we want them to kick the hell out of us at our own game. We don't want to play their game. We try to do what we can do best; we make our stuff simple, and if they beat us, well, they beat us. It's going to happen. But we won't offer them any gifts. They'll earn whatever they get."

When Sherman says simple, he really means it. Sometimes we go into a ball game with just six running plays, just six, and maybe two or three pass patterns, off which we can use individual moves as the game progresses. But we know those six plays inside and out,

247

against any defense they throw at us. And our receivers can run those few pass routes blindfolded. When the other club goes into a weakside roll defense, I do not have to scratch around for a pass play that will beat it. Sherman has done that for me on Wednesday. All I have to do is call the play. I know it will work if we execute properly. Keeping everything simple gives us the maximum percentage shot with whatever we use.

A simple offense builds confidence in a ball club. We know, for instance, that seldom will a red-dogger come through there uncovered; rarely will a looping, stunting tackle cross the line without someone picking him up; at no time will a rival safetyman be allowed to come through there on a safety blitz without a halfback or some other guy picking him up before he gets to the quarterback. There is such simplicity in our offense, in our approach, that we seldom allow ourselves to start scrambling and deviate from our pre-game pattern.

I think Sherman's approach to the running game reflects this attitude.

"We're going to go at them—slash!—with straight stuff. We won't run wide double reverses and flow plays because those plays can get you into trouble."

In passing, too, we try to minimize the possibility of mistakes. There are four things that can happen on a forward pass, and three of them are bad—an incompletion, an interception, or a long loss. Our aim is to reduce the percentage of these things happening.

No linebacker should get through our line completely uncovered. If one does, it is because of a physical breakdown, which is part of the game, and not because we were unprepared to pick him up and block him. They beat us physically sometimes but this is the only way we want to get beat. We do not want them to go scott free and knock the hell out of someone because we blew an assignment. If they beat us, we want to force them to do it by knocking us down and running over us. If we can't win, we do not want to make it easy for them to win. Victory costs a lot in pro football, and those who beat us have to pay the price.

Sherman's preparation has made me a better quarterback. But, by golly, I can't overlook the fact that we get the ball more with the Giants than any club I have ever played for. We get more chances to do something with the football because Huff and Katcavage and those fellows are always getting it back for us. No team, and this is something I want to stress, can be successful in our league without a great defense. And I don't mean just a good defense, I mean a *great* defense. You can have the fastest runners, the best passer, the top offensive line, but none of it is any good if that defense can't go out there and get the ball for you.

There is probably only one exception to this rule and that was the Philadelphia Eagles in 1960. The Eagles had Norm Van Brocklin at quarterback and no defense, and yet they won the N.F.L. championship. It was a real tribute to Van Brocklin, who did it all by himself. But it does not happen like that too often. You still need defense to win in this league. The Detroit Lions had the best defense in football when they were winning titles in the mid-1950s. So did the Green Bay Packers. Shoot, those guys were murder on defense, Hanner, Jordan, Nitschke, Davis and all the rest of them. The old Baltimore Colts, even with Johnny Unitas throwing all those passes, won two league championships because of their defense. By gosh, you take Gino Marchetti, the greatest defensive lineman I have ever seen; Art Donovan and Don Joyce and three great linebackers and you can win in any league.

Defense builds confidence in the quarterback. You go into a game and you are able to bide your time and program your ideas better because you know you are going to get the ball back. And with the Giants I have been fortunate in being helped by a great defensive unit.

I remember my first game with the Giants in 1961, the game against Los Angeles when I hurt my back. We were beating them pretty good, and when the defensive team came off the field, I heard Sam Huff yelling, "C'mon, gang, we got to bear down. We got to get 'em!" This was in the second quarter. I looked up at the scoreboard in the Coliseum. The Rams had three points. Still, the defense had such great pride they thought they were letting down.

When it comes to throwing a forward pass, I am no better, physically at least, than I was with San Francisco years ago. But playing with the Giants has provided me with a new lease on life. The defense has given me more shots at completing passes and gaining yardage. I get the ball a lot more than I did in San Francisco or

Baltimore. I could not have thrown 33 touchdown passes in 1962 and 36 the next year if the Giant defense hadn't kept knocking the other teams loose from the football and handing it over to me. Sometimes I had hardly sat down on the bench after one offensive drive when the defense would recover a fumble or intercept a pass or hold on fourth down, and I would be out there again throwing the ball all over the lot.

So many times we start a ball game and things go bad and we fall behind. But the defense goes in there, gets the ball, and we come back.

Against Baltimore in the opening game of the 1963 season, the Colts got ahead of us by 21–3 at halftime and we were plenty worried. But defensive coach Andy Robustelli stood up in the locker room and told us, "They ain't getting no more." They didn't, either!

CHAPTER TWENTY-NINE

THE BIG ONES

"TITTLE DOESN'T win the big ones!"

This is something I have lived with for a long time. They said it when I was with San Francisco in 1957 and we lost the western division playoff to Detroit after leading by 24–7 at halftime. They said it in 1961 and 1962 when the Green Bay Packers beat the Giants for the league championship. They said it again when we lost to the Chicago Bears for the 1963 title.

"Tittle doesn't win the big ones!"

Every time I opened a newspaper this thing hit me in the face like a red-dogging linebacker. Every time I turned on the radio, the words bounced off my ears like a lot of Gino Marchettis. It was hard to escape the stigma of failure. The Giants had lost the big one, and of course they had lost it because Y.A. Tittle does not come through in the championship games.

Losing the big ones has been a bitter experience for me:

I wait thirteen years to get into the championship game—and then I go 0-for-3 with the Giants. Green Bay is a great ball club in 1961, maybe the greatest I have ever seen. They beat us, 37–0, shut us out like a bunch of schoolboys. Charlie Conerly and I can't get our ball club on the scoreboard. It is bitter cold and the field is icy and we are never in the game. They jump us early and pour it on and we are all very embarrassed. I am angry with myself

251

because this is my first championship and I want very much to win it. It has been a long wait.

The next year we are better but the Packers are still the greatest team in pro football. They whip us, 16–7, on that terrible windy day at Yankee Stadium. They do not walk all over us this time. We give them a hell of a battle. Our defense is just great. But they win it. Again, I can't even get a touchdown. Our only score comes when Erich Barnes blocks a punt and Jim Collier recovers in the Green Bay end zone. It is no day for passing, and every time I throw the ball into that wind, I wonder where the dickens it will come down. Now it is 1963 and we are playing the Chicago Bears for the title and naturally everyone is saying the Bears will win the thing because Tittle sure as hell isn't going to cop it, not with his record in championship games. Unfortunately, they are right again, and Chicago wins the ball game, 14–10.

The championship losses to Green Bay were hard to take. But the defeat by Chicago was even worse. I do not want to minimize the talents of the Bears or their right to the title of champions. But I was firmly convinced we were going to win that football game in Wrigley Field. There was no doubt in my mind. When we lost, I was tremendously let down. Not only for myself but for my teammates and for our fans. It bothered me because I wanted . . . but, wait I shouldn't say it like that, "I wanted. . . ." The Giants wanted it, we all wanted it. This thing was not just me. It was a lot of guys who had battled through a real tough season, had come from two games behind to win the division. It was a great coaching staff. It was a fine organization from top to bottom that had turned out this winning ball club. We all had a stake in it.

Personally, I wanted the Chicago game so badly because the memory of the losing title games with Green Bay was still green. I wanted it, too, because I was damned sick and tired of hearing about how I could not win the big ones.

And then to play as poorly, as I played, I felt I had let down millions of people. My teammates too, because I have to think that my two screen passes the Bears intercepted led to the winning touchdowns.

I realize football is just a game. But defeat galls me. This one was harder for me to shake than the others. So many people were counting on me, and I was counting on myself. The loss to Green Bay back in 1961 had been tough but that was only my first year and we had run into a red-hot ball club. In the 1962 championship, well, the weather made a day for runners, and I'm a passer. In 1963 it was going to be different. . . .

The week leading up to the Chicago game was an experience I shall never forget. Frank Gifford started it all by interviewing me on a CBS television show. It was sort of a "This is Your Life Y. A. Tittle" bit. After it was over, everybody in New York City knew I lived in Eastchester. I don't have an unlisted phone, so they all looked up my number and started calling to wish me luck against Chicago. Boy, it was wild. That phone was ringing day and night for a week. One kid would be on the phone telling me how much he liked the Giants, and another would be knocking on the door for an autograph. Others would come up and say, "Go get 'em, Y.A., we're pulling for you." There were kids all over, on the front lawn, in the backyard.

One morning I found a parking ticket on my car. As I was taking it off the windshield wiper, I noticed writing on the back. It said, "Forget the ticket, Y.A., just beat the Bears." Even the East-chester Police Department was rooting for me—and the Giants. I got a Christmas package with "Beat the Bears, Y.A." written across the front of it in black crayon by the local post office guys. All kinds of things like that. Gosh, I have never had so many people behind me for a football game. My two boys, Pat and Mike, attend the Immaculate Conception school in Eastchester even though we are not Catholics. The nuns over there have been simply great to them. Sister Marguerite was saying the Rosary for me every day leading up to the game. The whole school was praying for the Giants.

Everywhere I turned that week, I knew the people of New York, my neighbors in Eastchester, everyone, wanted this game almost as badly as I wanted it. A lot of them were rooting for me, I guess, because they kind of figured I was getting close to the end of my career and that I would not have many more chances.

I think all the people who were in their middle or late thirties were on my side. Not all of them were Giant fans. But this was an older ball club with a lot of guys like Robustelli and Stroud and

253

Webster who had been around for a long time. They were symbols to guys in that age group who never played football. We had a big sentimental following all over the country. I could tell by the letters I received.

Everything seemed to have fallen into place. It had been a tough season with injuries, disappointments, comebacks and the good Lord seemed to say, "Now you fellows are going to get your reward."

I am not sure I should be saying all these things because I am certain the Chicago Bears had their tough times, their close ball games. While I was up in Eastchester getting ready to win this thing, they must have been saying, "This is ours."

But, by golly, I thought it was mine!

With everything happening that week, it was too hectic at home, so I took Minnette and the kids up to a little lodge in Connecticut for the Christmas holidays. I just had to get away from it all. I had to unwind. This was the place to do it. The owner closed the lodge for Christmas but filled the ice box and gave us the keys. They baked us a fruit cake, built a log fire in the fireplace and fixed us up a Christmas tree. It snowed the first night we were there. Minnette and I put the kids to bed and then went down and raided the ice box and sat in front of the fire. Boy, I want to tell you, that was the way to relax. The next morning they sent a chef over and he cooked us up a wonderful Christmas breakfast, ham, sausage, eggs, hot biscuits, the whole works. It was still snowing. It was wonderful. The rest seemed to do me a lot of good, and I went back to work feeling fine, eager to get to the big one.

Back at Yankee Stadium, we worked to prepare ourselves mentally for the Bears. Physically, there's not much you can do at the end of the season. You are either in shape in December or you aren't! We watched those films until we had them memorized. I am speaking only for the offense because I do not know what the defensive guys were doing all this time. I am sure, though, that their preparations were just as thorough. Everyone worked like hell.

On the basis of what had happened to me in the previous two championship games against Green Bay, I was more than a little concerned about the possibility of bad weather in Chicago. I wanted to cover every angle that I might have missed in the 1962 title game at Yankee Stadium when the weather helped to beat us. I talked to Sherman about different kinds of plays we could use on a frozen field, on a wet field, on a windy day, on a freezing day.

"Maybe this pattern would be better if it is slippery, Al," or "We can run the ball in here if the footing is bad."

How did we plan to beat the Bears? We really did not plan anything special. Again, there is no magic to pro football. You win with solid fundamentals. Rarely do you win with surprise plays and razzle-dazzle stuff. We went into Chicago with the same basic offense which had won for us.

We have a simplified game plan in New York. We hold down our number of running plays. We use basically one formation, for which we have been criticized. From a quarterback's standpoint our offense is great because simplicity is the keynote. Maybe this is just my personal viewpoint because I recognize that I am not a brain. I do not believe football necessarily has to have great minds. You can't plan everything. Eleven guys on defense just don't react on the field the way they do on a blackboard.

Allie Sherman's philosophy is that football is won by the side that makes the fewest mistakes. Do what you do best, even if it is simple, and minimize your mistakes. Let the other guy get fancy and beat himself.

The Chicago defense was supposed to be damned near invulnerable. I must say it was very good. It had to be good because we got only 10 points. The Bears had size and experience and they played an alert ball game. They intercepted five passes on me. But any defense can be had, I don't care who it belongs to, the Bears or anyone else. There isn't a defensive man in the league who can cover man-to-man on Shofner or someone like him if he does not have help in that secondary, and if the pass is thrown correctly. The 14-yard touchdown pass I threw to Gifford in the first quarter was an example of that. Frank worked on Chicago halfback Bennie McRae for a couple of plays and then told me in the huddle, "Y.A., I can beat him easy on a zig-out." So, I threw a zig-out off play action and Gifford easily beat him for the touchdown.

But just as I got rid of that ball, Larry Morris blitzed through and hit me across the left leg. I felt a twinge behind my knee.

255

When I went over to the sideline, I said to Sherman, "Damn, I got a pretty good lick on that one."

He asked what happened.

"Morris rolled into me just after I threw the ball," I said.

"Keep walking on it," he told me. "Move around a little and see how it feels."

I jogged up and down in front of the bench for a few minutes and when we got the ball again, I went back in. Now I could feel something in the knee, and I did not like it. I said to Kyle Rote, "I hope I can last this out. My knee is starting to get stiff."

I was okay until late in the second period. The Bears had scored after Morris intercepted one of my passes and ran 61 yards, but Don Chandler had kicked a field goal and so we were leading them, 10–7. We had the ball on the Chicago 32, first down and ten. I dropped back to pass to Gifford, but I stumbled on the hard ground and fell as I got rid of the ball. Morris was shooting in there again, and he dove into my bad knee. This time the pain shot clear up my leg. It was like somebody stuck a knife in the knee joint. I could hardly limp off the field. Now I knew it was bad.

They took me into the dressing room and Doc Sweeny and Dr. Anthony Pisani, an orthopedic man, looked me over.

"It's killing me," I told them. "I can't even bend it."

Dr. Pisani asked me exactly where the pain was and I pointed to the spot. He froze it with a spray and then gave me a needle. I don't know what it was, and at the time I didn't give a damn. I was too busy cussing my luck. Then the guys came in at halftime and I tried to look like it wasn't so bad because I did not want them to see me looking as bad as I felt.

I knew there was concern about my condition. No pro club can lose its regular quarterback in a championship game and not feel his loss and my injury easily could have created a morale problem. Glynn Griffing was our only other quarterback, and a good one. But he was only a rookie of 22. It was to be a tough spot. Before the team filed out for the second half, I said to the guys, "I don't know if I can play on this damned thing. But even if I can't, I am convinced we can whip these guys. We're ahead now. We can stay there."

Anyway, out we go for the second half and my knee is shot full of novocain and it is heavily taped. I can walk but I don't know what else I can do. I feel like I have a wooden leg.

I am throwing some warm-up passes behind the bench and Sherman asks me, "How does it feel, Yat? What do you think? I don't want you to take any chances unless you are sure you can make it."

I did not know what to say to him. Injuries are funny things. Football is an emotional game and sometimes you can do amazing things when you are hurt. I remember once I went into a game with two sprained ankles. I could barely walk into the huddle. But once I got under that center and said, "Ready, set . . ." well, boy I was cured on the spot. In 1953 I played a ball game with a broken cheek and completed 29 passes. Then there was the time I came in for the Forty-Niners with a broken hand and won the game. With San Francisco in 1957 I pulled a hamstring muscle and was supposed to be out for three weeks. But John Brodie went bad in the first half against Green Bay and Red Hickey said to me, "Can you play, Tittle?" Now what does a ballplayer say in a spot like this? I never heard one say "no." So I tried. I got out there on the field and threw a couple of touchdown passes and we won the ball game, 27–20.

So this was not the first time a coach had asked me how I felt. I said to Sherman, "It could be worse, Al, let me give it a whirl." A couple of warm-up passes told me I was severely handicapped. I couldn't drop straight back to pass; I had to back-pedal, which is awkward and a lot slower. But on our first series I came up against a third and seven situation and now, by golly, I had to throw. I called a Green Bay special—one of our favorite patterns—and dropped back to throw to Morrison in the flat. Joe made a first down. Hot damn, maybe I can do it after all, I thought.

But a minute later I knew it wasn't going to be that simple. On the next play I overshot Gifford on a sideline square-out pattern. He was wide open waiting for the ball. But I could not plant on my front knee, the left one, and my pass was late. The next time I threw, they intercepted a pass intended for Shofner. Later that period, I tried a screen pass to the right and Ed O'Bradovich, the Bears' defensive end, intercepted it and ran it down near our goal-

257

line. Bill Wade scored on a short plunge making the score, 14–10, Chicago.

I kept trying but I was not maneuverable. I could not get back away from the center. I like to fly back there, plant myself, find my receiver, and get rid of the damned ball. Especially when I am playing a team like the Chicago Bears, who red-dog the daylights out of a quarterback. I want to throw the type pass where I can hit that seven-yard drop, get the guy open, and if he is not open, throw it away. I am not going to have time for anything else. They are going to be right on top of me, Williams, Jones, O'Bradovich and the rest of them. Against the Bears, I figure I am going to have some touchdown passes and some good plays but it is probably going to be something like fifty percent. In other words, they are going to get me half the time. I can't sit back there and look around for my receivers. I am going to drop back and throw that quick turn-in pass or a flare-in. But I am going to do it quick, right now, before I get clobbered.

I was still putting the ball in the air when the game ended. But it was no use. The Bears knew I had to throw and they were dropping everyone but George Halas into the secondary to cover my receivers. They knew darn well that because of my knee, I couldn't put any mustard on my passes. The ball was wobbling end over end. I felt so futile, and I couldn't do a thing about it.

The game ended when Richie Petitbon intercepted a pass in the end zone. I had been aiming it at Gifford but it never got there.

I had lost another "big one."

I felt as low as at any time in my career. No defeat had ever been as hard to take. In the dressing room I eased my aching frame onto a stool and cried. Yes, I bawled like a baby. So did Gifford, whose locker was next to mine. Two grown men, veterans of a lot of years in pro football, and we were blubbering because we had lost a ball game. As I thawed out, the defeat assumed even more bitter proportions. I pounded my fists and said aloud: "Damn it . . . Why did it have to happen today? Why did I have to get hurt? Why? Dammit, why?"

Glynn Griffing was there with Gifford and me. He stared at us. I don't think he had ever seen veteran pros in tears. He could not have known how we felt. For Griffing there were a lot of tomorrows; for Gifford and me it was different. Perhaps our tomorrow was today.

Sherman walked over to us. He showed the strain of losing the championship. He put his arm on my shoulder and whispered, "Y.A., you're still the greatest. We had them today. You had them, Y.A. It's not your fault. I know how much you wanted this one. I wanted it too. But there will be other chances—for you and me."

Allie walked over and touched Gifford on the shoulder. Frank was still leaning against the locker with his face to the wall. His body was shaking and I knew he was terribly upset. The coach said something to Frank. Then Sherman shook Griffing's hand and said, "I am proud of you, boy. You did a great job. They pressured you, but you stayed in there. We will be back, don't worry about that."

It had been a sorry day all around for us. I had not been the only casualty. We lost a whole bunch of our regulars. Tom Scott broke his arm in the first period. In the second quarter Phil King went out with a sprained ankle. Then Bookie Bolin was injured. We were half a team at the end and still they only beat us by four.

They only beat us by four, but four is as good as forty when the championship is on the line. All a lot of people will remember anyhow, I thought, is that "Tittle never wins the big one."

Maybe so, but I contend there were a lot of big ones on the way to Wrigley Field in 1963. What could be bigger than the second Cleveland game when we were behind by two games with half the season gone? Or the last one of the year against Pittsburgh, when it was "all or nothing?" Or, by gosh, even the Dallas game when they had us by fourteen at the half and Sherman told us in the locker room, "This is it, the end, unless you come back." And we came back to whip them in the last five minutes.

If we had not won these ball games, the big one in Chicago never would have been played, at least not by the New York Giants.

Cleveland was a great football team at the start of the 1963 season. The Browns won their first six in a row, including a 35–24 shellacking of the Giants, and they were two games ahead when we went out to Cleveland to play them on October 27th. The season was all over for us if we did not beat them that day, and up to that time nobody had been able to do this. Jimmy Brown, the greatest running back I have ever seen, was trampling everybody in the league. Frank Ryan had given the Cleveland club a fine job at quarterback. Boy, they were hot. So there we were in front of 84,213 fans, the biggest crowd in Cleveland history, and it was win or else. The Browns had a chance to up their seasonal record to 7–0 with a victory. If that happened, well, the rest of the clubs in the eastern division could forget it.

But Cleveland did not go 7–0. We whipped them by 33–6. It was the greatest game I have ever played in. It was great from an offensive standpoint and great from a defensive standpoint. It was a game of flawless execution by every man on the Giants' team. I never saw anything like it. It was the kind of game coaches dream about when they put those Xs and Os up there on the blackboard. No one made a wrong move. No one blew an assignment. Boy, it was something.

Actually, we won the Cleveland game on Wednesday back at Yankee Stadium. That is when Allie Sherman told me, "Y.A., we are going to control the football Sunday and we are going to beat them on defense. I think we have found a way to stop this club."

There was a question in my mind that bothered me: "How the hell are we going to stop them? They ran all over us the first time around?"

Up to that point, we had been a winning football team. But we had been winning mostly with our offense. We were scoring a lot of points—37 a game against Baltimore, Philadelphia and Dallas, 24 against Washington and 24 in a losing cause against the Browns. Defensively it was another story. We had not been outstanding. Our defensive ball club was a little older than most and sometimes it was slow getting started.

Sherman believed in a balanced game, that is, running the ball, holding it, making the other club respect you so your quarterback could open up with the pass when the time was right. This was fine. But I was always afraid of staying on the ground during the early part of the season. I was skeptical about grinding it out because I felt we had to score a lot of points, and score them early. Otherwise, the defense might not do it for us. Take the Dallas game. We go ahead of them in the first five minutes and, they tie it up. We go in front again and then Eddie LeBaron throws a

75-yard bomb to Frank Clarke for another Dallas touchdown. Every time we score, they score. No matter how hard we work at getting points, they are right there with us.

When Sherman told me of his plan to control the ball on Cleveland and to stop them defensively, I was not so sure this was the right approach. They had whipped us pretty good a couple of weeks before, and I thought the only way to win was to go out there and shoot for the points. Throw the damned ball, as Cecil Isbell would say.

"Allie," I said, "I am going to be truthful and tell you I am afraid to go out and run the ball at them. I do not want to make a couple of first downs running and then miss one and have to kick the ball over to them. If Brown gets his hands on the thing, we will be in trouble."

"Don't worry," he said. "Just do what I say. The defense will stop them this time. We have made some changes and Robustelli and his boys go for them. They will get the job done."

I never asked what defensive changes had been made. This was not my concern. But from the way Sherman spoke, I gained confidence. He sounded like beating Cleveland would be a cinch. He told me we would go out there and run at them right from the start. He said we would control the ball. When we threw it, we would throw it short, get rid of it fast. In the first Cleveland game at the Stadium, the Browns had given me a bad time with their pass rush. I was calling long patterns and I was not keeping enough backs in to block for me. Paul Wiggin and Bob Gain and Bill Glass worked me over pretty good that day.

But Sherman was not going to make the same mistake twice. His preparations for the Browns were thorough. And he made us believe in his strategy.

It happened just the way he said it would. Our defense was great, overpowering. Frank Ryan completed *one* of nine passes, and it was for a six-yard loss. Jimmy Brown was stopped in his tracks. He got his hands on the ball only nine times, and then he was held to 40 yards. We took charge of Cleveland right away, shattered their confidence—and their six-game winning streak. When it was over, the Browns had run 38 offensive plays. We had run 78!

261

I don't remember everything about the game, but I do recall the opening minutes when our defense beat Cleveland right into the ground. The first time Jimmy Brown carried, four guys clobbered him. He fumbled and Sam Huff recovered. Don Chandler kicked a field goal and we were up by 3–0. The next time Cleveland got the football, Ryan tried to pass. Jimmy Patton picked off his first throw and ran it back to the Browns' 29. They seemed demoralized. I took advantage of this condition by throwing one of my few long passes of the day, a 23-yard scoring shot to Del Shofner. It was 10–0 with less than three minutes gone. I felt that the Browns already were a beaten ball club.

Sherman's game plan worked to perfection. I threw 33 passes and completed 22. But for the most part I kept them short. The Browns played a zone type of pass defense, so I threw the ball into the holes—quick turn-in passes to Shofner, slants to Joe Walton and square-outs to Aaron Thomas. I got rid of the ball in a hurry and Cleveland's rush-line did not get to me as it had two weeks earlier.

We also controlled the ball on the ground. We ran it right at them. Quick traps and draws with Webster and McElhenny chewing out those five and six-yard gains all day.

Sherman's preparation was really something. We had been told that whenever Cleveland went into a weakside odd-man line on defense it meant they were going to red-dog. "Don't run against that formation," Sherman said. "Throw the ball—and throw it in a hurry." When I saw the Browns in that weakside odd-man line, I flipped a sideline or a turn-in pass to Shofner. It was a first down every time. This was a confidence builder, by golly—to know that everything was falling into place just like they told us it would.

The key to the whole thing was the ability of our defense to hold Jimmy Brown. He is Cleveland's big gun. If he is contained, they are in big trouble. Jimmy ran wild against us in New York but in Cleveland the defense did a job on him. The first time he carried, he was hit so hard he lost the ball. But the Browns were stubborn. After we went ahead, 10–0, they tried to re-establish their running attack. Brown went around the left side and Scott and Huff stopped him after two yards. They really belted him too. He got up kind of slow. Then Jimmy tried the middle. He got five but LoVetere and Tom Scott took a lot out of him on the tackle. On third down, Ryan called Brown's number and he tried right tackle. Dick Modzelewski and Jim Katcavage cut him down for a yard gain. This was the turning point of the ball game to my way of thinking. The Browns had thrown their Sunday punch and we had taken all the steam out of it. Brown could not run against the Giant line, inside or outside. Ryan could not throw passes against the secondary. Cleveland had no way to move the football. It was all over four minutes into the opening period.

It was the perfect game. I hope I see another one like it, but I doubt it. This one was a once in a lifetime job.

There was no bigger game for the Giants than the last one against the Pittsburgh Steelers at Yankee Stadium on a cold, windy December afternoon. After a long season, we came to the end of the line with everything riding on this one ball game. We had to win it. Talk about your pressure! Man, you could feel it in the air. It was winner-take-all. We went into the game with a record of ten wins and three losses. Pittsburgh had seven wins, three losses and three ties. We had won three more ball games than the Steelers but because of a screwy league ruling on tie games, they could take the eastern championship by beating us. A win would put them at .727 and us at .714. It did not seem right then and it still doesn't. I am glad we whipped them, 33–17, because there was no doubt as to which was the best team in the division in 1963.

This was another great planning effort by Sherman and his staff. They got us ready psychologically as well as physically. In the first game with Pittsburgh, they had shut us out, 33–0. This thing had been with us all year and most of the guys had a complex. They wanted to get even in the worst way. But Sherman fought this sort of an attitude.

"We are not going out there like a bunch of schoolboys to get revenge," he warned. "We are going to approach this game like we had never seen the Pittsburgh Steelers. What happened in that first game is of no importance. We are going to play them like we play every other team. And we are going to beat them, but without any of this rah-rah about getting even."

Getting ready for the showdown, I was convinced we were a better football team than the Steelers. But they had a lot going for them, not the least of which was that licking they gave us in Pittsburgh. They had come a long way by scratching out a win here, a tie there. We had scratched some, too, but at least we had been up there with Cleveland and St. Louis most of the year. The Steelers had been more or less country cousins. While we were taking the lead and then losing it, Pittsburgh was on the outside, close but not really in the picture. Now, all of a sudden, they were playing us for the whole thing.

One thing we knew: the Steelers would be coming at us with everything. It would be a hell-bent effort because they had it all to gain.

Sherman's plan was not to let them scramble us in the beginning. They figured to be fired up. This was their first chance for a title in a long time and they would be coming onto that field like a bunch of wild men. Allie did not want us stampeded by them. "We play our game and we stay with it and we let them do all the scrambling," he said.

At first, I thought maybe we could go out there and get off a big play and bust their bubble and run the score up on them right away. We had done it to a lot of other clubs that year. But Sherman told me it might work the other way too. "Give these guys one break," he cautioned, "and they can run us right out of our own ballpark. We'll let them run out of adrenalin first."

So we approached the game along those lines. We studied the films of our win over Cleveland. We saw the ball control, the defense, the solid execution.

The Steelers came clawing and scrapping, which is the way they always play against us. But we stuck to Sherman's game plan. We controlled the football and scored three times for a 16–3 halftime lead. Then in the third period Frank Gifford made one of the finest catches I have ever seen to put the game on ice. On first down, the Steelers rushed me so hard that my pass to Walton fell incomplete. Then Phil King got only two yards into the line. With third and eight, we were in danger of stalling. Gifford had told me earlier that Pittsburgh halfback Glenn Glass was playing him to the outside during the first half. "He's worrying about the down-and-out," Giff said. So I called a pattern that sent Frank down and in. He made a fake to the outside and Glass crossed his legs to go with him. At that second, Gifford broke to the inside. I threw hard into the wind but the pass was low. It was around Gifford's knees. On the dead run he reached down with *one* hand, and somehow grabbed the ball. It was a 30-yard gain. I will never know how Giff caught that ball. It was unbelievable. I threw to Frank again on the next play and he went all the way to the Pittsburgh 22. Then a touchdown pass to Joe Morrison gave us the points we needed to win the eastern championship.

Sure I was disappointed two weeks later when the Bears beat us for the title. Nevertheless the 1963 season provided some of the top thrills of my career, especially those "must" victories over Cleveland and Pittsburgh.

Actually, I guess I was lucky to be playing football in 1963. My career came mighty close to being ended in the first game of the season. In the fourth period of our game against the Baltimore Colts I went back to pass but no one was open. I scrambled around and ran for the Baltimore goal-line, about ten yards away. I just made it into the corner of the end zone by diving. But two tacklers hit me from opposite sides and drove me into the ground. I felt a sharp pain in my shoulder and I lost my breath. I thought at first it was a temporary loss of breath, but it got worse and they took me out of the game. Ralph Guglielmi finished up and we beat Baltimore, 37–28, after at one time trailing the Colts by three touchdowns. It was a hell of a start for the year, a comeback like that, but my start was less auspicious. On the train back to New York, I still could not get my breath. It was an awful feeling.

Doc Sweeny took me to St. Elizabeth's Hospital that night. They shot a lot of X-rays but did not tell me anything. I stayed in the hospital until Wednesday. I was starting to breathe better, so they let me out. I hopped a cab and went right to Yankee Stadium. Wednesday is first real day of practice during the season and I wanted to be there when Sherman blew the whistle. But Allie had other ideas. "No you don't Y.A.," he said. "You can hang around and watch but I can't let you work."

"But I feel great," I protested.

"Shoot for Friday," Allie said. "We'll see how you shape up by then."

So I stood around Wednesday and I stood around Thursday. I

265

was waiting for Friday because I really was going to show him I was ready. My legs were a bit wobbly from being in the hospital for three days. But otherwise I felt fine. I was anxious to face the Steelers on Sunday and, while I did not relish missing my turn in practice, I decided I could sacrifice it so Sherman would give me a shot on Friday.

But when Friday arrived, Allie said, "There's no use rushing this thing today, Y.A. Rest a little more and you can work tomorrow."

Damn, it was tough to miss all that quarterbacking the week of a big game. But I had no choice. I did not understand, however, why getting the wind knocked out of me the week before should have everybody so concerned. Hell, I had played with worse things than that all my life. But Saturday afternoon I was out there. I ran the club. I threw some passes. I felt great.

That afternoon we flew into Pittsburgh and I was ready for the Steelers. I could hear a little gurgling sound in my chest when I ran, but it did not worry me. I was okay. My legs had come back and my arm was strong.

Sunday morning I was getting taped by Johnny Johnson, one of our trainers, in the hotel when word came that Sherman wanted to see me. This was about 10:30. So I went up to Allie's room and he said, "Y.A., you are not going to play today."

"Not play!" I almost shouted. "What the hell do you mean, 'not play'?"

"Exactly what I said. You can't play. The doctors have decided you should not play."

"For Pete's sake, Allie, I have played with a lot worse things than this in my time."

I was being held out of an important game because I had had the wind knocked out of me the week before. It did not make much sense to me. I really tried a selling job. But Sherman would not budge. I said, "Well, I won't accept it, Allie. I have just got to play today. If you don't let me play, I swear I'll never tell you or anyone else when I get hurt again."

"Listen," he interrupted, "this is a long season. One game isn't going to make that much difference. We may lose it, but I would rather lose the game than lose you for another few weeks."

266

This was the same story he had given me three years before when I had my bad back in training camp. "We need you more in December than in August." That was the bit in 1961.

I could not buy this and I asked Sherman to get a doctor up there. He called Dr. Pisani. Only then did I learn what it was all about:

"You have a partially collapsed lung," said Pisani.

A collapsed lung! That just about knocked the wind out of me again. I could hardly believe it.

Pisani drew me a diagram to show how the lung had been collapsed by the blow in Baltimore, and how it had started to fill out again during the week.

"It has improved," he said, "but there is no use taking a chance by playing today. You could get through the game without a scratch. But you could get hit there again and wind up with a totally collapsed lung."

"Would that kill me, Doc?" I asked.

"No," he replied, "but it sure as heck would finish your football playing."

"But I feel great now," I said. "My arm is great. I think I could play some today."

"Sure you could," he said. "But that's up to Allie here."

This is where Sherman exercised a great deal of control. Things went bad that afternoon and the Steelers were beating us. Guglielmi was having a terrible time of it and things were getting worse. Still, we were only ten points behind in the last period. Two touchdowns would pull it out for us. Allie could have given in to the temptation to let me in there to throw a few, maybe from a shotgun formation where I could get rid of the ball and then duck the Steeler pass-rushers without getting hit. Pisani had said I could play if Sherman wanted to take the risk. I sure as hell was anxious to play. But Allie did not see it that way. Even though his ball club was being humiliated, 31–0, he sat me down.

Sherman was the National Football League's Coach of the Year in 1961, and he won the honor again in 1962. But in my book, he did his greatest job of coaching in 1963. Starting with my situation in Pittsburgh, he spent the whole season juggling an injured ball club, an old ball club, a bunch of guys who were held together by his brains—and two miles of adhesive tape. He was like a guy walking a high wire on a windy day. But he walked it all the way from 31–0 in Pittsburgh to the championship game in Chicago. We all fell off that day. . . .

The Bears beat us, and around the league they started saying again, "Tittle doesn't win the big ones." Maybe so, but all I know is that the guys who sing this tune are usually home watching the "big ones" on television. Thanks to Allie Sherman and a great Giant team, I play in them.

CHAPTER THIRTY

FATHER IS SUPERSTITIOUS

IT IS HIGHLY unlikely that I shall ever acquire an inflated opinion of myself around the Tittle household.

My wife Minnette is my severest critic. My two boys, Pat and Mike, are Del Shofner fans. And my daughter Diane, now 14, has discovered that rock 'n' roll records and pizza are even more fun than dads—or old quarterbacks.

All of which is natural, I guess, and I am kind of glad it is this way. I like to think my family is average. That's what Minnette and I strive for. We want the Tittles to be like the folks next door in our seasonal Eastchester home or in Atherton, where we live the rest of the year.

It is not always simple to keep things in their proper perspective when you are a public figure. But Minnette does a wonderful job with the kids—and with old Y.A., too. She is the level-headed one in our family. She keeps things on an even keel no matter what happens. I'm fortunate to have someone like her at my side. She is a real football wife. The game has been her life almost as much as it's been mine. I was a football player at Marshall Junior High when we first met at the annual Christmas dance where our parents matched us up. Today, 25 years later, I'm still at it.

Minnette has shared my roller-coaster ride all the way, taking the good with the bad. Baton Rouge, Baltimore, San Francisco and the adjustment to a new life with the Giants.

As Mrs. Tittle, Minnette has suffered her share of frustrations. Times were not always as good as they have been in New York. There were lean, hard years with the Forty-Niners, and she felt the sting of public criticism which was aimed at me. She heard the mean whispers around the neighborhood, and she read the biting stories in the press.

It wasn't easy for her to overlook this sort of thing. But she never has openly defended me in public because I never have wanted her to. But I know that many things have deeply affected her along the way from Marshall to Yankee Stadium.

Although Minnette is not well-versed in football techniques, she is a keen observer of the game, and she never hesitates to tell me when she thinks I have played poorly. I will walk out of Yankee Stadium after a bad game and get into the car for the drive up to Eastchester. At first the conversation will be very polite and then I will say, "Okay, Minnette, let's have it. Tell me what's bothering you."

And then she will say, "How can you be so poor, YA.? How could you do this, or how could you do that? You were just awful out there today."

Minnette doesn't pull any punches; she really lets me have it. If I have had a pass intercepted at a crucial point in the game, she asks, "Why did you throw the ball to that fellow? Why, it went right into his hands. That was terrible."

Usually, I don't like to talk about a bad ball game. But that doesn't deter Minnette. She demands an explanation of everything that happened. She won't let me forget the game until we have talked it over. Actually, I guess this is good for me. It gives me an opportunity to get things off my chest. But we never take the ball game home with us. We discuss it in the car or at dinner and Minnette criticizes the hell out of me. But when we walk through that front door, the game stays outside.

Minnette rarely talks football with anyone, especially the other wives. I don't want her to. Most of the trouble between pro football players start with the wives. They get together at a coffee klatch or something and they gossip and chatter and all of a sudden there's a quarrel. It's been that way on every club I ever played for, so I just tell Minnette to keep out of those post-game discussions among the women.

In addition to being my severest critic, Minnette naturally is my biggest fan. She saves clippings and trophies and plaques, and I like to believe she is proud of what I have accomplished in professional football. But still she is careful not to let me lose sight of the real values in life.

Coming to the Giants was the greatest thing that ever happened to me. And living in New York six months a year has opened a new life for Minnette and the children. They love the east. As Texans who have lived in California, everything in New York is different and exciting: the changing seasons, the bright lights, the theaters, the big restaurants. We have had a chance to see things we never saw before, and to visit places we had only read about. We have seen our first real snow and, believe it or not, this has been a big thrill. I know most people in the east don't particularly care for snow. But we certainly enjoy it. I come home from Yankee Stadium in the evening and Minnette and I go for a walk while everyone else seems to be inside. We walk down to the diner and have coffee. We enjoy the stillness and beauty of snowy nights in New York. Of course in December we fly back to California and so we miss much of the bad weather. This helps. We are not in the snow all year, just long enough to enjoy the change. Maybe if I had to drive to work in it for three or four months, I might feel differently.

It has been almost like a vacation for us in New York, and being with a winning team has helped too.

Although our real home is in Atherton, Diane, Pat and Mike have no trouble making the change to New York every fall. We have lived in the same house in Eastchester for the past two years. When we drive up to the door every September, the kids hop out of the car, run over to a neighbor's house and yell, "Hey, we're back!" Just like that, like they had never been away. They have their eastern friends; they know their way around; they know where to get their milk shakes.

I often have been asked why I named my boys Pat and Mike. As you might guess, there's a story to it. After suffering through school with a name like Yelberton Abraham Tittle, Junior, I promised myself that if I ever had sons of my own I would never saddle them

271

with fancy names. I kept that promise. I had them christened Pat and Mike—not Patrick nor Michael, just plain Pat and Mike. There couldn't be much simpler names than those. Trouble is, everyone thinks they are Irish when really we are Scotch and English.

Mike, who is twelve, and Pat, who is eleven, are average kids in most respects. They are proud of their old man, I guess, but they are even more interested in playing ball themselves. I like it this way. I want them to play everything, like I did, and to find their own game. Right now they are young and they like all sports. Like all kids, ours occasionally have problems. But much of the time these have been Minnette's problems because I've been away playing football six months a year since the day we were married. Minnette has done a good job on all of us. As for the children, I am as proud of them as any father would be. The boys are sometimes too casual about their school work, and sometimes they get rambunctious. But basically they are good boys.

I don't think being the sons of Y.A. Tittle has made them different than the other kids around the neighborhood. Mike is cocky but I don't think it's because I am a professional football player. It's just his nature. He's an extrovert. He would be this way no matter what his father did.

Mike is always ribbing Minnette. He will get into a taxi with her and ask out loud, "Mommy, tell me again, how did daddy get the name Y.A. Tittle?" Of course, the cab driver turns around and stares at Minnette and she gets very embarrassed and tells Mike to hush up. He just loves to do things like that. He's a real needler.

Pat is different. He's the quiet one, and more of a homebody. He comes home on the school bus, hangs around the house and does little chores for his mother. Meanwhile, Mike is out somewhere getting into mischief. But all in all, the two boys get along well together.

Sometimes I have the feeling neither of them is overly impressed with my achievements. One day I was standing near an open window and the kids were out back playing football. A big argument started, and I heard Mike say, "No, I hollered first." And then Pat's voice, "No sir, I hollered first."

"Like fun," said Mike. "I hollered first. I get to be Del Shofner. You're Y.A. Tittle."

"Okay," grumbled Pat, "but only for a while. Then *you* have to be Tittle."

Sportscaster Howard Cossell, a close friend, refers to me as a "Nineteenth Century father" because he considers me a strict disciplinarian. Maybe I am, too. But gosh darn it, I want my kids to be well-mannered and well thought of, and if it means clamping down on them once in a while, well, that's what I'm going to do.

I don't have to play the stern parent with Diane much anymore because now she is quite a grown-up young lady. But I do worry about her when she goes to dances and parties and things like that. I guess I am no different than other fathers in this respect. Sometimes, though, I worry because my concern for Diane leads to differences of opinion with Minnette.

I remember one day when our daughter was supposed to go to a pizza place with some friends, and then over to a boy's house to dance. It was all very proper, Minnette told me. The boy's mother would be there and Diane would be home early. But I still didn't like the looks of it.

"I'll take the four of them for pizza," I declared. "I don't have anything to do this afternoon anyway."

"Nonsense," she protested. "They don't want *you* along!"

"What do you mean they don't want me along?" I asked indignantly. "After all, I *am* her father."

"But the youngsters have a date, Y.A., and you would just be in the way. Why, you would embarrass Diane to tears. It just isn't done."

I was not about to be detoured that easily. "Well, what's this about going to a kid's house?" I demanded.

"It's perfectly all right," Minnette said. "His mother will be there. I just spoke to her on the phone."

I still didn't like this business but I had to back off and agree, reluctantly, to Diane's going. Later, Minnette and I went to Howard Cossell's home for dinner and I heard Minnette say to Howard's wife, "With Y.A. as her father, the only thing left for Diane is to become a nun."

For the most part, though, Minnette and I have a pretty good understanding on family matters. She even tolerates my football player's superstitions.

I wouldn't say that I am really superstitious, I mean superstitious to the point where I am afraid to walk under a ladder or worry if a black cat walks in front of me, or maybe get a little upset because it's Friday the 13th. I don't have an unlucky number or a favorite color and I don't throw salt over my shoulder. My superstition takes the form of not wanting to change anything that has worked for me, not wanting to alter a successful pattern by doing something different. I think most ballplayers are this way. Everybody kids me because I still wear old high-top football shoes that look like something Red Grange might have owned over thirty years ago. But I always have played well in those old cleats and I never have had any ankle trouble. So, I don't see any reason to stop wearing them now. The same goes for my shoulder pads. They are too small and too old. They are held together by adhesive tape. They might be the shoulder pads Joe Magrill gave me at Marshall Junior High. But gosh darn it, I have thrown a lot of touchdown passes in those pads, and I intend to wear them as long as I play football.

Football players are no different than any other professional athletes. They get on a hot streak and they don't want to change a thing, not even their socks, as long as they keep winning.

Sometimes these situations sneak up on you before you're even aware they are happening. Like two years ago when the Giants went on the road for four straight games at the start of the season. Getting on the bus in front of the hotel the first Sunday morning, I went to the back and sat in the last seat on the right. Joe Morrison was across from me in the lefthand corner of the bus. Well, we won the ball game easy and so the following week we climbed right back into the same seats again on the way to the ballpark. Another win! The third week, the guys who got on the bus first saved the two back seats for Morrison and me. It was sort of automatic. No one made a point of it, but it was understood that we would sit there because we had sat there the first two weeks and we had won both times. That afternoon we made it three straight. Boy, we were hot! Maybe it wasn't entirely because of the lucky seats, but Joe and I sure weren't about to change anything. We knew we had something good going for us. Things got so nutty on that damned bus that even Allie Sherman, the coach, had to sit in a certain seat and Alex Webster right in front of him. And when

274

we got off the bus, well, we got off in the same order every-time.

The fourth Sunday I got on the bus, walked to the rear and, to my surprise, found Jack Mara, our owner, sitting in Y.A. Tittle's lucky seat. A sense of panic seized me. What to do? I felt Jack was breaking our winning pattern. But, hell, he owns the ball club and who am I to put him out of a seat on the Giants' bus?

So, I found myself another seat—and we lost the ball game!

The next week Mr. Mara was about to take my seat again when all of a sudden everybody starts hollering. "Hey, that's Y.A.'s seat. You can't sit there."

Jack was kind of startled, I think. But he didn't put up much of a fight. He moved down the aisle and I hopped into my lucky spot for the ride to the stadium. We won that day.

I really don't want this to sound like I am some kind of a nut. All I want to say is that I believe a pro football player must pay a price in his preparation for a game. The coaches prepare you physically and mentally, but psychologically you have to get your-self ready. I get ready by doing things the same way and at the same time, by sticking close to a set routine. If things go wrong, I don't want to have to blame anyone or anything but myself. In other words, I don't want a crutch or an alibi. I don't want to have to say, "Shoot, if I hadn't broken curfew, I might have hit Shofner with that pass today." Or maybe, "Damn it, why did I watch Lawrence Welk last night instead of Gunsmoke?"

This inclination to adhere to a pattern of sameness has almost become an obsession with me.

Halfway through 1961 my first season with New York, Allie Sherman decided to try something different with the team during a long home stand. We had just lost a ball game to Dallas and things were not going well. So instead of letting us go home after the Saturday morning practice, he put us on a bus and took us downtown to the Hotel Roosevelt. The idea was to keep us there as a unit until game time Sunday. That's how we do it when we are traveling and, frankly, we play a hell of a lot better on the road than we do at Yankee Stadium.

Well, this kind of upset my usual routine but I didn't mind too much because we had lost the previous Sunday anyway. It's only when ballplayers are winning that they dislike changing the pattern—or their socks.

After checking into the hotel that first Saturday, Shofner, Morrison and myself went looking for a place to get a bite to eat. We walked into this one spot but the guy said he had no sandwiches because it was after four o'clock.

"What have you got?"

"There are some cold meatballs left over from lunch," he answered.

"Okay, some meatball sandwiches and a couple of beers."

I didn't particularly care for this menu. Neither did the others. But we were all so hungry we ate the meatballs anyway.

The next day we murdered the Washington Redskins by 53–0!

Boy, you have got to believe that we were back for meatball sandwiches the following Saturday, same time, same place. For fifty-three points a game, I'd eat horse meat.

Next, we whipped the Philadelphia Eagles, 38–21, and all of a sudden our Saturday afternoon group began to get bigger. By this time a lot of the other Giants were in there eating those meatball sandwiches alongside of Shofner, Morrison and myself. Well, we kept winning big. We beat Pittsburgh, 42–21, and then took Cleveland apart, 37–21. We rang up 170 points in four games.

And the more we won, the more meatball sandwiches we ate on Saturday. At the end of that hot streak almost everybody on the club was saying, "Let's go over and have a meatball sandwich." A lot of the younger guys started going to Leone's for real Italian meatballs.

Now this is what I mean by being superstitious. I just wouldn't feel right if I missed that regular Saturday afternoon ritual. If we lost the game the next day, I probably would say to myself, "It's your own fault, Y.A. You didn't have your meatball sandwich."

There are a number of things we do the same way on Saturday when we are at the Roosevelt. In the evening, Shofner and I go over to Kenny's Steak Pub with Huff and Chandler and a few of the others. Then we go back to the hotel and watch Gunsmoke and shoot the breeze for a while before going to bed. Every Saturday is the same, or at least we want it to be the same. I have been with a championship ball club for three straight years and I don't want to tempt the fates by changing my habits now. I know a good thing when I see it, superstitious or not.

I mention this here because it may help clear up a point if some of the San Francisco ballplayers read this chapter. The Forty-Niners came to New York in 1963 to play the Giants and naturally some of my former teammates called me at the hotel and asked me to have dinner with them.

"Can't make it," I lied.

"Why not, Yat?"

"Can't. I've got something else to do. I'm sorry. Give the rest of the gang my regards. I'll see you at the Stadium tomorrow."

Boy, I could almost hear them sizzle over the wire. They were mad. I could hear them saying, "Well, what do you know, old Y.A. has gone big-time on us since he came to New York."

In a way, I couldn't blame them. I could have gone over and spent a few minutes with them for old time's sake. But I just didn't want to. It is my personal belief that a ballplayer has no business hanging around with ex-teammates the night before a big game. I was friendly with all the San Francisco guys, and I hope they still consider me their friend. But I felt it would put additional pressure on me, especially as the Giants' quarterback, to go down there and sit around and drink coffee with them and have the West Coast sportswriters come up and say, "Nice to see you guys sitting together. Think you can whip your old ball club tomorrow, Y.A.?"

All this kind of stuff puts more of a mental burden on a fellow, especially a guy like me who is usually psyched up anyway. I just don't care to fraternize with opponents the night before a game. I would feel the same way about Shofner and Morrison and the other Giants if I were traded to another club tomorrow.

Besides, in the case of the Forty-Niners, it would have meant missing Gunsmoke on television that night. I would not have liked that. Neither would Shofner have appreciated my interrupting our winning Saturday routine.

I hope this explanation squares me with my old San Francisco buddies.

And I also hope this book, I PASS, has squared me with everyone who has taken the time to read the story of an old bald-headed quarterback.

CHAPTER THIRTY-ONE

DONE, FINISHED...
AND A NEW BEGINNING

AFTER THREE straight championship years, the New York Giants fell to last place in 1964. The Giants were a bad football team that year—a ball club that won only two games. And I was a bad quarterback. So bad, in fact, that I knew it was time to quit.

I will say, though—and in this respect I guess I'm no different than any other ballplayer who decides to "hang it up"—that to this day, I do not feel I was physically washed up despite the awful showing I made in 1964. To the very end, I felt I could throw the football as well as ever.

But there are other signs for an athlete—subtle, intangible signs. Sometimes a guy can't put his finger on them but they are there just the same, and he can sense them.

And so, one cold December afternoon as I knelt on the sideline at Yankee Stadium watching the Giants take another licking, it dawned on me that it was all over. "Y.A.," I said to myself, "it's time to get out!"

In retrospect, I realize there were several reasons for my sudden decision. First, and I guess most important, I did not like being mediocre. My three winning years with the Giants had given me an aversion to losing. I had almost forgotten what it was to lose, and

278

I did not like being reminded. At 38, I could not bring myself to face the prospect of starting all over again as I had done so many times in my career. I had too much pride to go through another season like 1964.

Another thing, too. It was time to get out because I was lucky that I had played pro football for 17 years without any really serious injuries. Oh, there had been the usual broken bones and such, and some minor things, but for the most part I had been fortunate. It seemed that the good Lord had blessed me for a long time, and had enabled me to make a living in a rough sport which 38-year-old guys with bald heads had no business playing; a sport meant for younger, stronger men. Maybe, as I thought, my throwing arm was as good as ever. But something told me my legs weren't what they once were. The bounce was missing; the extra step was gone. And when a quarterback's legs go, well, forget it, pardner. After the legs, the timing goes, and then the confidence. And when that happens, a smart quarterback gets out.

It was a decision I had long dreaded making—a decision I had put off, one way or another, at various times in the past. But, in 1964, it finally had to be made, and I made it.

Cleveland beat us by 52–20 in the last game of the year at Yankee Stadium, and later in the dressing room, angry and frustrated and a little sad, I indicated to owner Wellington Mara that I might not be back in 1965.

Wellington Mara has a fine understanding of men who play pro football, and this was not the first time he had heard an old veteran threaten to retire after a hard season. He knew that things usually looked brighter when the aches and pains had subsided and the bitterness of defeat was forgotten. Wellington heard me out, then put his hand on my shoulder and said, "Give it more thought, Y.A., and we'll talk about it again in a few weeks. There's no use making a rash decision now."

So I went home and thought it over. But I always came back to the same decision—it was time to quit playing football!

We had a horrible season in 1964 and it had left a deep scar on my pride. The few weeks that Wellington Mara had given me failed to heal the wound.

The downfall of the Giants in 1964 was created by many things.

279

First of all, a lot of us got old—all at once! Second, we had more injuries than any ball club I can remember. They were carting us off on stretchers every other play. It was murder. Third, everybody was shooting for us, saving their Sunday punches for the Giants. Every week was like the world championship. It's tough to repeat after three straight division titles.

Then again, and this may be the most important point, my own personality hurt me that final year. As I said earlier in this book, I am a stickler for the things that have been good to me. I stay with them. I never change the pattern. This is what made it difficult for me to accept some of the things that happened. The Giants had made several trades after the 1963 season—Phil King and Sam Huff and Dick Modzelewski—and this disturbed me psychologically. As early as May of 1964, I was worrying about what effect the trades would have on the private world of Y.A. Tittle. I am not saying I was right in working myself up like that. Obviously, I was wrong. It was the management's business to make trades—and they had made some great ones, including, I believe, the one for an old, washed-up quarterback named Tittle back in 1961. I was just a player and, looking back, I guess I should have been concentrating on football and not on what the front office was doing.

But again, it was my nature to try and keep a good thing going. If last week we won, this week I want to sit in the same seat on the bus, eat at the same restaurant, go to bed at exactly the same time. This way, everything is okay with me mentally; everything is rosy and ". . . we can't lose."

But when something happens to rock the boat, well, I sometimes use it as a crutch. I say to myself, "Gee whiz, I knew it, I knew it. I should not have changed, or I should not have done this differently because now we have gone and lost and it's my fault."

My own personality helped defeat me in 1964, as surely as the murderous blitz by the Philadelphia Eagles in the opening game; as surely as the tackle by Pittsburgh Steeler defensive end John Baker that cracked my ribs the following week—and started me on the way down.

I wanted—I tried like hell—to do everything exactly as we had done it in the winning years of 1961, 1962, and 1963 with the *same* guys. Why break up a winning combination? I asked myself that question a dozen times a day in training camp. All my life, championships had eluded me. I got to believing that I could never be a winner. Then I went to New York and Allie Sherman made me a winner. Sherman made me believe in myself and in his system and in the Giants' personnel. I believed, and we won three straight championships.

Typically, I told myself it would last forever. I fell into a pattern which was upset when the trades were made that spring. Huff went to Washington for Andy Stynchula and Dick James—and, while Andy and Dick were fine football players, Huff was a winner, a real winner. I wondered how we could win without him. I now realize, of course, that perhaps certain trades *had* to be made. I can now see the other side of it. A coach has problems. He must look to the future and plan. He's got to move ballplayers in and out to keep the thing going. He does not go home after practice like the rest of us and forget about everything until tomorrow.

So, when things started to go badly early in the 1964 season, this fixation of mine for clinging to a set pattern ruined me as an effective quarterback. I found myself using the trades to rationalize my failures as a player. If they got to me on a red-dog and dumped me, I would say to myself, "That would not have happened if old Phil King was in there blocking for me."

I was a good player while everything was in place, but when something was out of place, at least in my way of thinking, I was not a good player. I was mediocre. I was a loser. That's when I began to realize the time was near to retire.

In January, the Giants called a big press conference at Mama Leone's Restaurant in New York City to announce my retirement. It was one of the saddest and most touching experiences of my life. Well Mara and Allie Sherman said some wonderful things about me. They retired my jersey, and I felt my eyes fill with tears when Mr. Mara told the writers and television people that "as long as there's a team called the New York Giants, no one will ever wear number fourteen again."

Of all my years in football, the last four in New York were the most memorable. I had finally made it with a championship club, and those were wonderful years for me and for my family. They made all the losing years seem worthwhile. And I will say again in this final chapter that I think the New York Giants, with Well Mara and the *entire* family of Giants, is the finest sports organization in the world. I wish I could have continued to play for them.

I remained in New York several days after the press conference and it was fairly exciting—television appearances, more interviews, and so on. I was kept so busy running around town that I did not have time to think about not being in football anymore. I did not really feel anything until I climbed aboard a plane one night and headed home to San Francisco.

Then it hit me—"By gosh, it's all over!"

I don't want to sound like an old sentimentalist, but you can't put most of your life into something, even a game, and then walk away from it without feeling a sharp pain. I felt such a pain that night as the big jetliner carried me away from New York, and away from the Giants.

It was all over, I admitted, for old Y.A. I was done, finished, through, and I had no regrets.

When the plane landed, I stepped out—and all of a sudden I was just an insurance man.

Now don't get me wrong. Insurance is a fine business and it has been good to me. But, well, it's just not as exciting as football, and Y.A. Tittle is never going to be as good around the office or behind a desk as he was in the huddle. I think most of my insurance customers will agree with me on that point.

Nevertheless, I told Minnette I would settle down and give it a real good try that spring. Football was a thing of the past, I convinced myself, and it would not do me any good to daydream about the great days at Yankee Stadium. That was all behind me now. My future lay with the Tittle-Iverson Insurance Agency. Nine to five every day, and Sundays off. What would I do with a Sunday off?

The Giants gave me an opportunity to stay with them in a public relations capacity on the West Coast. It was a gesture I sincerely appreciated. But it wasn't exactly satisfying because to me football is throwing passes, not making speeches at off-season banquets.

Then one afternoon I got a phone call from Lou Spadia, the general manager of my old ball club, the San Francisco Forty-

Niners. Like the call I got from Allie Sherman four years earlier, it was to change the course of my life once again.

"Y.A.," Spadia began, "how would you like to be backfield coach for the Forty-Niners?"

The question caught me by surprise and I didn't say anything for a few seconds. Spadia quickly added: "I talked with Well Mara in New York, and he said they'd be happy to release you so you can accept my offer."

By this time, I had my answer ready. "When do I start?" I almost shouted into the phone.

Minnette did not exactly greet the news of Spadia's offer with a round of applause. I kind of think she was glad that I had finally gotten out of football and that maybe I would settle down to a normal life. But Minnette knew better than to try and talk me out of this new offer. The past seventeen years had taught her that football was my lifeblood.

So, here I am—out of football for only a couple of months and itching to get started again, this time as a coach.

It wasn't like going in cold with San Francisco. I knew all the men in the ball club. Jack Christiansen, the head coach, was an old Detroit Lion defensive back, and we had knocked helmets for many years. Bill Johnson, the line coach, was my old buddy from our Texas high school days. And Billy Wilson, who coaches the Forty-Niner ends, had been my favorite pass receiver for years before I went back to New York and started throwing to Shofner and Gifford. It was like old home week when I went to camp down the road at St. Mary's College that July.

It was great to be a part of the game again, especially with a fine organization like the Forty-Niners. And it was great to be working for a fellow like Lou Spadia. But looking back on my early experiences as a coach in 1965, I think maybe I started coaching too fast. There was a lot of fanfare in the press and on television when I joined the team. I was flattered by all the attention, and I felt obliged to coach the devil out of anybody wearing a San Francisco uniform. I tried to show everybody what all my years and my experience had taught me—and I was somewhat shocked to learn that I didn't know a helluva lot myself. In fact, it took only a couple of days to convince me that I was a lousy coach.

This was a new and puzzling experience. I had always had an instinctive feeling for football, and that's the way I had played quarterback. But now, as a coach, I discovered I did not know how wide to instruct the end to split—I mean in exact yards. I had to put myself in at quarterback, walk up there behind the center, take a look over at the end and say, "Yeah, that's it."

So, it was difficult for me at first. A guy would walk up and ask me, "How far do I spread on this one, coach?" and I would have to say, "I don't know. I gotta look at you."

It was really something those first few weeks. I was supposed to know how deep the backs line up behind center, but I didn't. If someone questioned me on it, I had to get in behind the center, glance over my shoulder at the backs and say, "You gotta move up six inches, Ken." I was playing quarterback more than I was coaching.

All I knew about coaching was the X's and O's, and the overall strategy. Suddenly I discovered I had to know quite a bit more. But it was a great experience for me and, no matter how dumb I was as a coach, I was back in the game. That's what counted most to me—being in football. If I were playing today, I am sure I would be a much smarter quarterback because of all I have learned as a coach. Also, I now feel a bit more compassion for all my old coaches—from Joe Magrill at Marshall Junior High to Allie Sherman in New York. I never understood their side of it until I became a coach myself.

In the beginning, I had one trouble—I kept telling everyone about New York. I had played with the Giants for four years, and we had been tremendously successful. Naturally, references to the Giants kept creeping into my talks to the Forty-Niner players. I would get up there at the blackboard and say, "Now, this is how we used to do it in New York." I went to bed every night asking myself, "Why in the hell did I say this about New York today, or that about New York, or how good we were in New York?"

But still I persisted in doing it. I was continually telling them how we did it with the Giants. After all, we had won three straight titles in New York, and San Francisco hadn't won any.

Bill Johnson, my good friend, told me I was overdoing the New York thing a little bit and, of course, I agreed with him. John-

284

son also told me I was overdoing my coaching and that this was having an upsetting effect on Billy Wilson, the Forty-Niner end coach.

This was not done intentionally. I had great respect for Wilson. But *I* was the quarterback—or at least I had always been the quarter-back—and I had always thrown the passes to the ends and now as a coach, I wanted everything done *my* way. I was wrong, how-ever, because Johnson and Wilson had several years on me as coaches and they knew more football. But being the quarterback, I had always been my own boss and if I wanted a receiver moved in closer or set out a little, I would waggle my hands at him and tell him to move in or split out. And when I stuck my bald head in the huddle, I was running the show. I was an old quarterback and not too many guys dared disagree with me—especially when we were winning.

So this is how I approached coaching in the beginning. If I felt something should be done this way or that way, I just did it. I never thought of asking the other coaches what they thought. I was not aware that I was doing it, but this was small consolation to Johnson and Wilson, the fellows who had to put up with me in camp that first summer.

Maybe because of the trouble I was having making the transition from quarterback to coach, I spent the 1965 season in the press box spotting the games with Wilson and Jim David, one of the defensive coaches. I guess Jack Christiansen figured I would be less of a problem up there than down on the sideline trying to play quarterback in my street shoes.

I remember my first day in the press box. We were playing Cleveland in a pre-season game, and I had some big ideas on how I was going to send in all the great plays and everything. What I did not realize was that things happen so fast you can't see that much from upstairs. But I went up there with all my charts and papers and pencils, and I was determined to run the whole show on the phones. I was going to check that sideline—because I am a great believer in the sideline pass—and I was going to think up all sorts of things for quarterback John Brodie to do.

"It's not that easy," Billy Wilson warned me, "but you are such a stubborn old guy I'm going to let you learn for yourself. You're

285

going to throw all those charts away because you won't be able to see a damned thing."

I did not believe him, of course, because as he said, I am stubborn. But he was right. I had all the charts and pencils going for the first few plays, but when we went down to the locker room at halftime, I didn't have a darned thing on paper. I had nothing.

Gradually, I got a better feel of my new role in football and as the season wore on, coaching became fun. At least it was fun until after every game; that's when I really missed not being a player anymore. It would hit me the minute I walked into the dressing room. As a quarterback, I had always been a part of everything that happened during a ball game, good or bad. And after the game, I was usually in the middle of whatever was happening in the locker room. I guess I had come to expect it would always be that way.

But now, as a coach, I walk in and there's really not much to talk about. Among the boys, action and body contact are a common denominator. But, hell, we coaches don't even have our shirts wrinkled from being up in the press box with all our charts and pencils. We go around and slap the players on the rear end and say, "Good game, John," or maybe "Nice try, Ken." And that's about the extent of our post-game participation. The boys are taking their pads off, and they are all muddy and beat-up and cut-up, and we coaches just stand around in a corner twiddling our thumbs and trying to keep out of the way.

This is when I miss not being a player. I'm just not a part of it after a ball game, and it hurts. Maybe, in time, it won't. But it does in the beginning. I am there but I haven't done anything. I haven't even been able to keep my charts or send in the great plays. I stand there with my papers, my pencils, and my clean shirt, and wonder how long I am supposed to hang around. Nobody pays any attention to me.

The noise and excitement are there, and all the old familiar sounds and smells that I know so well. But I am an outsider—just a guy from upstairs who used to be a quarterback.

Billy Wilson said it best one day when we were down on the sideline before a game watching the teams warm up. As usual, I was preoccupied with the quarterbacks from both sides. I check them out every week. I don't even see the halfbacks and ends and tackles—just the passers. This day, I turned to Wilson and said, "By gosh, Billy, I don't give a damn what anybody says, I still think I am the best thrower in the business!"

Billy smiled and said: "You're right, Y.A., but you and I are probably the only guys in the whole country who know it anymore."

Y. A. TITTLE'S PASSING RECORD

ALL-AMERICA CONFERENCE

Year	Atts.	Comp.	Yards	TDs	Inter.
1948	289	161	2,522	16	9
1949	289	148	2,209	14	18
Totals	578	309	4,731	30	27

NATIONAL FOOTBALL LEAGUE

Year	Atts.	Comp.	Yards	TDs	Inter.
1950	316	161	1,884	8	19
1951	114	63	808	8	9
1952	208	106	1,407	11	12
1953	259	149	2,121	20	16
1954	295	170	2,205	9	9
1955	287	147	2,185	17	28
1956	218	124	1,641	7	12
1957	279	176	2,157	13	15
1958	208	120	1,467	9	15
1959	199	102	1,331	10	15
1960	127	69	694	4	3
1961	285	163	2,272	17	12
1962	375	200	3,224	33	20
1963	367	221	3,145	36	14
1964	281	147	1,798	10	22
Totals	3,818	2,118	28,339	212	221

NATIONAL FOOTBALL LEAGUE RECORDS HELD BY
Y.A. TITTLE AT THE TIME OF HIS RETIREMENT

Most attempts (career)—3,817
Most completions (career)—2,118
Most yards (career)—28,339
Most touchdowns (career)—212
Most touchdown passes (one season)—36 in 1963

MOST VALUABLE PLAYER IN THE NFL

1957
1961
1963

INDEX